Studia philosophiae religionis 11
Editores: Dick Haglund et Hans Hof

Håkan Thorsén

Peak-Experience, Religion and Knowledge

A Philosophical Inquiry into some Main Themes in the Writings of Abraham H. Maslow.

"In the thirties I became interested in certain psychological problems, and found that they could not be answered or managed well by the classical scientific structure of the time (the behavioristic, positivistic, 'scientific', value-free, mechanomorphic psychology). I was raising legitimate questions and had to invent another approach to psychological problems in order to deal with them. This approach slowly became a general philosophy of psychology, of science in general, of religion, work, management, and now biology. As a matter of fact, it became a *Weltanschauung.*"

Abraham H. Maslow, Towards a Humanistic Biology, American Psychologist, 1969, 24, p. 724.

"It's possible now to make a completely coherent & comprehensive psychological & naturalistic theory of religion—far more clear & real than any theology or religion has ever been."

Abraham H. Maslow, The Journals of A. H. Maslow. 1979, Vol. 1, p. 6.

Doctoral Thesis at the University of Uppsala 1983

CWK Gleerup is the imprint for the scientific and scholarly publications of Liber Förlag Lund.

BL
53
.T46
1983

Abstract

Thorsén, H.: Peak-experience, Religion and Knowledge. A Philosophical Inquiry into some Main Themes in the Writings of Abraham H. Maslow. *Studia Philosphiae Religionis 11*, 202 pp. Uppsala. ISBN 91-40-05038-6

The main aim of this dissertation is to reconstruct Maslow's argumentation in favour of his assumption that human beings have a special cognitive faculty ("B-cognition") for knowledge of special aspects in Reality. In this reconstruction the following areas of Maslow's thinkings are analysed: (a) his motivation and personality theories (chapter 2), (b) his theory of cognition and his theory of peak-experience (chapter 3) and (c) his epistemology (chapter 4).

Chapter 5 deals with Maslow's theory of Religion. In the centre of this chapter we find a discussion on Maslow's use of William James' over-belief-theory and on Maslow's ontological theory. The ontology found in Maslow's theory of Religion is characterized as a middle way between supranaturalistic ontologies and a purely materialistic ontology.

In chapter 6 the main parts in Maslow's philosophy of science are discussed: his use of B-cognition in a constructive philosophy of science; his methodological innovation — a taoistic method; his methodological suggestions for Psychology of Religion, with special regard to transcendent experiences.

The main result:

(1) Fundamental criticism of Maslow's motivation and personality theories and of his research about self-actualizing people. (2) It is shown that Maslow uses James' over-belief-theory in a gratuitously way in his theories of peak-experience and of Religion, and in his suggested method in Psychology of Religion. (3) Some questionable hidden presumptions are found in his theory of B-cognition.

These and other criticisms make Maslow's argumentation in favour of his assumption of a special knowledge of Reality, through B-cognition, non-tenable.

Håkan Thorsén, Teologiska institutionen, Uppsala Universitet, Box 1604, S-751 46 Sverige

Printed in Sweden 1983
LiberTryck, Stockholm   298562

Contents

---

* CTR is an abbreviation designating the reality which exists independent of human consciousness (see further section 1.0.)

Chapter 4: Maslow's theory of knowledge

Chapter 5: Maslow's theory of Religion

Chapter 6: Maslow's philosophy of science

Acknowledgements

I would like to express my gratitude to:

Prof. Hans Hof, my supervisor, who has guided me in my philosophical learning and for his stimulation and encouragements.

Dr. Eberhard Herrmann for our many philosophical discussions through the years which have helped me a lot and forced me to articulate my philosophical opinions and reflect on the reasons I have for holding them.

Both Prof. Hof and Dr. Herrmann have read through my manuscript and their constructive criticisms have been of much assistence in the preparation of this dissertation.

I am also grateful to Dr. Erik Götlind and Dr. Lennart Nordenfelt for their valuable comments on sections 2.0. and 2.1.

I also cordially thank M.A. Ted Harris who has translated chapter 1 into English and who has checked the rest of my manuscript in English. I am very greatful for his help and careful work and for his kindly and accomodating attitude.

I also thank the members of the High Seminar in Philosophy of Religion for their criticism of my manuscript.

Lastly, I am very grateful to my dear Diana for her loyal support and for her (sometimes under protest) acceptance that I have taken so much time in finishing this dissertation.

Chapter 1: Introduction

1.0. General Aim of this Study

The Norwegian philosopher Arne Naess sets forth the following question in the title of a book: *What reality is the true reality?* (Hvilken verden er den virklige?).[1]

A. H. Maslow (1908 – 1970) has tried to answer this question. In his attempt in answering this perennial question, Maslow is influenced by the epistemological tradition which includes, among others, such philosopher as H. Bergson and the pragmatic philosophers W. James and J. Dewey.[2] Advocates of this epistemological tradition assume that human cognitive faculties serve, first and foremost, as practical instruments with regard to survival, satisfaction of needs, etc., in the reality which exist independent of human consciousness. *(This reality will hereafter be abbreviated CTR, see section 4.1. for a closer analysis of this term.)* They also assume that human beings have other cognitive faculites which can give us knowledge of some specific aspects of CTR.

Maslow assumes that human beings have two main types of cognitive faculties: type I, which he names Deficiency-cognition *(hereafter D-cognition)* and which serves, primarily, as an instrument with regard to the satisfaction of human beings' basic needs; type II, which he names Being-cognition *(hereafter B-cognition)* and which gives us knowledge of certain aspects of CTR.[3]

The epistemological tradition which, similar to Maslow, assumes that human beings have the ability to develop another type of cognitive faculty and which gives us knowledge of CTR is carried on by, among others, advocates of Transpersonal Psychology. The most well known advocates of this psychological movement are R. Ornstein, C. Naranjo and C. Tart.[4]

Maslow's argument in favour of another type of cognitive faculty which gives us knowledge of CTR can be *reconstructed* in the following way:

Argument A_1

(1) If a person P has the qualifications $X_1 \ldots X_n$, P will have cognition of type II

(2) If a person P has cognition of type II, P will have knowledge of Y

(3) There are persons Ps who have the qualifications $X_1 \ldots X_n$

(4) There are persons Ps who have knowledge of Y.

Maslow writes:

> "I once suggested the principle that self-actualizing people can and do perceive reality more efficiently, fully and with less motivational contamination than we others do, then we may possibly use them as biological assays. Through their greater sensitivity and perception, we may get a better report of what reality is like, than through our own eyes, just as canaries can be used to detect gas in mines before less sensitive creatures can. As a second string to this same bow, we may use ourselves in our most perceptive moments, in our peak-experiences, when, for the moment, we are self-actualizing, to give us a report of the nature of reality that is truer than we can ordinarily manage."[5]

> "To the extent that perception is desire-less and fear-less, to that extent is it more veridical, in the sense of perceiving the true, or essential or intrinsic whole nature of the object (without splitting it up by abstraction). Thus the goal of objective and true description of any reality is fostered by psychological health. Neurosis, psychosis, stunting of growth — all are, from this point of view, cognitive diseases as well, contaminating perception, learning, remembering, attending and thinking."[6]

By replacing the variables in the Argument A_1 with the terms used by Maslow in his argumentation in these quotations and in other contexts, we get:

Argument A_2

(1) If a person P's basic needs are satisfied and P can be characterized as a self-actualizing person, P has B-cognition
(2) If a person P has B-cognition, P will have knowledge of Y
(3) There are persons Ps who have their basic needs satisfied and who can be characterized as self-actualizing persons
_____
(4) There are persons Ps who have knowledge of Y

In argument A_2 the qualifications $X_1 \ldots X_n$ have been replaced by such terms as "basic needs" and "self-actualizing". Cognition of type II means the same as what Maslow calls "B-cognition". Y implies that on the occasion of B-cognition, P gets:
(a) a more complete and a more correct knowledge of CTR which can be had in both D-cognition and B-cognition
(b) a knowledge of certain aspects of CTR which is not to be had in D-cognition.

Argument A_2 has the following logical form:[7]

(1) $\forall x(Sx \wedge Tx \rightarrow Qx)$
(2) $\forall x(Qx \rightarrow Rx)$
(3) $\exists x(Sx \wedge Tx)$
_____
(4) $\exists x(Rx)$

10

The implications in (1) and (2) are, in this first preliminary interpretation, interpreted as sufficient conditions. In this logical form, Argument A_2 has logical validity.

The general aim of this study is to discuss whether or not this argument is tenable.

In this attempt we have

(a) to clarify the meaning of the terms "basic needs" and "self-actualizing" in Maslow's works (to clarify the qualifications $X_1 \ldots X_n$).
(b) to clarify the differences between D-cognition and B-cognition.
(c) to make clear the meanings of the statements which describe the contents of consciousness in the experiences which Maslow calls "peak-experience" (to clarify the contents of Y).
(d) to make clear and discuss Maslow's argumentation in favour of the statements in (c) having referents in CTR.
(e) to make clear and discuss various interpretations of the constants in Argument A_2.

The general aim of this study can be formulated in the following way: to clarify the premisses in Argument A and discuss whether or not the Argument A is tenable. By a tenable argument is meant an argument in which the premisses are true and which by themselves or in combination with other true statements, deductively, lead to the conclusion in question.

The disposition of the dissertation is made with regard to this general aim.

In order to clarify Maslow's theory of man, which implicitly influences the qualifications $X_1 \ldots X_n$, and *to make the qualifications in Argument A clear,* we shall make explicit, in *chapter 2,* the main theses in Maslow's motivation and personality theories.

In *chapter 3,* an analysis of the distinction between D-cognition and B-cognition will be carried out in order *to clarify the cognition of type II* in Argument A. Also in this chapter, we shall try *to clarify the contents of Y* by distinguishing between some of the different types of contents of consciousness in peak-experience.

In *chapter 4,* we shall *reconstruct and analyse Maslow's argumentation in favour of cognition of type II which gives us knowledge of Y.* In this context, we shall reconstruct Maslow's theory of knowledge, his theory of truth and his ontology. These precizations of the premisses (1), (2) and (3) in Argument A, which are carried out in chapters 2, 3 and 4, give us a basis for discussing various interpretations of the constants in Argument A and for discussing the tenability of Argument A. This will be done in section 4.5.

In *chapter 5,* we shall show how Maslow uses his theory of the different types of contents of consciousness belonging to peak-experience in *his theory of Religion.* Maslow is very critical of what he calls "supernaturalism" and other types of ontologies which assume a sort of two-world reality, one for God *and* the other for human beings and the rest of nature. He is also very critical of a purely materialistic ontology. His intermediary position between these types of ontologies will be clarified, and in doing so, we clarify his naturalistic theory of Religion. In this context, we shall also clarify the *term* "peak-experience" itself.

In the final chapter, *chapter 6,* we shall describe and systematize some of the fundamental positions in Maslow's *philosophy of science.* We shall also show how Maslow applies his view that human beings have a special type of cognitive faculty, namely, B-cognition, in his philosophy of science and discuss the reasonableness of his view on the criteria for objective scientific results. We shall also notice how some of his criticisms of what he calls "orthodox science" are in agreement with the criticism which "the hermeneutic-dialectic school" makes of "logical empiricism".[8] His constructive philosophy of science with regard to the study of transcendent experiences will also be discussed. We shall make clear whether or not Maslow has made some contributions to any methodological innovation in the sphere of Psychology of Religion.

In the rest of this introductory chapter, we shall present some biographical data about Maslow, and spell out the fundamental aims of his research programme (1.1.). It is our contention that these fundamental aims constitute an important background for an understanding of Maslow's argumentation in what we have reconstructed as argument A. These fundamental aims must be made clear. A general characterization of the Humanistic and Transpersonal Psychologies of which Maslow was one of the most important initiators and organizers will be presented (1.3.). We shall also present our method of interpretation and our method of analysis of Maslow's statements, and discuss the subordinate aim of this study (1.2.). We shall also give a survey of some earlier research about Maslow (1.4.).

1.1. Maslow's Earlier Research and his Normative Non-scientific Aims in his Later Research

The aims of this section are twofold: (1) to present a brief outline of Maslow's earlier research which can be dated 1928—1941, and, (2) to show the fundamental changes in his research programme after 1941. In 1941, an important event took place in his life which led him to formulate the normative non-scientific aims for his continuing research programme. In order to understand Maslow's research programme and the results in his works on Religion,

Philosophy of Science, Epistemology, Ontology and Ethics, it is important, in our view, to be aware of these normative non-scientific aims.

1.1.1. Maslow's earlier research

Maslow underwent a basic training in psychology from 1928–1934 (Ph, D. 1934).[9] Among his teachers were C. Hull, H. Harlow and W. H. Sheldon. During these years behaviorism dominated most of the psychological research in the USA, and Maslow, at least until he got his Ph, D., was very much under behaviorism's influence. During this period he carried out experiments in which he used dogs and apes.[10] From 1935–1937, he worked as an experimental psychologist together with E. Torndike. He carried out experiments on primates focusing his attention on the relationship between dominance and sexual behavior. He also carried out experiments concerning women's sexual behavior and dominance which he published in 1939 and 1942.[11] The results of the latter research show some important changes in his scientific methodological ideal. These changes were brought about by the influences which Maslow underwent during his participation in the confrontation between American psychologists and different European scientists who were forced to leave Europe because of the threats posed by Nazism.

Maslow studied Gestaltpsychology under M. Wertheimer and K. Koffka, Social anthropology under R. Benedict and M. Mead and Psychoanalytic theory under E. Fromm, K. Horney, A. Kardiner and D. Levy. He also had personal contact with K. Goldstein whose book *The Organism* (1939), its central theme being human self-actualization and a critique of the psychoanalytic theory of homeostasis, had profound influence on Maslow. His personal contact with A. Adler also influenced his thought, inter alia, his understanding of some of the weaknesses of orthodox freudian psychoanalytic assumptions.[12]

The published articles on women's sexual behavior and dominance (1939, 1942) show that Maslow had abandoned some of his earlier behavioristic standpoints. In this research he developed a method which he later used in his experiments concerning "self-actualizing people" (1945–1949) and "peak-experience" (1956–1959), the so called "taoistic method". In this method he combines clinical and experimental methods, i.e., he tries, first of all, to establish a cordial contact with the examinee in order to get a holistic view of the examinee. This is followed by an "intensive interview"[13] (see further section 6.3.).

An example which illustrates his dissociation with methodological behaviorism[14] is his distinction between "inner personality" (a person's experiences of himself) and "outer personality" (a person's behavior). Maslow main-

13

tains that one cannot unequivocally deduce from "outer personality" "inner personality".[15]

Maslow is also critical of psychoanalytic theory. He stresses the difference between neurotic and "normal" persons and claims that freudian concepts are not always applicable when studying "normal" persons. This is one of the reasons why he leaves out the term "unconsciousness" in his research from 1939.

In 1941 he published, together with B. Mittelmann, *Principles of Abnormal Psychology: The Dynamics of Psychic Illness.* It is difficult to establish which of the book's assumptions Maslow adheres to since we do not know in what way the authors collaborated.[16] Some of these assumptions appear, however, in Maslow's later works. The authors claim, for instance, to have presented a dynamic psychology and to have introduced the term "vital needs", i.e., "self-esteem", "security", and "love", in explaining the origins of neurosis and other more serious pathologies. They also stress a holistic view, not only with regard to the relationship between "mind" and "body", but also with regard to the individual's relationship to the socio-economic and cultural environment in which he/she lives. The book includes a description of what the authors consider to be characteristic for "the normal personality", but they refuse to give a description of "the ideal personality".

1.1.2. The normative non-scientific aims in Maslow's later research

Maslow's continuing research programme changed in a fundamental way during 1941 due to a specific experience. He tells us in a interview that on the day after the Japanese attack on Pearl Habour, he was passing a parade when he suddenly got an overwhelming experience in which he became aware of his life's telos. He was to spend the rest of his life developing a theory of human nature which would be the ground for human beings to live in peace and unity.

In the interview, he says:

> "That moment changed my whole life and determined what I have done ever since. Since that moment in 1941 I've devoted myself to developing a theory of human nature that could be tested by experiment and research. I wanted to prove that human beings are capable of something grander than war and prejudice and hatred".

> "I've tried to develop an entering wedge, the basis for an ideology that all human beings can accept. There should be no boundaries. What we need is a system of thought — you might even call it a religion — that can bind human beings together. A system that would fit the Republic of Chad as well as the United States, a system that would supply our idealistic young people with something to believe in. They're searching for something they can pour all that emotions into. And the Churches are not much help."[17]

Maslow tried to formulate a theory of human nature which would be the core of and the epistemological ground for a *Weltanschauung*, for "a system of thought — you might even call it a religion". This mission of Maslow, which was first motivated by experiences associated with the second world war, received additional motivation, in the 50's and 60's, from his comprehension of the ongoing cultural crisis in America and Western Europe. This crisis, according to Maslow, implies, inter alia, a growing relativism in ethics, growing experiences of loss of personal identity, hopelessness and meaninglessness.[18] This general trend in Maslow's research programme reveals his assumption that a theory of man plays an important role in bringing about social, economic and cultural changes.[19]

His general aim led him to formulate in 1968 two important problems ("The Big Problems") which he considered to be the objects for all human power: man must use all his powers and resources to solve these problems.[20]

1. "The first and overaching Big Problem is: making the Good Person". In order to bring about such a state, it is necessary, according to Maslow, to have a knowledge of man's "essential" nature, what causes man to act morally wrong and what characterizes "The Good Human Being". He tries in his motivation and personality theories to make a contribution in these areas of knowledge. In these theories, he assumes that human nature shows itself in the features of self-actualizing people, partly with regard to such identityfeatures as creativity, self-knowledge, etc., partly concerning moral actions and partly in relation to cognitive faculties. We can *reconstruct* the basis for these assumptions as follows:

(i)   Human beings have certain genetic and somatic based needs (basic needs)

(ii)   If these needs are satisfied, human beings actualize their potential essence or nature

(iii)   The people who succeed in satisfying their basic needs can be regarded as self-actualizing people

On the basis of (i) — (iii) Maslow thinks that he is justified in assuming:

(iv)   Human beings' potential essence or nature can be studied by observing the features of self-actualizing people.

2. "The equally Big Problem as urgent as the one I have already mentioned is to make the Good Society".

Maslow is very vague in his description of what characterizes the "Good Society".[21] His normative ideal for individuals, i.e., self-actualization, forms the basis for his normative goal for "the Good Society". He characterizes the good society as a society in which human beings can develop their potentials.[22] The relations between human beings will be "synergic" (a term which Maslow has taken over from R. Benedict) which means that human beings' individual spontaneous actions and goals in life will be in agreement with the collective goals of the society.[23] The society will be decentralized, and he recommends a pluralistic society in which each person's unique potentials will have a chance of being actualized.[24] The means for establishing "the Good Society" is through an interchange between individuals' ongoing fulfilment of their basic needs plus the personality changes which follow and social institutions' ongoing adjustments in relation to the circumstances which make it possible for human beings to satisfy their basic needs.

Maslow's understanding of these fundamental problems and his view that increased knowledge of human nature is the most important means for solving these problems is a background for understanding why he emphasized the need to formulate a theory of human nature. He believed that psychology plays the most important role in gaining such knowledge, hence his reason for attributing to psychology this central position in the world of science and its importance in bringing about social change.

> "I believe that psychologists occupy the most centrally important position in the world today. I say this because all the important problems of mankind — war and peace, exploitation and brotherhood, hatred and love, sickness and health, misunderstanding and understanding, happiness and unhappiness — will yield only to a better understanding of human nature, and to this psychology alone wholly applies itself."[25]

Accordingly, Maslow tries with the help of scientific methods and results to formulate a theory of human nature. However, he does not accept the established scientific methods in psychology. He even assumes that the established scientific ideal is a hindrance in an attempt to find a theory of human nature. Instead, he argues, in his constructive philosophy of science, in favour of a new scientific ideal which, inter alia, calls for the use of descriptions of phenomenological data in theories, less restrictive criteria concerning the validity and reliability of scientific results, the introduction of new methods, etc. Maslow's new scientific ideal opens up new areas for psychological investigations, for instance, love, creativity and different types of religious experience. Investigations in these areas will lead, according to Maslow, to a more complete understanding of human nature, not only quantitively but also qualitatively.

While one's judgement of the reasonableness of Maslow's philosophy of science, motivation and personality theories, epistemology, theory of Religion and ontology must be independent of one's judgement of his normative non-scientific aims, it is our contention that the latter is worth knowing in

16

order to understand Maslow's psychological background to his argumentation in these various areas of concern. His general aim is to create a *Weltanschauung* which has as its core a theory of human nature and which is based on scientific results. His reason for creating a *Weltanschauung* is to counteract the cultural crisis which, he thinks, plagues the Western world today.

1.2. Method and Subordinate Aim of this Study

One of the difficulties in studying Maslow's works is his vague and unsystematic style of writing. Generally speaking, he does not define his terms, and futhermore, he borrows terms from psychologists and philosophers without specifying whether or not his use of these terms carry the same meaning. This way of writing is due to, inter alia, the nature of his works. In a hitherto unused source in research about Maslow, namely, his journals from 1959—1970,[26] we can follow his struggles in writing his books and articles.

Maslow wrote only three completed books throughout his life: *Principles of Abnormal Psychology* (1941), *Eupsychian Management* (1965) and *The Psychology of Science* (1966). The rest of his production is made up of articles and compilations. Many of the articles are lectures and according to the journals, he often did not have time to revise them.[27] Other explanations for this vague and unsystematic style of writing are his personality and his general aim with regard to his scientific programme. He characterizes himself as a *theoretical psychologist* which means that he creates tentative hypotheses, theories and conclusions which are based on observable data, but which do not, as yet, have sufficient empirical justification.[28] Futhermore, he sees himself as a very creative formulator of hypotheses while possessing lesser abilities for subjecting his hypotheses to empirical analysis.

In one of his journals, he writes:

> "I'e been having too many ideas all my life. But lately it's more so. The whole Weltanschauung is bearing fruit, & apples keep popping out rapidly. Last week, in A. M. two big illuminations before lunch, really big. But no time to write them out at once, so just a few notes until I can catch up. Then later in day several good ideas — merely good — which I just had to pass by .... The whole thing reminds me again of the visual image of the chicken trucker trying all alone to catch hundreds of chickens flying in all directions."[29]

In attempting to interpret Maslow's statements, we have chosen, first and foremost, to establish *contextual reasonable interpretations* which mean:

(a) *semantic reasonableness:* The interpretations presuppose that an author's statements do not differ from normal rules of language

(b) *logical reasonableness:* (1) the interpretations try to present an author's statements in such a way that they do not logically contradict each other and (2) the interpretations try to present an author's values and norms in such a way that they do not contradict each other

(c) *internal reasonableness:* the interpretations are consistent with an author's other statements which are relevant in the given context.[30]

In attempting to establish contextual reasonable interpretations, notice will be taken of those beliefs which an author rejects (the so called "disbeliefs").

The reason for endeavoring to establish contextual reasonable interpretations is our intention to present Maslow's individual statements and theories in a reasonable way, given their context.

Besides this general attempt to establish contextual reasonable interpretations, we shall also endeavor to establish non-contextual reasonable interpretations which differ from the former in that they are, from our point of analysis, reasonable. These interpretation-hypotheses need *not* be in agreement with statements and theories which are explicit in Maslow's texts. They are reasonable reconstructions.[31]

The reason for using non-contextual reasonable interpretations is: Maslow, from our point of analysis, in certain areas of concern, for instance, Epistemology, by-passes important distinctions. A legitimate and fruitful aim in interpreting texts is to present a theory in its totality and as reasonable as possible (the principle of generosity).[32] Given this principle, Maslow's statements and theories will be more interesting from the point of view of justification, hence our choice, at times, to establish non-contextual reasonable interpretations. In the main text, we shall state when a contextual reasonable interpretation or a non-contextual reasonable interpretation occurs. Hereafter, *non-contextual reasonable interpretations are called reasonable interpretations.*

It is believed that interpretation-hypotheses should be supported with rational arguments, and thereby, be open to intersubjective testability. It is our contention that our interpretation-hypotheses of Maslow's statements fulfil this criterion.

Maslow requires that his theories should be presented in a systematic way. One of the subordinate aims in this study is to systematize parts of his *Weltanschauung.* A reason for this is the view that a systematic presentation is important for the clarification of his argumentation that B-cognition gives us knowledge of CTR and reveals specific aspects of CTR. He claims that his argumentation covers many parts of his *Weltanschauung.* He has a holistic view regarding his different hypotheses and theories within the various areas of concern. Maslow compares himself with Freud on this point.

18

"But the truth is that I'm relying less on answering specific questions or difficulties than I am on sweeping onward, paying little attentions to the difficulties but rather building a bigger & bigger, more & more inclusive & comprehensive system of interlocking facts & concepts. The whole big system is getting to be so impressive that the questions fade away or become obsolete — let's say, as they did with Freud and his system. He never proved much directly in answer to a posed difficulty. He couldn't because any one part of the system rested on other parts of the system rather than on separate, tested-out facts independent of the system. It was the system as a whole which "answered" each of the hundreds of questions — really, by not bothering to answer them individually but just by building an awe-inspiring structure."[33]

The primary aim in the analysis of Maslow's motivation and personality theories is that of clarifying and discussing Argument A, and a subordinate aim is that of clarifying the premises', in Argument A, interrelation with other topics in Maslow's *Weltanschauung*. Since Maslow's motivation and personality theories have had a profound influence on different areas of concern, especially within industrial management, such clarifications are in order.

The *method* to be used in the clarification of Maslow's theories on motivation, personality, religion, epistemology and philosophy of science is: *bringing into the open central assumptions, and subsequently, to interpret and clarify them, systematize and interpret some of the logical relations between them, reconstruct his argumentations and investigate their tenability.*

Chapter 2, and to some degree chapter 6, have a more reporting character than the other chapters in the dissertation. This is legitimate, partly because chapter 2 forms an important basis for explicating Argument A and partly because it is a scientific task in itself to structure Maslow's motivation and personality theories, as well as his philosophy of science.

As will be explicit in our analyses of Maslow's different theories, we use, as an analytical conceptual framework, concepts and theories discussed within analytical philosophy. The classification "analytical philosophy" covers a varied area of philosophical thinking, but we do not need to clarify it further in this context. The reader will, in our concrete analyses in the following, be acquainted with the concepts and theories within analytical philosophy which we think are reasonable and fruitful as an analytical conceptual framework for analysing Maslow's different theories. The contents in our position of analysis will also be explicit in some of our criticisms and judgements of Maslow's different theories.

Our point of analysis is somewhat different from Maslow's own philosophical position. This being so, there is always a danger that our analyses can be criticized for "*conceptual imperialism*"[34] by which we "filter" Maslow's statements into our analytical conceptual framework and in doing so distort the meanings in Maslow's statements. We take this risk, because Maslow's statements, theories, argumentation and hidden presumptions have been easier to understand when we have interpreted them with our analytical conceptual framework. The hope is that this will be the case for the reader too.

We can summarize the aims of the study as follows:

(a) to clarify the contents in different theories in Maslow's *Weltanschauung*
(b) to clarify Maslow's argumentation in favour of B-cognition giving us knowledge of CTR and revealing certain aspects of CTR which are not to be had in D-cognition.

1.3. Some Remarks on the Humanistic and Transpersonal Psychologies

Since Maslow belongs to the Humanistic and Transpersonal psychological lines of thought we shall *briefly* outline a few of the main features normally associated with these lines of thought. Around the end of the 50's and the beginning of the 60's, a group of psychologists came together and published *The Journal of Humanistic Psychology* (1961). They also organized *The American Association of Humanistic Psychology* (1962). Maslow was one of the initiators and played a leading role in the administration of this association.[35] Some of these psychologists had criticized for a long time some of behaviorism's and psychoanalysis' basic assumptions. This criticism received, inter alia, via the association, more attention and greater influence. The group regarded itself, due to its opposition to behaviorism and psychoanalysis, as "The Third Force in psychology".[36]

The group embraces a wide variety of theories and assumptions which makes it difficult to delimit it. That which the members do have in common, and which binds them together as a group, is their dissociation from the basic tenets of behaviorism and psychoanalysis. Several philosophers of science and psychologists have tried to establish some of the humanistic psychologists general and common assumptions.[37] In these contexts, the following characteristics are emphasized.

The humanistic psychologists disapprove of "pathology-centred" theories, i.e., those earlier psychological lines of thought which deduced motivations and personality theories, first and foremost, from more or less "psychic sick" people. The humanistic psychologists try to create motivation and personality theories which can also be applied to "psychic healthy" people. Accordingly, they are interested in areas of investigation which have been, in the past, neglected by psychologists, such areas as creativity, love and self-actualization.[38]

They claim that there are certain human needs which cannot be reduced to physiological needs, i.e., food, drink, sleep, etc., instead, they claim that human beings have other (genetic) needs. The endeavor to fulfil these needs must be taken into account in any attempt to understand human beings, for instance, in the psychotherapeutic process. These psychologists reject the homeostasis theory, i.e., the view that an individual strives to reach equilibrium. Instead, they argue that human beings constantly strive to surpass a given state. This assumption is coupled with the view that human beings have potentials which, when actualized, means that human beings have achieved self-actualization.

They assume that human beings have the ability to actively participate in the struggle to determine their future. They advocate that human beings are not only observers but also agents of their own lives. Human self-consciousness is emphasized in this context and is regarded as an unique (essential) human characteristic.

The humanistic psychologists study the human being as a total organism, i.e., from a holistic perspective, which means, inter alia, that they consider the human being's different functions, both mental and physical, as constituting an intergrated whole. Sometimes this holism is extended to include the study of the human being as a psycho-physical organism who functions in a biological, socio-economic and cultural context.

One often finds that normative non-scientific aims are explicitly stated in their scientific studies of human beings, partly because of an attempt to justify their normative ethics by naturalistic premisses, and partly, given these premisses, to recommend possible ideals, goals and directions for life.[39]

They have some common assumptions regarding certain methodological ideals for psychotherapeutic processes. They believe, for instance, that it is important that the therapist establishes a cordial contact with the patient, and through dialogue and empathy, try to understand the patient's experiences of himself/herself ("Eigenwelt"), others ("Mitwelt") and his/her surroundings ("Umwelt").[40]

Generally speaking, in the philosophy of science, one tries to complement a purely natural scientific ideal, at least with regard to the scientific ideal in clinical psychology, with the tradition from Dilthey, which, inter alia, advocates idiographic understanding as primary to nomothetic explanation of human nature.

They require that notice be taken of both the rational and irrational biases which are not even articulated in the non-scientific assumptions. This is seen as a contrast to the rational tendencies which are noticeable in Positivism, and for instance, in the works of Karl Popper. They think that in these contexts, there are possibilities for co-operation between Psychology of Science and Philosophy of Science.[41]

Many humanistic psychologists' basic assumptions have their historical roots in, or, agree with ideas, reaching far back in the history of ideas. It is difficult to establish some general connections due to the group's heterogenous nature. However, many of these psychologists do state, quite explicitly, that they have been influenced by the phenomenological and existentialistic traditions.

A large number of humanistic psychologists have not distanced themselves completely from behaviorism or psychoanalysis for they continue to make use of concepts which are generally associated with older psychologists such as Freud, Adler, and to a great extent, Jung. They also borrow concepts from representatives of other lines of thought, for instance, W. James, M. Wertheimer and K. Goldstein. Among the most influential humanistic psychologists of the past decades are: G. Allport, C. Bühler, V. Frankl, A. Maslow, R. May and C. Rogers.

Some of the humanistic psychologists were also initiators of Transpersonal Psychology which Maslow regarded as the successor of, and a higher development of Humanistic Psychology.[42] Representatives of Transpersonal Psychology are, with regard to the view of man and philosophy of science, in agreement with the advocates of Humanistic Psychology, but they have, first and foremost, concentrated their investigations on "higher states of consciousness". Representatives of Transpersonal Psychology claim that their aim is, given scientific methods, to investigate "phenomena directly relevant to the ultimate positive nature of man".[43] They endeavor to describe and map-out different types of transcendent experiences, investigate different methods with which to arrive at such experiences and find out what stops human beings from having such experiences. By and large, they study states of consciousness which are different from "'waking' ordinary consciousness and 'ordinary' subconsciousness".[44]

In psychoterapy, they sometimes make use of different techinques of meditation and drugs.[45]

1.4. Earlier Research about A. H. Maslow

The works on Maslow with a philosophical approach are few.[46]

I. Franck has in *The Concept of Human Nature: A Philosophical Analysis of Human Nature in The Writings of G. W. Allport, S. E. Asch, Erich Fromm, A. H. Maslow, and C. R. Rogers* (1966) analysed Maslow's assumptions concerning man and his criticism of Freud's view of man. He shows Maslow's normative purpose in his motivation and personality theories.

C. Saussy has in *A Study of the Adequacy of Abraham Maslow's Concept of*

The Self to His Theory of Self-actualization (1977) tried to precizate Maslow's various meanings of "the self" and she relates these meanings to his view on self-actualization. The book also contains a precization of Maslow's various meanings of "the Unconscious".

The Swedish philosopher of science J. Bärmark has in *Världsbild och vetenskapsideal. Några ledande temata hos Abraham Maslow* (Worldpicture and Ideal of Science. Some leading themes in the works of Abraham Maslow) (1976) analysed Maslow's critical and constructive philosophy of science and its relation to Maslow's psychology of science, ontology and view of man. Bärmark interprets Maslow from another perspective than we do, and our study and Bärmark's have different foci, our on Argument A and the areas of problems related to this argument, Bärmark's on the extent to which Maslow has succeeded in his attempt to create a new paradigm in psychology.[47]

The work of F. Elmo *The Concept of Self Actualization in the Theology of Paul Tillich and the Psychology of A. H. Maslow* (1974) is also to be mentioned. Elmo tries to find the agreements and disagreements between Tillich and Maslow regarding their view of man and to some extent their ontology.

The works by C. Wilson, *New Pathways in Psychology. Maslow and the Post-Freudian Revolution* (1972), R. Lowry, *A. H. Maslow: An Intellectual Portrait* (1973), F. Globe, *The Third Force: The Psychology of Abraham Maslow. A Revolutionary New View of Man* (1972) and R. Poelling, *A Developmental study of Abraham H. Maslow's Self-actualization Theory* (1971) have a popular approach, but they can be useful for biographical data and for their attempt to describe Maslow's intellectual development.

There are also a lot of articles from a psychological point of view on Maslow's theories or special topics in his theories. Some of these articles will be mentioned in the current text.

Against this background, we think, that this dissertation can be motivated. The reconstructed argument A and the discussions around this argument are, principally, philosophical matter. Our systematization, explication and analyses of Maslow's motivation and personality theories are more detailed than any of the foregoing analyses. This is also the case concerning the differences between B-cognition and D-cognition, Maslow's ontology and concerning the contents of consciousness in peak-experience. Furthermore these latter topics have not been analysed from a philosophical point of view before. Maslow's theory of Religion has not been discussed before, except to a small extent by Elmo. Maslow's philosophy of science has been discussed by Bärmark, but we think, our analyses supplements Bärmark's analyses and in some topics we and Bärmark come to different interpretations of Maslow's opinions. Maslow's philosophy science's relevance for Psychology of Religion has not been discussed before.

Chapter 2: Some Main Theses in Maslow's Motivation and Personality Theories.

Our main aim in this chapter is to give an account of and systematize some of the main theses in Maslow's motivation and personality theories. This account functions as a basis for the precization of the qualifications $X_1 \ldots X_n$ in premiss 1 in argument A. In the account, we shall also make explicit some of the features in Maslow's view of man.

The general outline of this chapter is as follows: (2.0.) a reconstruction of the structure of explanation in Maslow's theory of motivation, (2.1.) an account and systematization of some of the main theses in Maslow's theory of motivation and (2.2.) an account and systematization of the main theses in Maslow's personality theory. At the end of the chapter (2.3.), we shall give, on the grounds of the results of our analyses in 2.1. and 2.2. a precization of premisses (1) and (3) in Argument A.

2.0. Introduction

In his theory of motivation, Maslow attempts to explain human actions in terms of intentions, beliefs and satisfaction of needs. He gives explanations to inner factors which can be regarded as both mental and somatic factors. These inner factors *activate* human actions, i.e., they bring about a general state of activity. Maslow also suggests a theory of learning which is supposed to explain the *direction* of human actions.[1]

The following overreaching structure of explanation, in the form of a *practical syllogism* (in von Wright's meaning), is our reconstruction of a methodological presumption in Maslow's theory of motivation.[2]

Explanadum: A person P performs the action A (in situation S_1).

Given a large number of human types of action, Maslow presupposes a structure of explanation which can be reconstructed along the following lines:

Explanans: (1) P intends to attain the goal M_1
               (2) P thinks that P is in situation S_1
               (3) P thinks that in order to attain M_1, in situation S_1, P has to preform the action A

Explanandum: (4) P performs the action A in situation S_1

In his theory of motivation, Maslow attempts to elaborate on this explanation. He does so, with regard to *premiss 1*, by attempting to answer the question: Why has P to attain M_1? Maslow is primarily dealing with the inner factors, i.e., somatic and mental factors. The outer incentives or factors are dealt with very briefly.

When he attempts to elaborate on the explanation in the practical syllogism, he introduces in his answer to the question concerning premiss 1, a means-goal-reasoning which can be formulated as follows:

(I) M_1 is a means for P to attain some of the universal human fundamental goals, $FG_1 \ldots FG_n$.

According to Maslow, human actions can often be analysed in terms of means-goals-hierarchies.[3] Concerning *many of the large number* of human types of action which can be explained in terms of intentions and beliefs, the following is valid: intentions can, in turn, be explained as means to attain some universal human fundamental goals. A complication in Maslow's theory is that he also assumes that human beings have other intentions which are *not* means to attain these universal fundamental goals.[4]

In (I), Maslow subsumes P's intention in premiss 1 under the general assumption: a large number of human types of action is a means to attain some universal human fundamental goals. It is worth noting that, according to Maslow, these goals are not, generally speaking, consciously intended.

(I) can be interpreted as a teleological explanation. According to teleological explanations, P's action at time t_1 can be explained in terms of the fulfilment of goals at time t_2.[5] This type of explanation is, however, *not* in agreement with Maslow's opinion. Instead, he falls back on (at least in his later writings, see 2.1. thesis (i)) his freudian background and puts (I) in relation to:

(II) Every human being strives to attain the fundamental goals $FG_1 \ldots FG_n$ because the fulfilment of $FG_1 \ldots FG_n$ gratifies the universal, genetic and somatic based needs, the so called "basic needs".

In (II), Maslow connects the universal fundamental goals with universal, genetic and somatic based needs. He makes this connection by assuming that the genetic and somatic based needs are the inner somatic factors which bring about human actions, and the gratification of these needs is simultaneously the universal human fundamental goal.[6]

Maslow attempts, in (I), to explain human actions in terms of intentions and beliefs can be seen as a manifestation of his humanistic scientific perspective. His attempts, in (II), to explain human actions in terms of somatic based needs can be seen as a manifestation of his naturalistic scientific perspective.[7]

Maslow's answer to the question concerning premiss 1: Why has P to attain M_1? is twofold: in (II) the answer is related to an activated general variable which is understood in terms of somatic based needs, and in (I) the answer is related to a directed variable which is understood in terms of intentions, beliefs and fundamental goals. We shall clarify the relation between (I) and (II) in the following section.

2.1. Maslow's Theory of Motivation

Our course of analysis in this section is to make explicit and precizate some of the main theses in Maslow's theory of motivation, and to state some of his arguments in favour of these theses. We shall also analyse how some of these theses are logically related and, at the end of the section, we shall also give some critical remarks. Maslow revised and complemented his theory of motivation throughout the course of his writings. Our account will concentrate on versions of his theory of motivation after 1949, and the reason for this will be given below (see thesis (i)). Our account aims at giving contextual reasonable interpretations of Maslow's statements in his theory of motivation with special reference to the additions which he made after 1949.

We have in (II) above (2.0) made a freudian component explicit in Maslow's theory of motivation and a basic thesis in his theory of motivation is:

(i) Every human being has some "instinctoid" basic need

As we mentioned in section 1.2., Maslow does not generally define his terms, even basic terms, in his theory of motivation. We shall make the following contextual reasonable interpretations of the following basic terms. The term "drive" designates physiological nerve-impulses.[8] Other terms used by Maslow as synonyms for "drive" are "impulse" and "instigation". "Need" designates physiological nerve-impulses *and* a general state of activity (Maslow calls the latter "goalless urge"). Accordingly, the terms "drive" and "need" overlap each other. We must also note that "need" designates both latent and manifested needs in Maslow's writings. "Basic needs" designates needs which are universal, genetic and somatic based. With a "somatic based need", we shall, in the following, mean a need which has a physiological genetic drive as one cause for its manifestation.

Maslow assumes that human beings also have what he calls "non-basic needs" which primarily designate neurotic, learned and so called habit-needs. Maslow does not define the features which characterize these needs, but claims that they are not related to any genetic and somatic based basic needs.[9] (See critical remarks, point 1). Maslow describes the basic needs as instinctlike

26

and connects his theory of motivation with instinct theories. However, he does not put human needs in the same category as animals' needs. This was, according to Maslow, the big mistake of earlier instinct theories.[10] Maslow's characterization of animals' instincts is: drive, instrumental behavior and goal object or goal activity are genetic in substance, which, among other things, means that animals have a disposition to react to special inner or outer stimuli in a non-learned constant or stereotyped way.[11]

Human beings have, concerning basic needs and in contrast to animals, only a few instinct-rests left, i.e., genetic and somatic based needs, which are not accompanied by any genetic ideas of goal or ideas of means. Maslow stipulates the term "instinctoid" to designate the character of these needs.[12]

With "ideas of goal" we mean intentional ideas which are directed towards the object or activities which a person P thinks will satisfy the manifested need.[13] Maslow's descriptions of these intentional ideas are very vague. He does not precizate his statements concerning the psychological character of this content of consciousness. He merely gives brief descriptions, for instance, "the drive as it appears introspectively in consciousness", "consciously felt wants", "conscious desire", "conscious motivations content", and "seen directly in consciousness". It is hard from these cryptic descriptions to ascertain Maslow's opinion concerning the psychological character of this content of consciousness. However, with the help of some of the examples he gives, the psychological character can, in some cases, be lucid mental pictures.[14] (We shall make a more ambitious attempt to clarify his statements concerning intentional ideas in chapter 3). We must in these contents note that ideas of goal are not primarily ideas of objects, we have a desire to *eat* a steak, not only of a steak, or a desire to *cuddle* a person Q, not only of person Q.[15] It is not clear if Maslow makes this distinction. His statements are too vague for any contextual reasonable interpretation.

Statements concerning intentional ideas of means refer to P's ideas regarding which behavior P thinks will lead to the attainment or realization of the intentional ideas of goal. We must in this case also note that intentional ideas of means are *related to premiss 3* in the practical syllogism above. We have to distinguish between the following levels:

a. Premiss (1): P intends to attain M_1. In his theory of motivation Maslow tries to explain this by: M_1 is a means to achieve fundamental goals.
b. Premiss (3): P thinks that in order to attain M_1, in situation S_1, P has to preform the action A. Intentional ideas of means are related to this premiss because these ideas set P to preform just A.

The first time Maslow characterized man's basic needs as instinctoid was in 1949.[16] Earlier, Maslow made use of what we shall call a functionalistic model of explanation when he went about explaining man's basic needs. Below, we shall describe and distinguish, very briefly, between this functionalistic model of explanation and what we shall call the freudian model of explanation; the later dominates Maslow's writings after 1949.[17]

The functionalistic model of explanation: In the expositions concerning relations between intentional ideas of goal and fundamental goals (see II in section 2.0) which we can find in *Principles of Abnormal Psychology* (1941), the fundamental goals are described as *solutions* to certain universal "main problems of life". Given these problems, Maslow (and Mittelmann) distinguish between the following main categories:

1. Problems which are caused by biological needs, i.e., to get food, shelter, warmth, etc.
2. Problems which are caused by learning, i.e., to get power, money, prestige, etc.
3. "Problems set by relatively internal psychological demands", i.e., to get self-esteem, independence, strength, safety, love, belongingness, etc.[18]

The genesis of these "main problems of life" cannot be explained only on the grounds that they gratify some genetic and somatic based needs, some of these problems are caused by cultural-learning, for example 2 above. Maslow regards human actions as means to find solutions to these "main problems of life" and he explains, for example, neurotic behavior and more serious psychopathological behavior as inadequate solutions to these "main problems of life".[19] (One basic assumption in Maslow's theory concerning psychopathologenesis is: these pathologies are caused by the frustration which human beings experience when they cannot find any solutions to these "main problems of life". Neurotic and psychotic behavior are reactions to this frustration or a holding of an inadequate behavior which P thinks is an attempt to find a solution to P's "main problems of life").

One important assumption in the functionalistic model of explanation is that not all of the fundamental goals are related to satisfaction of somatic localized drives.

In the articles *Preface to Motivation Theory* and *A Theory of Human Motivation* (1943),[20] Maslow describes this model of explanation simultaneously with a freudian model of explanation. The functionalistic model of explanation is, in these articles, alluded to in Maslow's assumptions that some of the fundamental goals are culturally dependent. He thinks that the classification of different motives, desires or wants would be very difficult if he did not postulate these fundamental goals, due to the fact that ideas of goal, instrumental behavior or goal objects show a great degree of variation in different cultures. Maslow also uses Allport's term "functional autonomy" which, in Maslow's contexts, means that some of the basic needs could primarily have been means to satisfy basic needs but they have, throughout an individual's life, gradually been liberated from these basic needs and developed into basic needs themselves.

The freudian model of explanation: In this model of explanation, the fundamental goals are regarded as satisfaction of genetic and somatic based needs (basic needs). Maslow is however very careful when he formulates this assumption. He writes:

> "... the foregoing considerations encourage us to the hypothesis that basic needs are in some sense, and to some appreciable degree, constitutional or hereditary in their determination".[21]

> "Our main hypothesis is that human urges or basic needs alone may be innately given to at least some appreciable degree. The pertinent behavior or ability, cognition or affection need not also be innate, but may be (by our hypothesis) learned, canalized or expressive ... This is to say that the hereditary component of basic need may be seen as simple conative lack, tied to no instrinsic goal-achieving behavior, as blind directionless demands, like Freud's id impulses ... What has to be learned is goal-bent (coping) behavior."[22]

This hypothesis, according to Maslow, cannot as yet be experimentally proved (1954), the reason being that the genetic and neurological sciences have not as yet developed so far (but he thinks the day will come).[23] Maslow asserts, however, that there are some arguments in favour of this hypothesis. His key argument is to disregard the alternative, which, according to Maslow, is the assumption that the basic needs are learnt and he questions, for example, if the need for love is learnt.[24] In this model of explanation, Maslow assumes that: (a) in the human organism certain needs emerge which, through learning, are associated with certain ideas of goals (see thesis (ii) below) and, (b) everyone of man's fundamental goals is ultimately satisfaction of the genetic and somatic based needs. In both of the above mentioned models of explanation, it is assumed that intentional ideas of goal are means to satisfy fundamental goals. The difference being that in the freudian model of explanation every intentional ideas of goal which is related to the fundamental goals is also related to satisfaction of genetic and somatic based needs. This is not the case in the functionalistic model of explanation.

The freudian model of explanation is the dominating one after 1949 and it is during this period that Maslow formulates the epistemological views which are the primary object of investigation in this dissertation. This is the reason why we shall in the continuing analyses of Maslow's theory of motivation only clarify the theses which Maslow makes in relation to the freudian model of explanation.

Another basic assumption in Maslow's theory of motivation is:

(ii) All of human beings' intentional ideas of goal and ideas of means are learnt.

Maslow explains the connection between the basic needs and intentional ideas of goal by referring to a special theory of learning. According to this theory, Maslow assumes that when P tests different goal objects and goal activities, P gradually makes the choice as to which objects or activities give P satisfaction of a given manifested basic need. The criterion for this choice is the degree of pleasure which P gets from different objects and activities. The one which gives P the greatest pleasure is the one which P selects.[25] When P has learnt this, and when P feels unsatisfied, P makes an association between this basic need and a learnt intentional idea of goal. This association is also caused by incentives from the environment. Maslow calls this kind of learning "canalization" (a term which Maslow took over from G. Murphy).[26]

In Maslow's argumentation in favour of the above mentioned learnt-relationship between pleasure and basic needs, he gets support from Cannon's hypothesis concerning "wisdom of the body". According to this hypothesis, the guidance of goal object or goal activity is through the degree of pleasure.[27]

Concerning all of the basic needs, Maslow also assumes a homeostasis model (with exception of the self-actualizing needs, see (viii), below). According to this model, a cycle of basic needs consists of an initial state of non-equilibrium which gives rise to nerve-impulses and which in turn is one cause for a person P experiencing some idea of goal. When P then performs an instrumental behavior and attains the goal, P gets satisfaction, which, physiologically, can be understood as a solution to a tension in the organism and which P experiences as a "relief"; the end of the cycle is when a state of equilibrium is established. This capability of self-regulation means that man has an ability to choose goal objects or goal activities which keep the organism in equilibrium, and in some cases develops the individual (for the latter see thesis (viii)).[28]

He attributes to people different degrees of ability to choose appropriate goal objects and goal activities which are connected with the basic needs. Similar to D. Levy, he distinguishes between "good" and "bad" choosers. He uses this distinction later on in his theory concerning self-actualizing people. Such people are "good" choosers and they provide the normative ideal for the type of goal objects or goal activities which people ought to choose.[29]

An important consequence which follows from the assumption of the human being's self-regulating capability, and which Maslow emphasizes, is his stress, in education, on various individuals' development through their spontaneous choice. The leading motto in education is "let him be".[30]

30

Maslow suggests that the ideas of means are to be learnt through "trial-and-error".[31]

Which intentional ideas of goal or ideas of means a person P has in different situations is dependent on the learning P has received. Maslow is inclined to ascribe behavior and ideas of means greater influence by cultural-learning than ideas of goal.[32] He states that there are no genetic intentional ideas of goal connected with a given basic need, but he distinguishes between "proper-gratifiers" and "non-proper-gratifiers". One possible interpretation of this distinction is that the realm of variation for objects or activities which can satisfy a given basic need is limited and they can vary, but the vagueness of his statements do not permit a contextual reasonable interpretation of his standpoint.[33]

(iii) The basic needs are unconscious

Maslow characterizes the basic needs as unconscious[34] and asserts that knowledge of these basic needs is often achieved through some form of analysis in which the "conscious motivation content of everyday life" is analysed.

According to Maslow, we shall find in these analyses that many of the learnt ideas of goal only serve as means to satisfy more fundamental goals. Maslow gives the following example of an analysis of this kind: P has a desire to earn more money which P needs in order to buy a car. The unconscious need in this case can be that P wants to keep his self-esteem, since his neighbour has a car, and if P shall keep his self-esteem, P has to buy a car in order not to feel inferior to his neighbour.[35]

Maslow varies his formulations of the relation between the basic needs and our learnt ideas of goal. Sometimes he uses the description: our learnt ideas of goal are means in order to satisfy basic needs which he, in this case, calls "ends in themselves". The most frequently used formulations are in accordance with the freudian model of explanation: ideas of goal represent or symbolize the basic needs and the attainment of the goal object or goal activities gratifies the basic needs which the ideas of goal represent or symbolize (see also thesis (iv) below). The vagueness of the statements concerning the determination of the relationship between the basic needs and the learnt ideas of goal can be explained as a result of Maslow's oscillation between the above mentioned models of explanation. Concerning the meaning of the term "unconscious" in relation to the basic needs and in the freudian model of explanation, we shall make the following contextual resonable interpretation: the term "unconscious" designates that P does not have any insight, that P's learnt intentional ideas of goal ultimately aim at satisfying some special somatic based needs. According to this interpretation, Maslow uses the term "unconscious" in order to designate that P does not have insight of what the ultimate goals for P's intentional ideas of goal are, that is, satisfaction of genetic and somatic based needs (the basic needs).[36]

This contextual reasonable interpretation of the term "unconscious" can be contrasted with Freud's meaning of the term. At least in his *Interpretation of Dreams* (1902), this term designates a drive's idea of goal which is repressed to a level in the human consciousness called "The Unconscious". This idea is of a psychic character, but inspite of this, it cannot be within reach for introspection.[37]

As a corollary to (iii), the following assumption can be formulated:

(iv) Some of man's intentional ideas of goal are means to gratify basic needs

Maslow characterizes many of man's intentional ideas of goal as representations or symbols for the somatic based basic needs. It is hard to determine the psychological character of these representations or symbols due to the vagueness of Maslow's descriptions of the psychological character of the intentional ideas of goal. These representations or symbols are means to gratify the basic needs in the sense that the attainment of these ideas of goal implies gratification of the somatic based needs.[38] In Maslow's example above, P buys a car as a means to gratify P's self-esteem need. The idea of goal expresses basic needs and when P attains the objected goal, it gratifies the expressed basic needs.

Another assumption which Maslow asserts in this context is:

(v) An intentional idea of goal often symbolizes several basic needs.

Maslow assumes that several basic needs can be channelled in one intentional idea of goal, the so called "multiple motivation". It is very seldom that an idea of goal symbolizes only one basic need. One consequence of this is: if two persons have a similar idea of goal, this idea of goal can channel different basic needs.[39]

The difference between the terms "canalization" and "channel" is that the first designates *one need* which can be symbolized by several different ideas of goal (see (ii)) while the later designates *one idea of goal* which represents or symbolizes, simultaneously, several basic needs, that is, multiple motivation.

One variation of thesis (v) is Maslow's opinion that ideas of goal, for, a person P, can have a double meaning, i.e., "intrinsic meaning" and "symbolic meaning".[40] This opinion is a consequence of the earlier mentioned vague distinction between "proper gratifiers" and "non-proper-gratifiers". Proper gratifier is connected with intrinsic meaning in the sense that Maslow thinks there is a more "direct" connection between a basic need and a goal object/

activity with an intrinsic meaning, than between a basic need and a goal object/activity with a symbolic meaning.

(vi) *The basic needs can be classified into two categories — deficiency needs and growth-needs*

Maslow states necessary and sufficient criteria for distinguishing basic needs from non-basic needs. He also asserts certain preconditions for the basic needs' gratification, for example, freedom of speech and a certain freedom of action. One necessary and sufficient criterion for a need to be a basic need is: if a need is not gratified, the frustration causes neuroses or more serious psychopathologies.[41] Maslow also states other criteria for example; these needs follow the individual throughout his life.[42]

Maslow differentiates between deficiency-needs and growth-needs. The deficiency-needs are common to all human beings and can be characterized in accordance with the cycle of needs described in (ii). When he characterizes the growth-needs, which he also describes as self-actualizing needs (see further (viii)), he does not use the model of homeostasis. In the growth-needs, we can find the following elements: a state of non-equilibrium, nerve-impulses, idea of goal, idea of means and instrumental behavior. The experiences of gratification can be described as joyful experiences, and P also experiences a "Funktionlust" when P is able to perform the activity which gratifies the growth-needs. These activities do not have any climax, they go on and on, and the gratification is given in the performance of the activity. This experience of gratification will be contrasted with the experience of gratification of deficiency-needs which is only a momentary experience of relief. Another difference is that the individual's reactions to the drives of deficiency-needs are negative or a tendency to repress the drives because they are not experienced as pleasurable. The drives of the growth-needs, on the other hand, cause the individual to react positively because the experience of gratification brings joy.[43]

Maslow's assumptions of growth-needs and the so called self-actualizing drive can be connected with the polemics which Maslow directs towards the theories of motivation which reduce *all* needs to deficiency-needs and which also assume the model of homeostasis. The reason why Maslow assumes the existence of growth-needs is: to explain activities which are not related to deficiency-needs, for example, creativity, problem-solving and struggle for independence. Earlier theories of motivation have been limited to deficiency-needs because their founders had only studied animals or psychic "sick" people. Maslow states that the assumption of growth-needs is necessary in order to explain and understand the actions of "healthy people".[44]

*(vii) The deficiency-needs can be classified into the following categories: physio-
        logical needs, safety needs, belongingness and love needs, and esteem
        needs.*

The interpretation of these categories is uncertain. According to the freudian model of explanation, it is not clear if the examples which Maslow gives under each category express *one* or *several needs*. The question is: are the examples which Maslow gives under one category only different expressions for *one* deficiency-need, for example, safety need, *or* are they expressions for *several* needs which Maslow only classifies under one common category? He explicitly classifies several sorts of needs under the category of physiological needs. Concerning the other deficiency-needs, Maslow uses plural forms, e.g., "safety needs", "the belongingness and love needs", and "the esteem needs".[45] This is a reason for us to make the following contextual reasonable interpretation: in every category there are several kinds or sorts of needs which Maslow only classifies under one category.

The above mentioned vagueness is a consequence of Maslow's oscillation between the two models of explanation. In the functionalistic model of explanation, we can interpret these categories as *sets* which have as their elements different drives, needs and ideas of goal and which are means to gratify needs, but not of necessity somatic based needs. In the freudian model of explanation, the examples which Maslow gives under each category can be interpreted as needs and ideas of goal which express or is a representation of *one* or *several latent needs*. As we stated above, there is reason to interpret Maslow's standpoint as: he assumes several needs. A contextual reasonable interpretation is not possible because Maslow's statements on this topic are too vague.

Categories of deficiency-needs:

Physiological needs: for example, needs for food, liquid, sleep, activities of the body and sexual needs.

Safety needs: for example, needs for safety, security, shelter, freedom from fear and anxiety, need of feeling of homeliness, rutine and possibilities to control and predict events in the future.

Belongingness and safety needs: for example, needs of affectionate relations with people, i.e., husband/wife, children and friends, and the need of feeling that one belongs to a group, community, etc.[46]

Self-esteem needs: Maslow divides these needs into two subsets:

a. need of high self-esteem which is psychologically grounded in one's own knowledge of one's competence.

b. need of high self-esteem which is psychologically grounded in other people's esteem of onseself, for example, the need to have prestige, status and a good reputation.[47]

(viii) Every human being has self-actualizing needs

The deficiency-needs are common to every human being and their realms of variation of proper gratifiers are fairly limited. Every human being also has so called "self-actualizing needs" which Maslow characterizes as more specifically directed for every unique individual than the deficiency-needs.[48] Our contextual reasonable interpretation is: these needs have for every individual a more limited realm of variation than the deficiency-needs.

The self-actualizing needs express themselves in the following ways:
1. P has needs to actualize P's special-talents. The examples which Maslow gives are, for instance, music-, sport-, mathematic- and art-talents.
2. P has needs to be engaged in social-ethical topics which P experiences as a mission. This mission is primarily directed towards other human being's welfare. The examples which Maslow mentions are: the struggles against nuclear warfare and overpopulation.

   Maslow develops this social-ethical direction in his later writings. He assumes that self-actualizing people, that is, people who have their deficiency-needs gratified and who in their activities try to gratify their self-actualization needs, are struggling to actualize some non-moral values, the so called "Being-values" (concerning Being-values, see section 3.2.).[49]
3. P is engaged in trying to get more self-knowledge and get more knowledge in order to go through P's *Weltanshauung* thoroughly.[50]

In his statements concerning self-actualizing needs, we can reconstruct the following two implicit assumptions:
a. every human being has one or several special-talents
b. if a person P has a special-talent, P also has the interest to develop this or these special talents.

It is uncertain whether he thinks (1) that P will actualize only one of his talents (for instance, the strongest or the one which P, in relation to other people, is best at), this opinion will be called the *ideal of specialization*, or (2) that P will actualize several of his talents even if P has different aptitude for some of them. This opinion will be called the *ideal of versatility*.[51]

Our contextual reasonable interpretation is that Maslow on this topic assumes and (note!) recommends the ideal of versatility. One reason for our interpretation is his holistic view of man which assumes that all human beings' abilities or talents ought to be actualized; the emotional life, for example, ought not to be repressed in favour of the intellectual life.[52] In Maslow's

35

judgement in favour of the ideal of versatility, we can see that his normative ideal is connected with his descriptive aim.

Maslow also assumes that the basic needs stand in a certain relation to each other:

(ix) The basic needs stand in a dominance-hierarchical relationship to each other

According to this assumption, one basic need has to be gratified to a certain degree before a "higher" need in the dominance-hierarchy asserts itself and claims to be gratified. There is a certain proportional relationship between the degree of gratification of the "lower" needs and the degree of strength of the "higher" needs.[53] Maslow assumes that man always struggles for gratification of needs because as soon as one need is gratified another "higher" need in the dominance-hierarchy asserts itself and claims to be satisfied. The basic needs have the above reported to order of dominance, that is, most dominating are physiological needs, followed respectively by safety needs, belongingness and love needs, and self-esteem needs. Maslow also gives criteria for this hierarchy of dominance.[54]

When the deficiency-needs are gratified the self-actualizing needs assert themselves and claim to be gratified. However, Maslow's description of the relationship between the deficiency-needs and the self-actualizing needs vary. In some texts, he describes the gratification of the deficiency-needs as necessary and sufficient conditions for the actualization of self-actualizing needs, in others, the gratification of the deficiency-needs are only necessary conditions, and in still others, he describes the gratification of the deficiency-needs as not even necessary conditions.[55]

(x) The basis needs are ethically neutral

A great difference between Maslow's theory of motivation, and, for example, Freud's, is Maslow's characterization of human instinctoid basic needs as ethically neutral.[56] Maslow asserts that many theologians, Freud and even Darwin have explained, in a wrong way, the genesis of many of man's moral evil actions by their view of man's instincts. They have identified man's instincts with the instincts of animals, and Maslow calls this view "bad-animal-interpretation". This view has led to fatal consequences, for example, the opinions that man's manifested instincts express themselves very clear in criminals' and mentally deranged persons' behavior, that there is a necessary conflict between the interests of various individuals and the interests of the community, and that there is a conflict between man's reason and his instincts.[57]

Maslow states that there is no necessary moral evil in the need for food, safety, belongingness, etc., and he asserts that aggressive behavior can be said to emerge when these basic needs are not gratified. Aggressive behavior, according to this view, is a defence for gratification which failed to appear.[58]

Maslow also distinguishes between "healthy aggression", for instance, as a reaction to exploitation or unjust behavior and "unhealthy aggression".[59]

A very important application of thesis (x) is Maslow's emphasizes that the aim of upbringing and education is to actualize man's potential basic needs.[60]

(xi) The basic needs are weak

The instincts of animals are strong, but man's instinctoid basic needs are weak, in so far as they can very easily be repressed, for instance, by the pressure of culture, learning, habit and negative attitudes. This means that the individual's content of consciousness will be dominated by learnt ideas of goal which do not channel basic needs. The basic needs are, however, strong in another respect, namely, their attempt during the individual's whole life to be gratified in a lot of different ways and they cause neurosis or more serious psychic sickness if they do not get this gratification.[61]

As we can notice from the theses (i)-(xi), Maslow has a potential-actualization model in his theory of motivation and view of man. Man has certain genetic potentials which Maslow describes as "inner-core", "inner-nature", "essence", "raw material", "Real Self", etc. Maslow's descriptions of the extension of this "inner core" is mainly the basic needs.[62] Maslow describes these as man's potentials and they demand their actualization via their innate drives which activate human actions. This actualization occurs in confrontation with CTR (in this context Maslow often uses the term "extra-psychic world"). The basic needs are channelled through learning of ideas of goal and the gratification of these needs are dependent on the surrounding people, culture and nature.[63]

If the basic needs are gratified P actualizes P's Real Self[64] (concerning the term "Real Self", see section 2.2.). If P does not try to gratify these needs, P is subjected to "intrinsic conscience". This term is taken over by Maslow from Horney and Fromm and in Maslow's contexts it designates a kind of conscience which registers and reacts if P does not really try to gratify P's basic needs. Intrinsic conscience emerges when there is a difference between what P is doing and what P can be doing — according to P's potentials. This kind of conscience is a theoretical supplement, Maslow assumes, to Freud's "super-ego". The latter has developed through other person's behavior, attitudes and judgements (internalization). This is not the way intrinsic conscience develops, according to Maslow. Our contextual reasonable interpretations is: it is innate and starts to function when P does not actualize P's Real Self.[65] In order to actualize one's Real Self and avoid intrinsic conscience, Maslow emphasizes the importance of self-knowledge. One aspect of self-knowledge is judging which ideas of goal channel basic needs and which do not. Maslow describes this ability as the ability to listen to "the inner signals".[66]

When P actualizes P's Real Self, P gets experiences of identity. These experiences of identity are given when P's activity is directed towards actualizing the basic needs and especially the self-actualizing needs. The experience of identity is not given through some cognitive content in consciousness, but in the experiences of P's endeavours to attain ideas of goal which P has set up and which expresses basic needs.[67]

Maslow states that freedom is the ability to be able to identify one's basic needs *and* to have the power to act in order to gratify these needs. Maslow touches, in these context, on Riesman's distinction between "other-directed" and "inner-directed" people. Maslow states that P is inner-directed and free, if P has the ability to identify P's basic needs and the power to act in order to gratify P's given potentials.

> "For if we assume that the healthy organism is, paradigmatically, basic need-gratified and therefore released for self-actualization, then we have thereby also assumed that this organism develops from within by intrinsic growth tendencies, in the Bergsonian sense, rather than from without, in the behavioristic sense of environmental determinism. The neurotic organism is one that lacks basic need satisfactions that can come only from other people. It is therefore more dependent on other people and is less autonomous and self-determined, i.e., more shaped by the nature of the environment and less shaped by its own intrinsic nature. Such relative independence of environment as is found in the healthy person does not, of course, mean lack of commerce with it; it means only that in these contacts the person's ends and his own nature are primary determinants, and that the environment is primarily a means to the person's self-actualizing ends. This is truly psychological freedom."[68]

2.1.1. Some critical remarks

Below, we shall note very briefly some critical remarks which can be made with regard to Maslow's theory of motivation.

1. A great lack in his theory of motivation is the basic terms' vagueness, for example, "need", "drive", "motive", "desire" and "satisfaction". He does not define his terms and perhaps he presupposes that the reader knows their meaning through ordinary language or through contemporary usages in different theories of motivation. This is one reason why our contextual reasonable interpretations of these terms have a certain unreliability.

In our contextual reasonable interpretations, we have distinguished between the following needs in Maslow's theory of motivation:

38

I. Basic needs	a) Deficiency-needs	1. physiological needs
		2. safety needs
		3. belongingness and love needs
		4. self-esteem needs
	b) Growth-needs	1. self-actualizing needs

II. Non-basic needs, that is, the needs which Maslow describes as not being related to any genetic and somatic based needs. Maslow gives us the following examples, neurotic, learnt and habit-needs.

The criteria which Maslow states for distinguishing between basic needs and non-basic needs are reported in thesis (vi). In this thesis we also reported how Maslow characterizes deficiency-needs and growth-needs. Maslow does not state, however, any criteria which distinguish between the four categories of deficiency-needs. We can conjecture that the degree of psychic sickness is one criterion. The more serious psychic illness which P has, the lower down in the dominance-hierarchy is the basic need which is frustrated. (Naturally we also had to count the degree of frustration of a given deficiency need.) In these assumptions and conjectures, we can note how Maslow connects his theory of motivation with his theory of personality. This connection will be clarified some more in section 2.2. However, we shall mention one connection in this context. In the theory he sets forth in order to explain psychopathogenesis, he makes the assumption that frustration of safety needs causes more serious psychic problems than frustration of self-esteem needs, and this is one reason why Maslow classifies the safety needs as lower down in the hierarchy of dominance.

2. An important conceptual vagueness which makes contextual reasonable interpretations of his theory of motivation very unreliable is the vagueness of the term "basic needs". In our account, we have distinguished between two models of explanation (the functionalistic and freudian). But even within the freudian model of explanation the term "basic needs" is vague. Is there one need *or* are their several needs which are channelled in different ideas of goal and which express a named basic need? A contextual reasonable interpretation is that there are several needs (see (viii)).

3. The explanation which Maslow gives for a great number of P's actions is that their ultimate aim is to gratify some fundamental goals. Maslow identifies these fundamental goals in the freudian model of explanation as gratification of some somatic localized basic needs. But others of P's action can aim at gratifying other ideas of goal which are learnt and not related to the fundamental goals. One important criticism is that Maslow does not formulate any criteria which enable us to know if an action aims at gratifying:

a) one basic need *or* several basic needs, or
b) either one or several basic needs *or* one or several non-basic needs, or
c) one or several basic needs *and* one or several non-basic needs, or
d) in the case an action aims at gratifying one or several of the basic needs, *which one or ones* of these is the case?

Such criteria are in fact almost impossible to formulate because in our thesis (v) (multiple motivation), Maslow assumes that one intentional idea of goal often channels several basic needs, and sometimes several basic needs and non-basic needs. Maslow is consistent when he states that non-basic needs cannot be introspectively differientiated from basic needs.[69] These factors make Maslow's explanations of P's particular actions as ultimately aiming at some fundamental goal almost impossible to verify.

4. Another difficulty in close relationship to 3 is that people's actions and intentional ideas of goal do not show any invariance. But Maslow states that he can explain many of these actions as aiming at some fundamental goal. He does this by characterizing these fundamental goals as unconscious. One weakness in his theory is that this latter assumption can be described as an *ad hoc*-assumption to save his assumption concerning fundamental goals.

5. In 1949, Maslow switched from the functionalistic model of explanation to the freudian model of explanation. By this he assumes that every human being has genetic and somatic based needs, and that ultimately every human being strives to gratify these needs. This changeover can be critically described as follows: a heuristic model (in the functionalistic model) which is constructed in order to explain human actions and which contains an assumption of some universal fundamental goals becomes a model in which Maslow assumes that these fundamental goals are some genetic and somatic needs. The heuristic assumed fundamental goals are transformed from a heuristic assumption to the assumption of the existence of universal, genetic and somatic based needs.

We can now clarify the relation (see section 2.0.) between the statements (I), M_1 is a means for P to attain some of the universal human fundamental goals, $FG_1 \ldots FG_n$, and (II), every human being strives to attain the fundamental goals $FG_1 \ldots FG_n$ because the fulfilment of $FG_1 \ldots FG_n$, gratifies the universal, genetic and somatic based needs, the so called "basic needs". Firstly, Maslow had a funtionalistic model of explanation, but after 1949 he more and more applied a freudian model of explanation. In the latter, he explains one activating general causal factor in physiological terms of genetic and somatic based needs. People learn (a) different ideas of goal which channel these genetic and somatic based needs, and (b) different ideas of means, and by this Maslow states that people have common fundamental goals in spite of the fact that people perform varied actions and have varied ideas of goal. The fundamental goals can be identified as the gratification of the ideas of goal which channel the genetic and somatic based needs.

6. The vagueness of Maslow's term "fundamental goal" is another critical point in Maslow's theory of motivation. Is the fundamental goal the experience of pleasure which emerges when the basic needs are gratified? If such is the case, Maslow's theory of motivation can be classified as a hedonistic theory. Another possibility is that these goals, at least concerning the deficiency-needs, can be described as an attainment of a state of equilibrium. There is also a possibility that these two proposed fundamental goals can be combined. The state of equilibrium concerns the physiological level and this state causes the experience of pleasure on the psychological level.

7. Another vagueness is how to interpret the relationship between a drive of a basic need and the state of activation which it is supposed to cause. The drive, that is, on the physiological level, is a cause of a general state of activation on the psychological level. It is not clear if this drive is (a) a necessary causal condition, or (b) a sufficient causal condition, for this state of activation to emerge.[70] Another vagueness is whether or not the physiological drive only brings about a general state of activation or if it also has a directing determination. Maslow's terms "proper gratifier" and "intrinsic meaning" suggest a directing determination.

8. With regard to the mind-body problem, Maslow states a dualistic view which can be classified as an *interactionism.*[71] One reason for this classification is Maslow's assumption that genetic and somatic based needs are causes for man's ideas of goal to emerge. Another reason is Maslow's stress on the close relationship between mental health and somatic health. Two difficulties of principle matter emerge from this view:
a. Maslow does not explain how a physiological process can be a cause of a psychological process, for instance, how a drive can be a cause of P's ideas of goal at time t.
b. Maslow does not explain how P's ideas of goal and ideas of means can be a cause of P's bodily movements at time t, for example, how P's idea to get some water can be a cause of P's bodily movements in order to get some water, for instance, to put one leg before the other, to raise one arm, etc.

9. Maslow's theory of motivation has had great influence, not least within industrial management. A number of psychologists have tried to test the theory or parts of the theory experimentally. Wabha & Bridwell have done a survey of these investigations (35 different investigations). Their conclusion is that Maslow's theory of motivation gets little experimental support.[72] Mas-

low formulated his theory primarily from theoretical considerations and from his clinical experiences.[73] Maslow's theory had to be very difficult to test experimentally, and one reason for this is the vagueness of the basic terms in his theory (see especially our critical remark in point 3 above). The psychologists who try to find experimental support for Maslow's theory of motivation have to consider these serious conceptual vaguenesses.

2.2. Maslow's Theory of Personality

2.2.0. Introduction

Maslow assumes that different effects emerge from the gratification of the basic needs, *one* being changes in the personality. The following account reports and systematizes Maslow's statements concerning some of these changes in the personality.

This account aims at giving a background to:

a) our analyses of Maslow's descriptions of what a person P experiences during and after peak-experience and

b) our precizations and analyses of the qualifications $X_1 \ldots X_n$ in premiss 1 in Argument A.

Maslow asserts that when P gets gratification of his basic needs, P develops certain personality traits. This relation between Maslow's theory of motivation and his theory of personality can be expressed with the help of the following schema:

Schema I: (1) P strives to gratify the needs $B_1 \ldots B_n$
(2) P gets gratification of the needs $B_1 \ldots B_n$
From (1) and (2) Maslow concludes: (3) P develops the personality traits X, Y, Z ...

Maslow applies schema I, inversely, when he explains neurotic and more serious psychopathological behavior, hence premiss (2) is transformed:

Schema II: (1) P strives to gratify the needs $B_1 \ldots B_n$
(2) P *does not* get gratification of the needs $B_1 \ldots B_n$
From (1) and (2) Maslow concludes: (3) P develops the personality traits R, S, T ...

"My conclusion was, speaking very generally, that neuroses, as well as other psychic illnesses, were due primarily to absence of certain gratifications (of objectively and subjectively perceivable demands or wishes). These I called basic needs and called them instinctoid because they had to be gratified or else illness (or diminution of humanness, i.e., loss of some of the characteristics that define humanness) would result. It was implied that neuroses were closer to being deficiency diseases than had been thought."[74]

"However we define threat, certainly there is one aspect that we must never neglect. An ultimate definition, no matter what else it might include, must certainly be related to the basic goals, values, or needs of the organism. This means that any theory of psychopathogenesis in turn must rest directly upon theory of motivation."[75]

The needs $B_1 \ldots B_n$ can be identified as the basic needs. The personality traits X, Y, Z ... will be described under section 2.2.2. below. Schemata I and II express a "gratification and frustration"-theory of personality which Maslow compares with "association"-theories of personality. He suggests that the latter had to be complemented with a gratification and frustration-theory.[76]

The term "personality trait" designates not only behavior, but even thought, feeling, impulses to act, disposition and attitude. In some contexts, Maslow also assumes one general structure of personality which can be described as the sum total of a person P's particular personality traits. In his earlier writings, he names two examples of such general structures of personality namely "high or low self-esteem" and "high or low security".[77]

Schemata I and II are very general and can therefore be misleading. Below, we shall make an attempt to clarify these schemata in the following way:

1. There are special relations between gratification and frustration of the basic needs *and* the development of specific personality traits. One example which Maslow mentions is the so called "meta-pathologies" which express themselves as feelings of emptiness, hopelessness, rootlessness, existential boredom, etc. These meta-pathologies arise when the self-actualizing needs are not gratified.[78]

   In general, Maslow does not assert any specific relations between particular deficiency-needs and particular personality traits. He discusses these relationships at some length in the article *The Role of Basic Need Gratification in Psychological Theory*.[79] We shall not describe these relationships further here, it suffices to merely state that Maslow does not qualify these relationships in any precise way.

2. In his research about self-actualizing people, Maslow tries to investigate the relationship between the gratification of the needs $B_1 \ldots B_n$ and the personality traits X, Y, Z ... He is, however, very careful when he formulates these relationships, and he states that the gratification of the basic needs are a necessary causal condition but not a sufficient causal condition for the genesis of the personality traits X, Y, Z ...[80] This has relevance for our interpretation of premiss (1) in Argument A (see, 2.3.).

3. The relationships between the non-gratification of the basic needs and the genesis of the personality traits, R, S, T ... are stated in Maslow's theory of psychopathogenesis. He does this mainly in *Principles of Abnormal Psychology*. We shall not describe these theories here because they are not relevant for the realms of investigation in this dissertation.

43

Maslow connects his theories of basic need with his theory of self-actualization. He uses the terms "self-actualization" and "self-actualizing" in several ways and in the following we shall distinguish between:

I.   Self-actualizing as a process
II. The characteristics of self-actualizing people
III. Self-actualizing as a normative ideal of life

2.2.1. Self-actualizing as a process

We can make the following contextual reasonable interpretation of Maslow's description of self-actualizing as a process. When P, in P's process of life, gets gratifications of the deficiency-needs, P can direct P's activity to the gratification of P's self-actualizing needs. This means that in every choice situation, P actualizes P's potentials and P makes, in Maslow's terms, a "growth-choice" or "progression-choice" and not a "safety-choice" or "regression-choice". In the latter case, P stays in well known circumstances because P is afraid to leave a safety situation and face a new situation. If P makes safety-choices, P does not actualize P's potentials, instead, P satisfies other people's wishes and demands and these decide P's choices. In this way P loses his Real Self and P is forced to form P's personality after other people's demands. If P instead, in P's process of life, makes growth-choices, P actualizes P's Real Self. P then listens to the inner signals and a self-regulative process begins (we described this under thesis (ii) in section 2.1.). In this way P "discovers and uncovers" P's Real Self.[81]

Maslow describes the conflict between safety-choice and growth-choice as follows:

> "This basic dilemma or conflict between the defensive forces and the growth trends I conceive to be existential, imbedded in the deepest nature of the human being, now and forever into the future."[82]

Self-actualizing is a continuing endeavour, a dynamic process of gradually actualizing one's potentials. With a term borrowed from G. Ryle, we can characterize Maslow's term "self-actualizing" as a "process-verb".

> "To make the growth choice instead of the fear choice a dozen times a day is to move a dozen times a day toward self-actualizing. Self-actualization is an ongoing process."[83]

2.2.2. The characteristics of self-actualizing people.

Maslow devotes plenty of space in his works to descriptions of characteristics which he finds in people whom he judges to be self-actualizing people.

44

During 1946—1949 he carried out a research in order to determine these characteristics.[84] The result of this research will be reported and systematized below. We shall, in an initial systematization, distinguish between the following categories of descriptions:

1. The self-actualizing people's relation to themselves
2. The self-actualizing people's relation to other people
3. The self-actualizing people's cognition of CTR

The characteristics under 1 and 2 will be briefly described below. We shall deal with 3 along with our analysis of the problems in Psychology of Knowledge and Epistemology in chapters 3 and 4 because Maslow's descriptions of self-actualizing people's cognition of CTR primarily concern these topics.

1. The self-actualizing people's relation to themselves

I. They have great self-knowledge which means:
    a. they can distinguish between which of their needs are basic needs and which are non-basic needs,
    b. they can distinguish between their own opinions, abilities and feelings and those which other people have forced upon them,
    c. they have identified and to a great extent removed their mechanisms of defense and recalled and lived through earlier traumatic experiences,
    d. they have discovered and are engaged in their mission.
II. They are self-accepting which means that they know and accept their nature ("inner-core") with its particular potentials and *shortcomings*. There is no, or a very little, conflict between "Real Self" and "Ideal Self" because they know their potentials. One cause for this is that they have uncovered other people's misconceptions of what other people think are the self-actualizing people's potentials.
III. One consequence of their degree of self-knowledge and self-acceptance is that they develop a spontaneity and naturalness in their behavior. They do not play any games, but express in their actions their potentials without any blockages or inhibitions.
IV. They are autonomous. Maslow describes this in various ways:
    a. They are agents, self-determinated and inner-directed which means that they have the power to act in accordance with their own opinions.
    b. They are independent of other people's judgements concerning themselves. Their self-esteem is build upon their own knowledge of their competence and is to a less degree dependent on other people's judgements.

c. They have worked through their opinions and are less influenced by fleeting feelings. They have a stable normative ethics and a readiness to act in accordance with it, even if they have to make personal sacrifices. Maslow asserts that the content in their normative ethics have great similarity, inspite of their cultural differences.[85]

d. They are creative. Maslow distinguishes between what he calls "self-actualizing creativeness" which designates a general creativeness and which every human being has innate, and what he calls "special talent creativeness" which designates specific talents which only some people have. Every human being actualizes self-actualizing creativity when their deficiency-needs have been gratified and it expresses itself in activities and products not primarily associated with traditional creativeness, but it can be expressed in, for example, cooking, teaching, taxi-driving and gardening. Maslow confesses that his designation of these terms is vague and he describes only some examples of self-actualizing creativity, for example, easy to improvise, flexibility and adaptability in new situations, capability to combine ideas and knowledge from various fields in an original and fruitful way, and a spontaneity and naturalness in the performance of the activity. This type of creativity is distinguished from "special talent creativeness" which says that a person P has talents for a specific activity. This activity does not necessarily need to be associated with creativity of the type: to create music, art, poems and books, but includes other special talents for sport, dance, etc.[86]

VI. They have capabilities to distinguish between goals and means in their lives and when the goal is stated, to adjust the means accordingly. They have also the capacity to transform means-activity to activity which is an end in itself. This capacity is designated by Maslow as "ontification".[87]

VII. They are integrated which means that they do not experience any conflicts within themselves, for example, between feeling-rationality, volition-knowledge, egoism-altruism, duty-pleasure and instinct-reason.[88]

2. The self-actualizing people's relation to other people

I. They experience a "Gemeinshaftsgefühl" with other people. They experience an identity-expansion which makes them feel the good and bad for other people as concerning themselves. This identity-expansion is a cause for their sympathy and attachment to other people, and it gives rise to a genuine wish to help the human species.[89]

II. They are "problem-centered" and not "ego-centered" which means that they are engaged in problems which primarily concern other people's welfare. They feel the duty and mission to work with these problems and feel a moral responsibility in doing so. They are trying to realize some non-moral values, i.e. Being-values in their mission, for instance, justice and freedom.[90] Maslow gives the following examples of this kind of problems: nuclear war and overpopulation.

III. They accept other people with their characteristics and do not judge them according to common cultural norms. Instead, they try to regard every person as a unique human being. They do not treat other people as means to gratify their own needs, instead, every person has his own end-value and everyone gets the same respectful treatment from them.

IV. They are democratic which means that they accept democratic changes. They have made the choice to work within the system and to change it from within.

2.2.3. Self-actualizing as a normative ideal of life

Maslow's normative ethics can be classified as a consequence-ethics, and the overriding norm in his normative ethics is (in one version, see critical remarks 2.2.4, point 3): an action is ethically right only if it leads to self-actualizing for the maximal number of people. This can be classified as *self-actualizing utilitarianism*.

> "Therefore I believe that medicine and physics, law and government, education, economics, engineering, business and industry, are only tools though admittedly powerful. They are means but not ends, the end is human betterment. The ultimate end to which they should all be bent, then is human fulfilment, growth and happiness".[91]

> "... the far goal of education — as of psychotherapy, of family life, of work, of society, of life itself — is to aid the person to grow to fullest humanness, to the greatest possible stature. In a word, to become actually what he deeply is potentially."[92]

In his theory of motivation, Maslow tries to show that every human being in fact strives to get self-actualizing, and in his theory of personality he describes the characteristics of self-actualizing people. Maslow's *meta-ethical opinion can be reconstructed as a naturalistic value-objectivism*. The overriding norm: an action is right only if it leads to self-actualizing for the maximal number of people, can be justified by the fact that people strive to be self-actualizing people.

> "My thesis is, then: we can, in principle, have a descriptive, naturalistic science of human values; that the age-old mutually exclusive contrast between 'what is' and 'what ought to be' is in part a false one; that we can study the highest values or goals

of human beings as we study the values of ants or horses or oak trees, or for that matter Martians. We can discover (rather than create or invent) which values men trend toward . . ."[93]

Maslow proclaims that self-actualizing is the ideal of perfectibility for man. We can distinguish two levels in self-actualizing:
a. the process in order to gratify the basic needs, and
b. through the gratification of these basic needs certain personality traits emerge.

Maslow's ideal of perfectibility for man can, with a term borrowed from J. Passmore, be classified as a *teleological perfectibility* which means that perfectibility consists of the actualization of man's potentials.[94] The import of this opinion is dependent on the determination of the content in man's potentials. As we stated above, man has two levels of potentials, the basic needs *and* the personality traits which develop when these basic needs are gratified.

Maslow criticizes the freudians who describe man's potentials as ethically evil, the behaviorists who assume that man's potentials are of secondary importance, and Sartre whom Maslow interprets as denying the existence of any human potentials.[95]

Maslow assumes that every man has a capability via the self-regulative processes to actualize his potentials. This actualization proceeds continuously and perfectibility proceeds gradually and not in one single moment. Any definite end or any absolute perfectibility is not possible, but perfectibility takes place in the process of life, in the continuous endeavors to gratify the basic needs. Perfectibility can therefore, in Maslow's view of man, be described as a dynamic state in contrast to a static state of perfectibility.[96] In the latter respect Maslow's view on teleological perfectibility is not in agreement with "classical" views, for instance, Aristotle's or Thomas'. They think that the teleological goal can be reached in a static state.

One line of thought in Maslow's works is to distinguish between different degrees of perfectibility. In this context, Maslow applies R. S. Hartman's definition of "good" when he describes the perfectibility of man. The ideal of perfectibility is to develop all the characteristics which Maslow attributes to self-actualizing people. From this ideal we can distinguish different degrees of self-actualization, by estimating how many of these characteristics a certain person P has.[97]

We cannot classify Maslow's ideal of perfectibility as individualistic since he stresses the social ethical direction in the self-actualizing needs. Maslow's view of perfectibility of every individual man is therefore related to every other man's welfare and self-actualizing. P's gratification of P's basic needs and especially the self-actualizing needs, Maslow assumes, is related to other

48

persons' possibilities to gratify their deficiency and self-actualizing needs. Bühler & Allen make a distinction between the humanistic psychologists who

a. assert that self-actualizing consists of the actualization of man's potentials, for example, C. Rogers
b. assert that self-actualizing consists of the struggle to realize some non-moral values, for example, C. Bühler and von Bertanlaffy.[98]

We can describe Maslow's opinion as a combination of these two views of man's self-actualizing.

Maslow's ideal of perfectibility also contains a possibility of experiencing a transcendent reality. The content in these experiences will not be described until chapter 3.[99]

The main cause why people do not reach this described ideal of perfecti-bility, according to Maslow, is that they do not get their basic needs gratified. In his suggestion of means which can remove these causes, he concentrates his attention on changes within each individual. Maslow states that the main impediment to self-actualizing is insufficient self-knowledge, and mainly the unability to listen to the inner signals which assert which intentional ideas of goal channel the basic needs and which do not.[100] Maslow emphasizes that the task of education is to teach people to discover their potentials. The teaching which aims at actualizing people's potentials he calls "intrinsic learning", in contrast to what he calls "extrinsic learning", that is, the teaching which aims at giving P knowledge and capabilities which other people think P must have but which do not help P to actualize P's potentials.[101]

> "Generated by the new humanistic philosophy is a new conception of learning, teaching, and education. Such a conception holds that the goal of education ... the human goal, the humanistic goal ... is ultimately the 'self-actualization' of a person, the development of the fullest height that the human species or a particular individual can come to. In a less technical way, it is helping the person to become the best he is able to become. Such a goal involves very serious shifts in learning strategies."[102]

According to E. Ryding[103] who describes some criteria which opinions of self-actualization usually satisfy, we can characterize Maslow's opinion of self-actualizing as satisfying:

a. *the criterion of universality.* This means that Maslow assumes that all human beings have self-actualizing needs and an inclination to actualize them, and Maslow asserts that everybody has the right to get the chance to actualize these needs.
b. *the social criterion.* This means that Maslow asserts that from the perspec-tive of the community it is desirable that all its members actualize their potentials. Maslow can state this because he assumes (1) that all of man's potentials are ethically neutral (or good) and (2) that when all members of

the community actualize their potentials their actualized potentials are not in conflict with each other but co-operate in harmony for the best of the community.

c. Maslow's opinion of self-actualizing does not satisfy the third of Ryding's criteria, namely, *the criterion of pleasure*. According to this criterion the process of self-actualizing must be pleasurable. It is true that the self-regulative process of the gratification of basic needs must be directed by P's experiences of pleasure, but Maslow also asserts that frustration is a necessary condition in order to develop into a self-actualizing person.[104]

2.2.4. Some critical remarks

Below, we shall, after this short account of Maslow's theory of personality, add some critical remarks.

1. When Maslow in 1951 describes the results of his research concerning self-actualizing people, he makes the claim that the results describe characteristics of people who have their deficiency-needs gratified and who spend most of their time trying to gratify their self-actualizing needs. He has, however, very serious problems finding criteria which determine whether or not the people in his research really have their deficiency-needs gratified and if they really act in order to satisfy their self-actualizing needs. [105] He has in fact great difficulty in determining these criteria logically independent of his descriptions of their characteristics. In 1967 he confessed the metodological fallacies in his research and states that some of the characteristics which he attributed to self-actualizing persons were in fact criteria for selecting the people whom he described as self-actualizing persons. These characteristics served as analytical specifications.[106] A consequence of this fact is that Maslow's descriptions of the characteristics of self-actualizing persons transform from descriptive characteristics to a normative ideal what characteristics people ought to have, according to Maslow.

2. Maslow describes the characteristics of self-actualizing persons as if these were independent of historical and cultural contexts. Maslow describes them as effects which emerge when the basic needs are gratified. However, in the article *Self-actualization and Beyond* (1967) he restricts the cultural independence of his described characteristics and states the possibility of cultural and social variation of these characteristics.[107]

We think it is a mistake to explain peoples' personality traits *only* as some effects which emerge when people get satisfaction of their basic needs. The cultural learning is also very important, according to our view. It is hard to see how Maslow's gratification and frustration-theory complements an association-theory in his descriptions of the characteristics of self-actualizing people.[108]

3. Maslow uses the term "self-actualization" in different ways.[109]

A. He uses "self-actualization" as a *descriptive term*.

> "I think I have shown that the concepts of psychological health and of self-actualization need not be based on implicit value judgements, when properly defined, they are derived from scientifically observed facts. They are descriptive concepts".[110]

He uses the term in order to describe people who have some special characteristics (see 2.2.2. above) and who strive for self-actualizing.

B. He uses "self-actualization" as an *explanatory term*.

> "I have published in another place a survey of all the evidence that forces us in the direction of a concept of healthy growth or of self-actualizing tendencies. This is partly deductive evidence in the sense of pointing out that unless we postulate such a concept, much of human behavior makes no sense. This is on the same scientific principle that leds to the discovery of a hitherto unseened planet that *had* to be there in order to make sense of a lot of other observed data."[111]

In his theory of motivation he gives causal explanations for certain types of actions in terms of self-actualizing needs (see thesis (vi) section 2.1.). These explanations can be subjected to the criticism which we gave of Maslow's theory of motivation (section 2.1.1.), that is, other assumptions in Maslow's theory of motivation (for instance, multiple motivation) make these explanations almost impossible to verify.

In his theory of personality he gives explanation for the characteristics of self-actualizing persons which we reported in section 2.2.2. above and which were described as some effects which emerge when people have their deficiency-needs gratified and they act in order to gratify their self-actualizing needs. This explanation can be subjected to the criticism which we gave in point 2 above, that is, Maslow uses some of these characteristics when he picks out self-actualizing people.

C. He uses "self-actualizing" as a *normative term*.

> "... what is good? Anything that conduces to this desirable development in the direction of actualization of the inner nature of man."[112]

Maslow's application of the term self-actualizing in his normative ethics is ambiguous.

I. In one line of thought, as we reported above 2.2.3., his overriding norm in his consequence-ethics is: an action is ethically right only if it leads to self-actualizing for the maximal number of people (self-actualizing utilitarianism).

Maslow's determination of self-actualizing, understood as a process, is the highest non-moral end-value. He justifies this opinion with his proposition that human beings in fact strive to get self-actualization. We classified this opinion, in 2.2.3. above, as a naturalistic value-objectivism. A criticism which we can make of this is: Maslow commits the *naturalistic fallacy*. We shall, in accordance with M. Moritz, use the term *axiological fallacy*.[113] The reason for using this term is: the term "naturalistic fallacy" is connected with an ontological and meta-ethical opinion which we reject, that is, an intuitionistic value-objectivism. The *axiological fallacy* consists of Maslow's claim, in our reasonable interpretation of Maslow's opinion, that value statements (for example, "P ought to strive to get self-actualization") can be completely translated into or identified with factual statements (for example, "Everybody strives to get self-actualization"). From our point of analysis, we think that this translation is not correct on the assumption that value statements have an a-theoretical meaning and mainly another semantic function to that of factual statements which have a theoretical meaning and mainly an informative function.

Another critical point, in close relationship to the *axiological fallacy* is, from our point of analysis, that one cannot from a "be-statement" deduce an "ought-statement". From the fact that most or all people strive to get self-actualization, one cannot conclude, according to our view, that all people ought to strive to get self-actualization.[114]

II. The other line of thought in Maslow's normative ethics has another overriding norm: an action is ethically right only if it leads to the realization of Being-values. These Being-values are the highest non-moral end-values. Examples of these are: truth, goodness, justice, life and oneness (see further, section 3.2.)[115]. Maslow's opinion can still be classified as a consequence-ethics, but he has another overriding norm and other end-values.

That the maximal number of people get self-actualization suggests an ethical value, but only an instrumental value. Self-actualizing people's actions are, in greater degree than other people's, directed towards the realization of Being-values, according to Maslow. When Maslow, in the meta-ethical topic, tries to state conditions for the justification of the overriding norm: an action is ethically right only if it leads to the realization of Being-values, we can classify his opinion as an intuitionistic value-objectivism.[116] (The reason for this classification will be given in chapter 3).

The relationship between these two lines of thoughts (I & II) in Maslow's normative ethics is ambiguous. We can only state that the latter one is dominating in Maslow's later writings, that is, during the 60's.

4. The term "self-actualization" or "self-actualizing" reveals that a self is to be actualized.

When Maslow determines the content in this self, he uses Horney's term "Real Self" and in doing so he develops the theories about intrinsic conscience and inner signals. Maslow's determination of the content in the "Real Self" were reported in section 2.1. He includes, primarily, in this term the genetic and somatic basic needs. A human being bears in its biological organism its Real Self as a potential. Human beings strive in the process of life to actualize their potentials and when this happens they get experiences of identity. Maslow assumes a connection between the actualization of man's potentials and an *experience* of identity "to be oneself", a psychological identity-experience.

Maslow's use of the term "Real Self" has, however, little similarity with Horney's term "Real Self". She does not localize her concept in the biological organism. Instead, her term designates an "original force": "The real self, which I have defined several times, is the 'original' force toward individual growth and fulfilment, with which we may again achieve full identification when freed of the crippling shackles of neurosis".[117]

5. Maslow determines his term "Real Self" in terms of basic needs and intentional ideas of goals. He thinks that he can judge when P actualizes his Real Self by interpreting if P's action is directed towards the gratification of intentional ideas of goal which channel self-actualizing needs.

Given our criticism of Maslow's theory of motivation in point 3, in section 2.1.1., Maslow cannot give any criteria with which he can judge if P actualizes his Real Self or not, because Maslow cannot judge if a given intentional idea of goal channels basic needs or not and *mutatis mutandis* whether or not P's actions are directed to gratify P's self-actualizing needs.

6. Some of the assumptions in Maslow's theory of personality and opinions on self-actualization are not argued for and can be questioned.
a. He assumes that if P has a potential special talent, P has an inclination and finds pleasure in actualizing this potential special talent. It is however not unreasonable to think that sometimes and for some people this correlation does not exist.
b. Maslow's limitation of the inner-core is vague. This is important because Maslow asserts that all of the potentials in this inner-core must be actualized. We can ask: must all the potentials be actualized or *is there a limitation,* for example, only the basic needs must be actualized? In the first case, we can imagine that P's genetic given disposition to develop schizophrenia can be developed which we do not think is in accordance with Maslow's opinion.
c. Maslow assumes that if people can actualize their self-actualizing needs, their actions in order to actualize these needs take place in co-operation

53

and harmony with what is best for the community.[118] We can imagine that different people's actions in order to gratify these self-actualizing needs can be in conflict with each other. Maybe Maslow can meet this criticism by his assumption of self-actualizing people's ability to experience a "Gemeinshaftsgefühl" with other people, which makes them willing to adjust their individual self-actualizing needs in relation to other people's needs.

2.3. A First Precization of Argument A

After our account and systematization of Maslow's motivation and personality theories, we can clarify premisses (1) and (3) in Argument A_2. Argument A_2 was formulated in 1.0 as follows:

Argument A_2

(1) If a person P's basic needs are satisfied and P can be characterized as a self-actualizing person, P has B-cognition
(2) If a person P has B-cognition, P will have knowledge of Y
(3) There are persons Ps who have their basic needs satisfied and who can be characterized as self-actualizing persons

(4) There are persons Ps who have knowledge of Y

The logical form of Argument A_2 is:

(1) $\forall x(Sx \wedge Tx \rightarrow Qx)$
(2) $\forall x(Qx \rightarrow Rx)$
(3) $\exists x(Sx \wedge Tx)$

(4) $\exists x(Rx)$

After our account in 2.1. and 2.2., our contextual reasonable interpretations of premisses (1) and (3) are as follows:

Argument A_3

(1) If a person P's deficiency-needs are gratified and P's actions are directed towards gratifying P's self-actualizing needs, P will actualize some characteristics X, Y, Z . . . . , and if P actualizes some characteristics X, Y, Z . . . . , P will have B-cognition
(2) If a person P has B-cognition, P will have knowledge of Y
(3) There are persons Ps whose deficiency-needs are gratified and whose actions are directed towards gratifying their self-actualizing needs and who have the characteristics X, Y, Z . . .

(4) There are persons Ps who have knowledge of Y

The logical form of Argument A_3 is:[117]

(1) $\forall x(Sx \land Tx \rightarrow Px) \land (Px \rightarrow Qx)$
(2) $\forall x(Qx \rightarrow Rx)$
(3) $\exists x(Sx \land Tx)$

(4) $\exists x(Rx)$

In our interpretation of the logical form of A_3, we have interpreted the relation between the gratification of P's deficiency-needs, P's direction towards gratifying P's self-actualizing needs and the actualization of the characteristics X, Y, Z . . . in premiss (1) as a *sufficient* condition. This is necessary if the argument is to have logical validity. The complication mentioned in 2.2.0. (point 2) will be discussed in 4.5. In the logical form in A_3, the argument has logical validity. In 2.2.2. we have described the characteristics X, Y, Z . . . A more precizated relationship between the characterstics X, Y, Z . . . and B-cognition will be given in section 4.5. The other variables and constants in the argument will be gradually clarified in chapters 3 and 4.

However, we have in this first precization to anticipate that the conditions in premiss 1 seem, after our account in 2.1. and 2.2, to be *causal* conditions and not *logical* conditions. We can precizate the causal conditions as (a) a necessary condition, that is, p is a necessary condition of q means that whenever q is, p has to be there too, or (b) a sufficient condition, that is, p is a sufficient condition for q means that whenever p is, q will be there too.[120]

These *causal* conditions are not symmetric with the *material implication* $(\rightarrow)$ used in argument A. Because material implication is true in all cases, without in the case when the implicans (that is, "the component statement between the 'if' and the 'then' ") is true and the implicate (that is, "the component statement which follows the 'then' ") is false.[121] We shall discuss this problem in section 4.5. We shall, in this dissertation, also use sufficient and necessary in relation to logical criteria, that is, (a) *sufficient logical criterion*, which means the same as material implication $(\rightarrow)$, (b) *necessary logical criterion*, which means that p is a necessary criterion for q when one can conclude: that whenever q is, p has to be there too. This can be formulized as $(\neg p \rightarrow \neg q)$ and (c) *necessary and sufficient logical criterion*, which means the same as logical equivalence $(\leftrightarrow)$.

Chapter 3: Peak-Experience

Maslow's descriptions of the contents of consciousness in the experiences which he calls peak-experience are very unstructured and vague. One of the aims in this chapter is to structure these descriptions, and as a first attempt, we shall distinguish between the following kinds of descriptions:[1]

(1) descriptions of processes of cognition
(2) descriptions of how a subject experiences CTR during peak-experience
(3) descriptions of how a person experiences himself/herself during peak-experience
(4) descriptions of the emotional contents which a subject feels during peak-experience

The main aim in this chapter is to clarify these descriptions, and with the help of these clarifications, make explicit:

(a) the differences between the cognitive faculties B-cognition and D-cognition
(b) the meaning of the statements which describe the contents of consciousness in the experiences which Maslow calls peak-experiences.

With (a) and (b), we clarify cognition of type II and the contents in Y in Argument A.

In the introductory section 3.0., we describe Maslow's research concerning peak-experience and discuss some methodological problems with regard to this research. In 3.1., we analyse the differences between D-cognition and B-cognition. In 3.2., we make an attempt to structure Maslow's descriptions of how a subject experiences CTR during peak-experience. In 3.3., we describe briefly how a person experiences himself/herself during peak-experience. In 3.4., we describe briefly some emotional contents which a subject feels during peak-experience. In 3.5., we try to clarify the differences between the closely related terms "peak-experience", "mystical-experience" and "plateau-experience" in the writings of Maslow. The chapter finishes, 3.6., with an interpretation of Argument A following the clarification of processes of cognition in peak-experiences and the meaning of the statements which describe the contents of conciousness in peak-experience.

3.0. Introduction

In his research concerning so called self-actualizing people (1945−1949), Maslow discovered that such people often had a specific type of experience. When he published the research, he named this type of experience "oceanic feeling" (he took over this term from Freud)[2] or "mystical experience". Maslow also discovered that such people did not describe these experiences in "religious" terms.[3] He also states that these experiences could be of different intensity, and he distinguishes between calm and strong "oceanic feelings"/ "mystical experiences". The extension of the latter includes "any of the experiences in which there is a loss of self or transcendence of it . . . "[4]

During the end of the 50's, Maslow made a research of these oceanic feelings/mystical experiences. His method for getting descriptions of these experiences was:

(1) He sent out questionnaires[5] (These were answered by 190 college students).
(2) He made personal interviews (80).
(3) He studied books on mystical experience, religion, art, creativity, love, etc.
(4) He got about 50 spontaneously delivered letters containing descriptions of such experiences.[6]

One important source is, of course, Maslow's own experiences of this type of experience.

> "I have myself had the mystic experience . . . (in which) I experience a blind groping for something, an overwhelming sense of unsatisfied desire, a helplessness which was so intensive that it left me almost weeping".[7]

Before we give an account of his results, we shall make some comments of his view on the relationship between language and the contents of consciousness in peak-experience. This aims at giving a clarification of his method of interpretation when interpreting the descriptions in his sources.

His general view concerning the relationship between language and the contents of consciousness is: the contents of consciousness are more differentiated than is possible in linguistic articulation and therefore the contents of consciousness cannot be completely described in language.[8] Maslow touches upon the relationship between language and the contents of consciousness in peak-experience when he discusses whether or not the contents in these experiences are ineffable. His answer to this question is: the contents in these experiences are *not* ineffable. However, he oscillates between different answers in replying to this question.

In some contexts, he states that the contents in these experiences are ineffable in the sense that they cannot be communicated with a theoretical-descriptive language. A theoretical-descriptive language is our contextual reasonable interpretation of his "cool, analytic, rational, abstract language". But these contents can be communicated if both the sender and the receiver have had experiences of this type and if they use analogous language.[9] Analogous language is our contextual reasonable interpretation of Maslow's "metaphoric, poetic, rhapsodic language". The contents in these experiences can, according to Maslow, be regarded as communicable if these two conditions are satisfied. Necessary conditions, and which also seems to be a necessary logical criterion, for the contents in these experiences to be regarded as communicable are: (a) both the sender and receiver must have had experiences of this type, and (b) the sender has to use analogous language.

When he describes his method of interview in his research another view appears. In this context, he states that the theoretical-descriptive language can be used in order to communicate the contents in these experiences, if and only if, both sender and receiver have had experiences of this type. If the receiver does not consider himself/herself to have had experiences of this type, the sender can use metaphors and analogies in order to actualize repressed memories of experiences of this type and get the receiver to identify, with the help of these metaphors and analogies, these as peak-experience.[10] Communication is however impossible if the receiver cannot identify any experiences to which the words refer. Maslow writes:

> "That is, what we must do is to make him become aware of fact that peak-experiences go on inside himself. Until he has become aware of such experience and has this experience as a basis for comparison, he is a non-peaker; and it is useless to try to communicate to him the feel and the nature of peak-experience. But if we can change him, in the sense of making him aware of what is going on inside himself, then he becomes a different kind of communicate. It is now possible to communicate with him. He now knows what you are taking about when you speak of peak-experiences; ... "[11]

> "Until that point is reached at which he has a conscious, objective, detached awareness of the relationship between a particular name or label or word and a particular set of subjective, ineffable experiences, no communication and no teaching are possible; ... "[12]

In both views above, Maslow states a necessary criterion for the contents of consciousness in peak-experiences to be regarded as communicable, namely, both the sender and the receiver must have had "similar" experiences of this type independent of whether or not they use theoretical-descriptive language or analogous language.[13]

58

In order to clarify the problems in this view, we shall use the following example:

1. At time t_1, P has a content of consciousness X_P which consists of an aggregate of different elements. (This illustrative example primarily concerns the contents of consciousness which Maslow classifies as peak-experience, and in these experiences we can make the distinction between cognitive and emotional content.[14] The following remarks primarily concern the cognitive content because the main object of this study is epistemological problems).

2. At time t_2, P expresses verbally or in writings X_P. We name this semantic statement X_{PS}.

3. At time t_n, Q hears or reads X_{PS}. If Q is to understand X_{PS}, according to Maslow, Q has to associate X_{PS} with a content of consciousness X_{M2} which in some way is "similar" to X_P. To satisfy this claim, Q must have had a content of consciousness X_{M1}, at time t_{n-1} which is "similar" to X_{M2}, at time t_n.

We shall now consider some of the problems connected with Maslow's view:

I. What criteria can Q apply:
    (a) in order to state that Q's X_{M2} is "similar" to P's X_P?
    (b) in order to state that Q's X_{M2} is "similar" to Q's X_{M1}?

II. How must the term "similar" be clarified, and is it the same type of similarity in the different relations of similarity?

In these formulations of problems, it is not assumed that P, at time t_2 (see 2 above), must have had some content of consciousness which in some way is "similar" to X_{P1}, at time t_1. This would complicate the matter even more. We merely consider the receiver's understanding, not the possibility of some content of consciousness, that the sender has when he/she expresses X_{PS}.

In discussing I. a. we can make the following interpretation: Maslow assumes an *ideational theory of meaning*. According to this theory of meaning, the sender has a content of consciousness X_P when he/she expresses the statement X_{PS}, and the receiver understands X_{PS} when he/she associates X_{PS} with a content of consciousness (X_{M1} in our example) which is "similar" to the sender's X_P. The receiver makes unequivocal and regular associations from statements, concepts or names to contents of consciousness and these contents gives the meaning of the semantic statements.[15]

Critical remarks against this theory of meaning are, among others:

C1: In introspection, one cannot discover any unequivocal regular associations from statements, concepts or names to specific ideas in consciousness.

C2: The theory does not state what psychological character these ideas have, for instance, are they concrete pictures or do they have some kind of isomorphic similarity to the referent.

C3: One can wonder if there are any ideas when one understands statements, concepts or names.

C4: One can wonder if ideas exist independent of language which this theory presupposes.[16]

An unequivocal interpretation of Maslow's theory of meaning is hard to come by. He never discusses the problem of semantic meaning explicitly in his writings. However, we have reconstructed a basic assumption: a necessary criterion, in order for a receiver to understand a statement concerning the contents of consciousness in the experiences which Maslow embraces in his term "peak-experience", is: receiver R must have had experiences of this type.

This assumption has some important epistemological consequences. Scientists in psychology of religion and philosophy of religion must have experiences of this type in order to understand the descriptions of the contents of consciousness in peak-experience. This assumption is against a postulate which is formulated by the Swedish philosopher I. Hedenius, namely, the so called *semantic-theoretical postulate:* "The semantic-theoretical postulate states ... it should be possible for scientists in philosophy of religion who are either believers or unbelievers to understand the meanings and the semantic functions of Christian statements".[17] In this quotation, Hedenius uses his postulate in relation to Christian statements, but a reasonable interpretation is that this postulate ought to be applicable to all theoretical statements. This scientific methodological claim can be found among representatives of analytical philosophy. W. Stegmüller names it *the problem of communication.* He writes:

> "So long as everyone thinks his private thoughts about something, there is no such thing as science; science begins only when these thoughts become communicable so that they can be actively discussed with other people. Thus science must be intersubjective not only in the sense that there must exist generally agreed upon methods of testing scientific statements, but also in the sense that the expressions used in science must be intersubjectively understandable. Science exist only where discussion is possible, and a discussion can take place between myself and someone else only if I am in a position to explain to the other person with sufficient exactness the meaning of the expressions I use, just as he must be able to explain to me the meaning of the words he employs."[18]

This problem has relation to the claim of intersubjective testability. Others have first to be clear over what they shall test before they start their testing. We shall discuss these complications in 4.4., 4.5. and 6.5.

We shall discuss below the problem I. b.: how can Q know that Q's X_{M2} is "similar" to Q's X_{M1}? This problem touches upon Wittgenstein's criticism of *private language*. According to Wittgenstein, the statements in this language only refer to a person P's own private experiences. The referents of these statements cannot be intersubjective-ostensively defined. The private language is constituted by P's "inner ostension", that is, P focuses P's attention on a content of consciousness X_{P1}, and gives X_{P1} a stipulative name, for instance, "F".

Wittgenstein's main criticism is: P does not have any criteria to judge if P's content of consciousness X_{p1} at time t_1 is qualitatively identical or "similar" to P's content of consciousness X_{P2} at time t_n. We shall illustrate this by distinguishing between the following factors in the example below:

1. P has the content of consciousness X_{P1} at time t_1 and names it "F".
2. P has the content of consciousness X_{P2} at time t_n.
3. P has the memory of X_{p1} at time t_{n+1}. The content of this memory we name X_{MP1}.
4. P compares X_{P2} with X_{MP1} at time t_{n+2}.
5. P discovers that X_{P2} and X_{MP1} are partly "similar", and P asserts that X_{P2} can also be named "F".

Wittgenstein's criticism is, *inter alia*, that P only has the memory of X_{P1}, that is, X_{MP1}, and this memory cannot by itself justify if it is partly "similar" to X_{P1}. P does not have any criteria to judge if X_{MP1} and X_{P1} are qualitatively identical or "similar". P cannot state any private rules regarding the use of "F". Such rules have to be justified by an objective instance outside P's private language.[19]

Maslow did not take the problem of private language into consideration in his research concerning peak-experience. This problem is relevant in our analyses of Maslow's method in his investigation because Maslow gives descriptions of the experiences he investigates to the examinee. He gives these descriptions in order to actualize memories of experiences which the examinee may think can be described in similar ways. It is a great risk that the descriptions which Maslow gives to the examinee direct or shape the examinee's descriptions of his/her memories of these experiences and thereby distort these descriptions.

The problem concerning I.a and I.b. touch upon the general problem concerning the meaning of statements which express "mental states". Their specific problem is that these states cannot be directly defined along intersubjective-ostensive lines. One suggested solution is: it is possible to correlate certain content of consciousness with certain behavior or physiological data, that is, indirectly, one can assume that when behavior X or physiological data

Y are present, content Z is present in consciousness. Maybe it is possible to establish correlations of this type i.e., between some types of content of consciousness and certain types of behavior or psysiological data, for instance, in the case of certain kinds of pains.

In such contents of consciousness, as for instance, anguish, love and happiness, we think this correlation is difficult to state in an unequivocal way. Concerning the contents of consciousness in peak-experience, we find it very hard to state such correlative in an unequivocal way. One of our reasons is that the descriptions of contents of consciousness which Maslow embraces in his term "peak-experience" have a great and varied extension (see section 3.2. and 3.3).[20]

Another important problem is how the *term* "peak-experience" itself can be interpreted in Maslow's writings.

> "I use one term — peak-experience — as a kind of generalized and abstract concept because I discovered that all of these ecstatic experiences had some characteristics in common. Indeed I found that it was possible to make a generalized, abstract schema or model which could describe their common characteristics. The word enables me to speak of all or any of these experiences in the same moment."[21]

What are the relationships between the general term "peak-experience" and the various descriptions of contents of consciousness which Maslow embraces under this term? Our heuristic interpretation is: these various descriptions are part-descriptions which Maslow embraces in a model he has constructed in order to systematize these part-descriptions, and subsumes them in his general term "peak-experience". Some of these part-descriptions occur quite frequently in Maslow's sources while other part-descriptions occur less frequently. In this introductory section, we shall not discuss this problem further. Let us only remind the reader *not* to interpret these part-descriptions as analytical specifications of the term "peak-experience". Whether or not it is possible to define "peak-experience" in terms of different conjunctions of these part-descriptions will be discussed in chapter 5.

Another problem in Maslow's research is the following: what is the relationship between the part-descriptions which Maslow presents and the descriptions in Maslow's sources? Maslow has undoubtly an ontological, epistemological and semantic reductive tendency in his interpretations of the descriptions in his sources. For example, descriptions of contents of consciousness which use supernaturalistic terms, that is, terms which, according to Maslow, refer to a personal entity who is distinct and separate from the material world but who inspite of this separateness can direct events in this world,[22] can, according to Maslow, be interpreted in such a way that they do not refer to any supernaturalistic entity.

Maslow considers it possible to make these recommended interpretations because he has a theory of *over-belief.* This is a theory of cognition which Maslow has taken over from W. James. According to this theory, the subject is assumed to interpret the contents in consciousness with terms which are culturally dependent and which determine the contents of consciousness in some important ways. This theory is a presupposition which Maslow uses when he makes his recommended reductive interpretations of the descriptions in his sources. The problems concerning the over-belief-theory will be discussed further in chapter 5.

3.1. Maslow's Theory of Cognition

3.1.1. Some terminological remarks

In this section, we shall clarify some of the terms which we intend to use as instruments of analysis in our attempt to clarify Maslow's theory of cognition and his epistemological view.

Maslow assumes that there exist a reality independent of human beings' consciousness (*ontological realism*).[23] In 1.0., we named this reality CTR. He also assumes that there is some correspondence between human beings' contents of consciousness and CTR (*epistemological realism*). He belongs to empiricism within epistemology whose advocates assert that the genesis of knowledge of CTR is brought through sense-experience and that this knowledge of CTR is justified by sense-experience.

> "In a certain sense I see the acceptance of the prepotency and the logical priority of experience as another version of the spirit of empiricism itself. One of the beginnings of science, one of the roots from which it grew, was the determination not to take things on faith, trust, logic, or authority but to check and to see for oneself. Experience had shown how often the logic or the apriori certainly or Aristotle's authority failed to work in fact. The lesson was easy to draw. First, before everything else comes the seeing of nature with your own eyes, that is, experiencing it yourself."[24]

When we in section 3.1.3. analyse Maslow's meaning of "sense-experience", we shall find that he assumes that human beings have a capability to use an intuitive cognitive faculty. In chapter 4 we shall discuss whether he considers this faculty, not only as a faculty for the discovery of knowledge but also as a justification for knowledge.

Since Maslow assumes an ontological realism and a dualism between CTR and human beings' consciousness, all the "classical" problems in this view emerge. For example; what is the relation between P's content of consciousness and CTR?; to what extent does P's equipment shape the sense-experience of CTR and to what extent do the ontological objects shape P's sense-experience of CTR?; how does P's sense-experience stand as a mental entity to P's physiological sense-organs? In chapters 3 and 4 we shall try to interpret Maslow's opinions on these classical epistemological problems. We shall also find how he hints at an ontology which transcended this dualistic ontology.

A contextual reasonable interpretation of Maslow's theory of cognition is: he presupposes a version of the so called *sense-data-theory*. This theory states that we have to distinguish between P's experiences of CTR (sense-data) and CTR itself. This theory will be analysed in the following way: relation R_1 is a relation between person P and the sense-datum S, and relation R_2 is a relation between sense-datum S and entities x, y, z . . . in CTR. We can analyse the statement "P perceives x" as: "there is a sense-datum S and P experiences S and S is in relation R_2 to x".

Entities in CTR will hereafter be called *ontological objects*. Relation R_1 will be analysed in terms of acts of consciousness and contents of consciousness, that is, P has acts (that is, the actual state of experience) which have different contents.

One type of element in this content will be called *intentional objects,* and these objects are of another ontological category than ontological objects. Ontological objects exist independent of human beings' acts of consciousness. Intentional objects exist only in relation to human beings' acts of consciousness.[25]

Acts of consciousness are psychological states which can have different qualities of acts, for instance, perception, memory, wish and expectation. These acts can also have different intensity. P's qualities of acts and intensity vary, naturally, from time to time.

Maslow's view on relation R_2, that is, the relation between intentional objects and ontological objects, we interpret as follows: there exist a causal relation between ontological and intentional objects. In the process of cognition the subject of knowledge works, in different ways, upon proximal stimuli, that is, the stimuli which appear in the receptors.[26] Proximal stimuli are assumed, by relation R_2, to be caused by ontological objects (in perception indirectly via the light waves). The content which P experiences in a given act of perception is the result of this causal relationship and the subject's work upon the proximal stimuli. A contextual reasonable interpretation of Maslow's view on the relation between intentional objects and ontological objects is that he assumes a sort of *representative realism* (we shall clarify this further in chapter 4).[27]

We have used above the term *"subject of knowledge"*. This term will in this study designate the logical subject for: (a) the activities, such as interpretation of proximal stimuli, selection and focusing of attention which Maslow assumes take place in P's consciousness in the process of cognition, (b) acts of consciousness and (c) contents of consciousness. We shall hereafter use the abbreviated subject$_k$ for this logical subject.[28]

The term *"object of knowledge"* will in this study designate the entities which P claims to have knowledge of, for instance, particular ontological objects, relations among ontological objects, and contents in P's consciousness, (for instance, P knows that P at a given moment has an idea of the Cathedral in Uppsala).

Maslow also uses a distinction concerning the self, and he distinguishes, on psychological grounds, between *"experiencing-self"* and *"observing-self"*.[29] We use Sartre's terms "unreflective consciousness" and "reflective consciousness" in order to make reasonable interpretations of Maslow's terms. Experiencing-self is comparable with unreflective consciousness where the contents are apprehended without any reflection. Observing-self is comparable with reflective consciousness. The content in unreflective consciousness is the object of knowledge for the reflective consciousness. By this a distance to the content in the unreflective consciousness can be at hand, and judgements, concerning these contents, can be made by the reflective consciousness.[30]

As we stated above, Maslow assumes a causal relationship between intentional objects and ontological objects. A contextual reasonable interpretation concerning perception is: Maslow assumes an information-working-model in the process of cognition.[31] Accordning to this model proximal stimuli are assumed to go through various working phases before they are transformed into a psychological sense-experience. This working process will be called, the *process of cognition*. In 3.1.2., we shall analyse which phases Maslow assumes in his theory of cognition. The result of this process, that is, the psychological sense-experience, will in this study be called *percept*.[32] This is in agreement with Maslow's own term. The percept is a subset of P's total content of consciousness at time t. The total content of consciousness can, including the percept, also embrace, for instance, certain emotional feelings, tactile sensations and auditive sensations.

Another terminological abbreviation will be stipulated, namely, the process of cognition and percept in D-cognition we shall name D-process and D-percept respectively, and the corresponding terminology in B-cognition we shall name B-process and B-percept.

In Maslow's theory of cognition, we can find hypotheses concerning the content in the various phases in the process of cognizing which the subject$_k$ makes, and hypotheses concerning psychological factors which determine the content in these phases. Maslow states these hypotheses, mainly with regard to descriptions of peak-experience, because a characteristic of peak-experience is changes in the process of cognition. He describes these changes by contrasting the process of cognition in peak-experience (B-process) with what he regards a "normal" process of cognition (D-process). One important factor in his explanation of these changes, which the term "deficiency" in Deficiency-cognition hints at, is: D-process is determinated — in several ways — by non-satisfaction of the deficiency-needs.[33] This hypothesis orginates from Maslow's psychoanalytic background and from the so called New-Look-school. The latter appeared in the 40's and advocates of this school stated that perception is in great degree determinated by such factors as needs, motives, neuroses and anguish.[34] B-process, on the other hand, is not determinated by these factors to the same degree, and this is one of Maslow's explanations for the differences between D-percept and B-percept. As we mentioned in sections 1.0 and 1.2., these changes are: (a) B-percept gives a more complete and correct knowledge of CTR which can be experienced in both B-percept and D-percept and (b) B-percept gives experiences of specific aspects of CTR which cannot be had in D-percept.

A vagueness in Maslow's writings is that he does not distinguish between (a) percept *qua* content of consciousness, that is, P's psychological sense-experience, and (b) the statements which describe the percept *qua* content of consciousness, that is, P's description of P's sense-experience. We shall name (a) percept on the level of consciousness and (b) percept on the semantic level. The same distinction can be made concerning processes of cognition, that is, processes of cognition on the level of consciousness and processes of cognition on the semantic level. When we in 3.1.2. and 3.1.3. analyse Maslow's theory of cognition, our contextual reasonable interpretation is: Maslow's terms "percept" and "processes of cognition" in these contexts refer to percept and processes of cognition on the level of consciousness.

3.1.2. D-process

We shall give below some more terminological clarifications before we give an account of Maslow's descriptions of D-process. The intentional objects can be of different kinds, for example, stones, cars, clouds, rainbows, shadows, people and TV-pictures. These examples are different in various ways but they can all be intentional objects and be part of P's percept.

The attention can be directed to certain properties of a given intentional object, for example, the colour of a car or the make of a car. These properties can be given more specific properties, for example, colour-red or make-Volvo and these can be given more specific properties in turn, for example, red — brick red, or Volvo — Volvo 343. In order to handle these hierarchies of properties, the terms "determinable-determinat" will be used. "*Determinable*" designates the most general property, for example, red. "*Determinat*" designates the less general property, for example, brick red. The terms are relative in the sense that the properties which are called determinable in one description of an intentional object x can be called determinat in another description of x.[35]

Determinable-determinat have to be distinguished from the term "complex of properties" ("Bestimmungskomplex"). Intentional objects can be described as complex of properties, as for example, a red, round table top. The description contains the properties red, round and table top. These properties do not stand in a determinable-determinat-relation to each other. Instead they are a complex of properties.[36]

As we mentioned above, Maslow is influended by the so called New-Look-school. This is easy to notice because Maslow very strongly emphasizes that the process of cognition is to a high degree determined by different states of motivation. This will be clear when we report below on the different forms of cognizing which take place in Maslow's information-working-model of the process of cognition.

A. Selection

P's attention at time t_1 is directed to intentional objects or determinables-determinates of these which P thinks are relevant for P's activity at t_1. According to Maslow's theory of motivation, P's activities are caused and directed by non-gratified needs. P's attention is therefore directed to information in P's visual field which P thinks are relevant for P's need-gratifying activities.[37] Maslow naturally asserts that P's attention can also be determinated by factors other than states of motivation. In cognitive psychology, one often names factors such as, intentional objects with strong intensity of light and/or high level of sound or certain changes in the visual field, for instance, an intentional objects which suddenly emerges. Besides these factors, Maslow mentions sets of different kinds, but he does not describe these in any way. These sets arise partly from earlier experiences and partly from different inclinations. The extension of the latter can vary greatly from theories within a specific topic to general ontological assumptions.

D-percepts are selective because of the direction of attention, and it is organized in sharp figure-ground-relation. P tends to notice intentional objects or determinables-determinates of these which P thinks are relevant. Two different phases of selection can take place: (a) the process of organization in figure-ground where certain intentional objects are assigned to the ground and others to the figure and (b) selection of determinables-determinates of the intentional objects which are in the center of attention (that is, in the figure).

Selection also takes place in the so called perceptual defence, that is, the center of attention is directed from intentional objects or determinables-determinates of these which can give rise to anguish or other negative emotions in P.

We shall hereafter call *organization* and *selection* two *forms of cognizing* in the process of cognition. These two forms of cognizing can be in action simultaneously as in clear from the above.

B. Projection

Maslow used Rorschach's test quite often in his various research. According to this test, the examinee is supposed to interpret certain ink-blots. One of the assumptions in the test is that the examinee uncovers certain unconscious needs when the examinee interprets the ink-blots. The examinees are assumed to project certain repressed intentional ideas of goals and certain emotional feelings (which are assumed to be connected with the unconscious needs) when they interpret the ink-blots (as, for example, big birds or the masks of natives). The examinees are assumed to externalize or localize repressed ideas of goals or emotional feelings in their interpretations of the ink-blots.

Maslow assumes, in agreement with traditional psychoanalytic theory, that these projections also take place in "normal" perception inspite of the fact that proximal stimuli, in most cases, are not so ambiguous as Rorschach's ink-blots. These ink-blots do not have any conventional limits concerning the extent of their interpretations.

One example of projection and its co-operation with selection is: P perceives another person Q, and P interprets Q as very aggressive (this interpretation is groundless, in our example). P has then localized certain repressed ideas of goal to Q, instead of confessing P's own unconscious aggressive ideas of goal. This projection means that a selection in the visual field takes place, some determinables-determinates are noticed, some are distorted and some are not noticed at all.[38]

Projection can also take place in the sense of anthropomorphism, that is, P interprets a purpose in the events of nature, P regards things as living beings, etc.[39]

Projection will, in the following, be called *a form of cognizing* in the process of cognition.

C. Organization of wholeness

Maslow is also influenced by Gestaltpsychology. We can see this, inter alia, in his assumption that every intentional object in the visual field is perceived in relation to the other intentional objects in the visual field, *and* that all these intentional objects are included and organized in a Gestalt of wholeness. The Gestalt of wholeness and the relations which are determinated from this Gestalt of wholeness determinate the perception of a given intentional object x in this visual field, and x, in turn, determinates the perception of each of the other intentional objects in this visual field.[40] In short, the Gestalt of wholeness and the intentional objects in the visual field determinate the interpretation of x; x is not perceived *per se* but in relation to the other intentional objects and the Gestalt of wholeness.

Organization of wholeness will be called, hereafter, *a form of cognizing* in the process of cognition.

D. Rubricizing (identification of objects)

Attention, organization, selection and identification of objects are determinated by a learnt abstract system of categories, constructs, rubrics, etc, which are developed by the concepts which P has learnt in P's culture.[41]

> "Most of our cognitions (attendings, perceivings, rememberings, thinkings and learning) are abstract rather than concrete. That is, we mostly categorize, schematize, classify and abstract in our cognitive life. We do not so much cognize the nature of the world as it actually is, as we do the organization of our own inner world outlook. Most of experience is filtred through our systems of categories, constructs and rubrics . . . "[42]

> "What is more to our point, however is the fact it is possible to discern in the attending responses the difference between fresh idiosyneratic attending to the unique event, and stereotyped, rubricized recognition in the outside world of a set of categories that already exist in the mind of the attending person. That is, attending may be no more than a recognition or discovery in the world of what we already put there—a sort of prejudging of experience before it happens."[43]

> " . . . he may respond to the experience not as unique, but as typical, i.e. as an example or representative on one or another class, category, or rubric of experience. This is to say that he does not in the strictest sense examine, attend to, perceive, or even experience the event: his reaction is rather like that of the file clerk who perceives only enough of the page to be able to file it under A or B etc. For this activity the name 'rubricizing' might be suggested."[44]

The quotations are about the so called *problem of recognition or identification.*[45] Many theories in cognitive psychology have tried to solve this problem. One possible interpretation of Maslow's opinion concerning this problem is: he assumes the *template-matching-theory.*[46] According to this theory, proximal stimuli are in the information-working-process, matched against specific information in the memory and this information are called "templates". These templates identify proximal stimuli and shape P's experiences of intentional objects. In connection with a polemic against a certain type of scientist, Maslow contrasts this type with the artist about whom he writes: "He is in no way interested in classifying the experience or placing it in any mental card catalogue that he may have."[47]

One difficulty with the template-matching-theory is that of clarifying the meaning of, and the referent of these templates. Maslow is very vague on this topic and we can only assert a reasonable interpretation. Our interpretation follows that of U. Neisser who, in a discussion of the template-matching-theory, identifies these templates with general terms, that is, templates in cognitive psychological terminology mean the same as general terms in philosophical terminology.[48] This hypothesis of interpretation has to be clarified, by in the term "general term" distinguishing between:

(1) logical extension, that is, the elements (in set-theoretical meaning) which are embraced in the term
(2) logical intension, that is, the property or properties which all elements in a given extension have, (analytical specification)
(3) the psychological function of the intension
    a. in the interpretation of semantic statements
    b. in the interpretation of proximal stimuli (perception)
    c. in the interpretation of content of consciousness as, for example, in dreams and wishes.

According to our interpretation, the meaning of "template" is: the logical intension of general terms. The ontological status of these intensions are one of the classical problems in the history of philosophy. We shall, in this study, refrain from taking up this problem, since neither Neisser nor Maslow discusses this problem, and furthermore, it is not of importance for our attempt to clarify argument A.[49] In short, we have followed Neisser in our attempt to interpret Maslow's opinion concerning the problem of recognition or identification. We have interpreted Maslow's terms "categories", "constructs" and "rubrics" as logical intension of general terms.

On the problem of identification or recognition, Maslow emphasizes very strongly the distinction between abstract and concrete identification.[50] In D-process there are only abstract identification, and Maslow names this *rubricizing*. He explains the occurrences of rubricizing by asserting that in D-process there is a strong connection between the process of identification and selection because P's attention is directed to relevant information in P's visual field in order to find information relevant for P's need-gratifying activity. In this case, the only information P needs is sufficient information to identify the intentional objects. This has the effect that P only notices the analytical specifications of the intentional objects. When P rubrices, P does not notice certain determinables-determinates of the intentional objects, others P distorts and others are created by P. The unique intentional object is

70

only experienced as one element (in set-theoretical meaning) in a given set. P does not notice it's various determinables-determinates, only the ones belonging to the analytical specifications.

In order to illustrate Maslow's theory of rubricizing, we shall give the following example, P perceives x and recognizes x as a car. In not-rubricizing identification, (that is, concrete perception), on the other hand, P perceives x and recognizes x as a blue Volvo 343, a 1977 model with sliding roof, extra headlights, a dent on the left wing, etc.

In repeated rubricizing perception of x, P does not perceive x's hitherto unnoticed determinables-determinates. Instead, P has a strong tendency to keep the first classification of x. This leads to a static and abstract perception of CTR.[51] The borderline between abstract and concrete perception is blurred (see further concrete perception 3.1.3.).

Identification of objects will be called hereafter a *form of cognizing* in the process of cognition. In D-process this identification can be characterized as rubricizing.

In summing up, Maslow asserts that D-process is characterized by:

(A) D-process is very *selective,* P only notices the intentional objects or determinables-determinates of these which P thinks are relevant for P's need-gratifying activity.

(B) P only perceives the intentional objects *as means* in order to attain certain goals.

(C) P *projects* certain repressed ideas into the intentional objects. This contributes to the selectiveness and distortedness of D-percept.

(D) When P identifies the intentional objects or determinables-determinates of these, P does this with the help of *general terms.* This has as one of its effects P's failure to notice the unique determinables-determinates of a certain ontological objects x. P only notices the determinables-determinates belonging to the analytical specifications.

(E) The visual fields is organized in *a Gestalt of wholeness* which makes it impossible to perceive a unique intentional object *per se.*

3.1.3. B-process

In this section, we shall give an account of Maslow's description of changes in the process of cognition in B-process compared with D-process. The basic explanation of these changes are, as we mentioned earlier, satisfied basic needs. These satisfactions can lead to a changed attitude towards intentional objects, for example, love or interest, which also influence the process of cognition. With "attitude" we mean emotional feelings and value judgements concerning intentional objects which also imply a disposition to act in certain ways in relation to a given intentional object.

A. Changes in attention

Maslow describes different types of changes in attention. One type is more intensity in attention which has the following as a result: the organization of figure-ground does not have a sharp contrast. The intentional objects which are presented in the visual field, are noticed in the same degree.[52]

In other cases, intensity in attention is so strong and focused that the figure dominates the whole visual field. The intentional objects in the background shift out of the visual field and are not noticed anymore.[53] An intentional object x which in this case is a figure, is not perceived in relation to other intentional objects in a Gestalt of wholeness. This is one reason why the ground and Gestalt of wholeness only to a small degree determinate the perception of x. The attention in this case, is not selective and the various determinables-determinates of the intentional objects are perceived simultaneously or in rapid succession.[54]

B. Passive process of cognition

Since B-process is not an instrument for satisfying some deficiency-needs, only a rather small selection or none at all take place in B-process. Intentional object's determinables-determinates are equally important/unimportant.[55]

B-percepts are organized in figure-ground-relation but this organization is not as sharp as in D-percept. One reason for this is that the intentional objects which will be in the figure and the ground are more flexible in B-cognition.[56]

There is either no or only an insignificant selection and organization of the intentional objects in the visual field which is caused by projection. The intentional objects are not attributed properties from the human point of view, for example, terrible and dangerous. Intentional objects are perceived with minimal human projection.[57]

Different sets of earlier experiences or different inclinations determine to a small degree, the selection of intentional objects or determinables-determinates of these.[58]

One change which Maslow very strongly emphasizes is the overcoming of rubricizing. In B-process, the subject$_k$ does not only identify the intentional object in its characterizing properties, the subject$_k$ also notices the main part of determinables-determinates of an intentional object. There is an individualization with a more complete and less distorted percept of the ontological object.[59] In order to clarify the differences between rubricizing and non-rubricizing cognition, the earlier car example will be used. (Maslow uses the terms "concrete" or "innocent cognition" for this non-rubricizing cognition). P has D-percept and Q has B-percept. P's and Q's percept are different in two principle ways:

a. P perceives a car. Q's percept contains a more specific classification, which can be analysed by set inclusion, for instance, car, Volvo, Volvo 343 and Volvo 343 DL. In our example Q, for instance, interprets proximal stimuli as a Volvo 343.
b. P does not notice or notices to a very small degree the details of the car. Q's percept contains properties which can be analysed in terms of part-wholeness. Q notices: 1) more parts of the car than P, for example, the car has a sliding roof, extra headlights and a dent on the left wing, 2) determinates of these parts, for example, the extra headlights is of the mark Hella.

Maslow does not assert any definite limit between rubricizing and innocent cognition. This borderline is blurred, but he states that it is possible to give unambiguous cases of rubricizing and innocent cognition.

Maslow asserts a difference in degree between rubricizing and innocent cognition. A contextual reasonable interpretation is: in the extreme case of innocent cognition, he assumes that in the process of cognition, proximal stimuli are apprehended independent of concepts. In these cases, the onto-logical objects are perceived more completely and less distorted than in other forms of cognition.

Maslow's general view is that every classification with concepts in the process of cognition eliminates the particular and unique characteristics of an ontological object. Concepts are created by a process of abstraction where common characteristics among intentional objects are abstracted to a logical intension. When a unique intentional object x, in rubricizing, is compared with other intentional objects, x's unique characteristics are not apprehended, only the characteristics which x has in common with other intentional objects are apprehended.[60] One example of this is: x is attributed the characteristic a, y is attributed the characteristic a, but according to Maslow, x's a is different from y's a because x's a is determined by x's other characteristics and y's a is determined by y's other characteristics and therefore, x's a and y's a are perceived in a distorted way when they are identified with the same general term. Interpretation with concepts in the process of cognition is a hindrance to a complete and undistorted percept, while, through an intuitive conceptless process of cognition, P can apprehend CTR in a more complete and less distorted way.

Maslow asserts that the writings of H. Bergson has influenced him concern-ing his view of innocent cognition. We shall, in this section, take up very briefly Bergson's view of intuition. Bergson characterizes intuition as follows: "Intuition is the kind of intellectual sympathy, through which one goes into an object in order to merge into the unique and consequently ineffable the object entails."[61] Bergson thinks that human beings are not able to apprehend the true reality with the help of concepts.[62] The true reality can only be apprehended by intuition in which the objects of knowledge are apprehended independent of concepts. Another characteristic of intuition is that the experiencing-self and the object of knowledge are not experienced as separate but form an experienced unity.

The primary examples which Bergson gives as objects of knowledge for intuition are: motion, "la durée réellé" and one's own personality.[63] The extreme case of innocent cognition, in Maslow's theory of cognition, is very similar to Bergson's view of intuition. There is however one important difference. The objects of knowledge which Maslow names in connection with innocent cognition are things and human beings (see the type of peak-experience, named suchness in section 3.2.). A more exhaustive comparison between Bergson's view on intuition and Maslow's view on innocent cognition will be made in chapter 4, section 4.2.

We can summarize, in Maslow's theory of cognition, the following hypotheses:

(a) hypotheses concerning which forms of cognizing can be present in the process of cognition. The most important ones are: organization, selection, projection and identification.
(b) hypotheses concerning the time when these forms of cognizing actually are at work and why they work as they do. These hypotheses refer to states of motivation.
(c) hypotheses concerning the results of the activity of the different forms of cognizing.

We shall in the next section (3.2) turn to (c).

3.2. Descriptions of How the Subject$_k$ Experiences CTR During Peak-Experience

This section aims at clarifying the content of Y in argument A. An interpretation of argument A, after the clarification of cognition of type II and the content in Y, will be presented at the end of this chapter, in section 3.6. The descriptions below refer primarily to how the subject$_k$ experiences CTR during peak-experience, that is, descriptions of the cognitive contents of consciousness. These descriptions also claim to describe states of affairs in CTR and are therefore in the second instance descriptions of CTR.

"I want to stress that these [peak-experiences] are claimed to be descriptive characteristics; the reports say these are facts about the world. They are descriptions of what the world appears to be, what it looks like, even they claim, of what it is. They are in the same category as the descriptions that a newspaper reporter or a scientific observer would use after witnessing some event . . . They are not hallucinations; they are not merely emotional states, lacking cognitive reference. They are reported as illuminations, as true and veridical characteristics of reality which previous blindness has hidden from them."[64]

Maslow's distinction between D-process and B-process aims at explaining changes in the percepts of the experiences which he embraces in "peak-experience". As we have mentioned earlier, one change is that CTR is perceived more complete in B-cognition than in D-cognition. Another change is that other aspects of CTR are apprehended in B-cognition which are not to be had in D-cognition. Maslow's descriptions in distinguishing between different types of cognitive contents in peak-experiences are very vague. He distinguishes explicitly between "Cosmic consciousness" and "the narrowing-down-kind of peak-experience".[65] He also names two other distinct descriptions, namely, "Unitive consciousness" and "suchness". We can add descriptions of CTR in non-moral value-terms, namely, "Being-values" as another distinct description of cognitive content in peak-experience.

The analysis below is an attempt to classify and clarify the cognitive contents in Maslow's descriptions of peak-experience.

A. Suchness

P perceives particular things, vegetables, animals and human beings in their suchness (in some contexts Maslow uses the term "realness"), that is, "Suchness . . . refers to the peculiar and characteristic defining whole-quality, or Gestalt, of the object which makes it exactly what it is, gives in it's particular idiographic nature, which differentiates it from everything in the whole world".[66]

One clarification of this is that intentional objects are individualized. They are perceived as unique complete wholenesses with great richness concerning their details, much nuance concerning their determinates, (Maslow calls this "intra-object richness") and independent of the characteristics of relations such as, usual-unusual and beautiful-ugly.

Maslow assumes that there are degrees of suchness, and a contextual reasonable interpretation concerning the extreme case is: proximal stimuli are not interpreted with concepts at all. Instead, the objects of knowledge are apprehended in an intuitive conceptless way (innocent cognition).

"An experience of redness or of pain it's own definition, i.e., it's own felt quality or suchness. It is what it is. It is itself. So ultimately is any process of classifying that is always a reference to something beyond the suchness of an experience. Indeed, this holds true for any abstracting process whatsoever, which by definition is cutting into the suchness of an experience, taking part of it and throwing the rest away. In contrast the fullest savoring of an experience discards nothing but takes it all in."[67]

A contextual reasonable interpretation is: Maslow implicitly differentiates between content of consciousness and an interpretation of content of consciousness through concepts. He assumes that a process of cognition independent of concepts is possible and that the ontological object is directly apprehended, that is, the ontological object is apprehended without any intentional object as an intermediary between the subject's$_k$ content of consciousness and ontological objects. According to Maslow, the ontological object is in this case apprehended more correct and more complete than in any other process of cognition. (We shall clarify this further in section 4.2.) These cognitive contents of consciousness are not completely communicable because they cannot be completely described in language due to the conceptless process of cognition.

In suchness, P apprehends the unique nature of the object of knowledge. This unique nature can be interpreted as a unique organization of the object's properties and the properties are, in a strict sense, also unique or non-comparable. This unique organization cannot be completely caught in concepts. In order to apprehend this unique organization a cognitive faculty which works without concepts has to take over.[68]

If P succeeds in maintaining the ability to apprehend ontological objects in their suchness, this gives P a feeling of closeness to CTR. This feeling Maslow calls "freshness" and can be clarified by an analysis of the description of the contents of consciousness in peak-experience which Maslow calls "the narrowing-down-kind of peak-experience". In these descriptions, the relation between the experiencing-self and the object of knowledge are emphasized and he found that the examinees expressed that the visual field was limited to one single intentional object. A vivid example which Maslow often uses is works of art and some loving person.[69] In these experiences, other realities outside the visual field are "forgotten". An expansion of identify takes place and the object of knowledge is not apprehended as distinct from or separated from the experiencing-self. Maslow denies the existence of a substantial self, that is, the existence of an unchangeable self "behind" the momentary contents of consciousness and which in itself can never be an intentional object but only indirectly inferred.[70]

The relation between experiencing-self and the object of knowledge can, in the narrowing-down-kind of peak-experience, be described as follows: self-consciousness is dissolved and the separateness between the experiencing-self and the object of knowledge is experienced as abolished and they are experienced as integrated into a unity.[71] This is one context in which Maslow states a transcendence of the dualism between experiencing-self and the object of knowledge. A contextual reasonable interpretation is: this transcendence is on the psychological level only. In his description of suchness he is still assuming a dualistic ontology. The reasons for this interpretation will be given in section C. below and in section 4.2.

B. Unitive consciousness

This term designates a type of experience in which the subject$_k$ experiences simultaneously an object of knowledge, from two aspects, that is, partly as an aspect with concrete properties and partly in a symbolic aspect or quality.

> " ... namely the unitive consciousness. This is the ability to simultaneously perceive in the fact—that is—it's particularity, and it's universality; to see it simultaneously as here and now, and yet also as eternal, or rather to be able to see the universal in and through the particular and the eternal in and through the temporal and momentary."[72]

In Unitive consciousness the symbolic aspect is not determined in relation to the subject$_k$. It is determined in relation to the object of knowledge, that is, the object of knowledge can show itself from different aspects (see quotation from Wittgenstein, below). Aspect should accordingly be distinguished from perspective. Perspective is related to, literally speaking, the subject$_k$'s point of view.

Not long before his death, Maslow states that Unitive consciousness can, in some people, be a permanent experience. The other types of experiences embraced in "peak-experience", that is, suchness, Cosmic Consciousness and B-values, are momentary experiences.[73]

The objects of knowledge which are apprehended from the symbolic aspect are described in two main ways:

I. The object of knowledge is experienced simultaneously as a concrete individual and as a manifestation of an "archetype", for example, a particular woman is experienced as a symbol of Mother Earth or the Life-giver.[74] The object of knowledge which is apprehended in the symbolic aspect is then experienced as sacred and eternal. The content given in this symbolic aspect is not hypostasized as existing in any ontological "place" outside the object of knowledge.[75] Maslow does not attribute this content any independent existence as we find in conceptual realism. In this type of Unitive consciousness, we can distinguish between the following factors in the process of cognition:

a) perception of a concrete object, for example, woman W
b) a kind of non-sensory apprehension of the symbolic aspect, for example, the Life-giver

c) an activity of synthesis in which the relation between an object (woman W) and the symbolic aspect (the Life-giver) is apprehended.

A variant of this type of Unitive consciousness is when a person experiences himself/herself from the symbolic aspect, and then as participator in a universal eternal role or in a universal mission in life. Maslow illustrates this variant of Unitive consciousness with an experience of his own:

> "For example, my experience of being bored in an academic procession and feeling slightly ridiculous in cap and gown, and suddenly slipping over into being a symbol under the aspect of eternity rather than just a bored and irritated individual in the moment and in the specific place. My vision or imaging was that the academic procession stretched way, way out into the future, far, far away, further than I could see, and it had Socrates at its head, and the implication was, I suppose, that many of the people far ahead had been their and in previous generations, and that I was a successor and a follower of all the great academics and professors and intellectuals. Then the vision was also of the procession stretching out behind me into a dim hazy infinity where there were people not yet born who would join the academic procession, the procession of scholars, of intellectuals, of scientists and philosophers. And I thrilled at being in such a procession and felt the great dignity of it, of my robes, and even of myself as a person who belonged in this procession. That is, I became a symbol; I stood for something outside my own skin. I was not exactly an individual. I was also a 'role' of the eternal teacher, I was the Platonic essence of the teacher."[76]

We can, in this experience, distinguish the factors mentioned above:

a) an experience of ourselves
b) an apprehension of a universal role (for example, the Teacher)
c) an apprehension of the relation between ourselves and the universal role.

Maslow does not in this variant of Unitive consciousness attribute the role any independent ontological existence.

II. The other type of Unitive consciousness which Maslow describes is as follows: the subject$_k$ apprehends the potential of the object of knowledge, that is, the content in the ideal actualization of the *object's* potential. The content in the symbolic aspect, in this type, is the potential properties as actualized. Maslow gives as an illustrative example the little child's potentials for development.[77]

In this type of Unitive consciousness the following factors, in the process of cognition, can be distinguished:

a) perception of an object's, for example, a child's, actual properties
b) an apprehension of an object's potentials, for example, a child's potential
c) an apprehension of the relation between an object's (the child's) actual properties and it's potential properties

Maslow uses the terms "aspect" and "attitude" in order to explain the contents of consciousness in Unitive consciousness. By gratification of basic needs and a changed attitude, the subject$_k$'s aspect blindness disappears and the subject$_k$ can apprehend the symbolic aspect. According to our view, there is a difference between "aspect in a narrow sense" and "aspect in a wide sense".

A stipulative definition of "aspect in a narrow sense" is:

aspect in a narrow sense = df. from a numeric identical proximal stimulus, a subject$_k$ forms two *inconsistent* Gestalts.[78]

A well-known example of this is Wittgenstein's rabbit-duck head.

A stipulative definition of "aspect in a wide sense" is:

aspect in a wide sense = df. from a numeric identical proximal stimulus a subject$_k$ forms two *consistent* Gestalts, one Gestalt (G_2) adds something to the other Gestalt (G_1).

Compare the following quotation from Wittgenstein:

> "Two uses of the word 'see'.
> The one: 'what do you see there?' — 'I see this' (and then a description, a drawing, a copy). The other: "I see a likeness between these two faces" — let the man I tell this to be seeing the faces as clearly as I do myself.
> The importance of this is the difference of category between the two 'objects' of sight. The one man might make an accurate drawing of the two faces, and the other notices in the drawing the likeness which the former did not see.
> I contemplate a face, and then suddenly notice its likeness to another. I see that it has not changed; and yet I see it differently. I call this experience 'noticing an aspect'."[79]

In this example, we can distinguish between the following factors:

a) perception of face A
b) perception of face B
c) an apprehension of the similarity between face A and face B

One Gestalt of this proximal stimulus is perception of face A and face B respectively (G_1). Another Gestalt is the apprehension of the similarity between the two faces (G_2). We shall introduce the stipulate term *"addition-Gestalt"* for G_2, that is, in Wittgenstein's example, the apprehension of the similarity between the two faces. In order to clarify Maslow's descriptions of contents of consciousness in peak-experience, we need this term in our language of analysis.

These addition-Gestalts are apprehensions of non-sensory properties, as, for example, development of potentials, participation in a universal role, and non-moral values. When Maslow states that P in B-cognition experiences other aspects of CTR than in D-cognition, we can describe this as: P experiences addition-Gestalts.

One problem is: how to interpret these addition-Gestalts? are these addition-Gestalts only subjective experiences or, do these addition-Gestalts also correspond to something in CTR? do descriptions of these contents of consciousness have claim to be knowledge and if this is the case what kind of ontology does Maslow assume? We shall deal with these problems at length in chapter 4. In this section, we shall give below some preliminary answers to these questions. Maslow writes:

> "I had better stress that talk of 'B' realm and 'D' realm is actually talk about two kinds of perception, two kinds of cognition, two attitudes toward the one world. It might also be better to talk about the unitive attitude, rather than about unitive consciousness. An example of the kind of confusion that could be eliminated by thinking of 'B' and 'D' cognition as simply two attitudes or styles of perceiving can be seen later in Suzuki's book where he finds it necessary to talk about transmigration, incarnation, souls, and the like. This is the result of hypostatizing these attitudes into real objective things. If I speak of these two kinds of cognition as attitudes, then these transmigrations, etc, simply do not apply, any more than they would to the new kind of perception that a person would have of a Beethoven symphony after he had taken a course in the structure of music. This also implies that the meaning, or the structure in the Beethoven symphony was there before the lesson took place; it was only that a certain blindness was lifted from the perceiver. He could now perceive, now that he had the right attitude, knew what to look for and how to look for it, and could see that the structure of the music and the meaning to the music and what Beethoven was trying to say, what he was trying to communicate."[80]

The analogy between Beethoven's symphony and Maslow's examples of addition-Gestalts has some differences. For example, while there is a given structure in Beethoven's symphony the problem is: we cannot *a priori* attribute any structure to CTR. We interpret Maslow's aim with this analogy as follows: if the subject$_k$ has some qualifications, the process of cognition is changed and the subject$_k$ can apprehend some specific aspects of CTR. The question is: what is the relation between these addition-Gestalts and the properties in CTR?

As a preliminary answer to this question, we shall, in a *reasonable* interpretation, make use of the classic distinction between primary and secondary properties. The statement: "The property E are attributed the ontological object A" can be interpreted in two ways:

I 1: P experiences the property E, and A has the property E (primary property)

I 2: P experiences A, and A has certain "possibilities" which make that when homo sapiens perceives A, homo sapiens experiences a property E (secondary property)[81]

A reasonable interpretation of I 2, in our analysis of Maslow's view, is to interpret secondary properties as disposition properties, that is, A has a disposition-base named "e" which makes it possible for P, when P has B-process, to apprehend E.

With the help of this terminology we can make the following interpretation of the addition-Gestalts. We do not attribute to the ontological object these addition-Gestalts as primary properties. The ontological objects have instead disposition-bases and when B-process is at hand homo sapiens gets experiences of these addition-Gestalts. If P has capabilities for B-process, P can apprehend several of the ontological objects' "possibilities" and in this sense other aspects of CTR open up for P. In chapter 4, we shall analyse further the distinction between primary and secondary properties and Maslow's arguments in favour of the existence of these disposition-bases.

C. Cosmic consciousness

Maslow names this type of peak-experience after R. M. Bucke.[82]

> "States tending toward ultimate holism, i.e. the whole cosmos, all of reality, seen in a unitary way; insofar as everything is everything else as well, insofar as anything is related to everything; insofar as all of reality is a single thing which we perceive from various angles. Bucke's cosmic consciousness".[83]

> "Also useful would be Bucke's use of cosmic consciousness. This is a special phenomenological state in which the person somehow perceives the whole cosmos or at least the unity and integration of it and of everything in it including his Self. He then feels as if he belongs by right in the cosmos".[84]

A contextual reasonable interpretation of these quotations is that they express a *Pan-en-hen-ism*.[85] In this view we can distinguish between the following factors:

(1) The experiening-self experiences that it belongs to or is united with everything that exist.
(2) Everything that exist is experienced as a whole.
(3) In this wholeness, there are no ontological categories besides matter and the consciousness of particular human beings.

We shall clarify these points below:

1. Maslow denies the existence of a substantial self (see, suchness, above). A reasonable interpretation of Maslow's descriptions of Cosmic consciousness is: the term "self" designates experiencing-self, that is, a non-objectifiable self-consciousness. In D-cognition this self-consciousness is experienced as distinct from and separated from the objects of knowledge. In Cosmic consciousness the experiencing-self is described as not being experienced as

distinct from and separated from CTR. Instead the experiencing-self is described as partly dissolved in and partly united with CTR. A reasonable interpretation is that self-consciousness has disappeared and the apprehension of the experience has also disappeared. CTR is directly apprehended, that is, without any intentional objects as intermediary. (See further chapter 4.)

2. CTR is experienced as a wholeness
(a) "insofar as everything is everything else as well"
(b) "insofar as anything is related to everything"
(c) "insofar as all of reality is a single thing, which we perceive from various angles".

Maslow does not clarify (a) and (c). In (b) Maslow asserts that the wholeness is the *experiences* (not through any theoretical model-description as in microphysis) of everything that exist, i.e., experiences of all entities in the universe being interrelated with each other and thereby forming a wholeness. The entities are not independent or distinct elements. They stand in an interrelation with each other and make a homogeneous connected wholeness. It is not clear whether or not this wholeness should be interpreted according to the theory of relation or as a wholeness in the Gestaltpsychological sense. According to the theory of relation, the wholeness is apprehended by the relations between the entities. In Gestaltpsychology, the wholeness is assumed to be something in excess of the entitites and the relations between the entitites, and therefore cannot be reduced to the sum total of the entitites.[86]

3. None of the entities in CTR are attributed any ontological category besides matter and consciousness of particular human beings. In Cosmic consciousness there is only a changed experience of (a) relations between the existing entities in CTR, and (b) relations between these entities and the experiencing-self. A contextual reasonable interpretation of Maslow's opinion is: he is against any assumption of there being an ontological entity or entitites "below" or "behind" matter in CTR of which these entitites are only different manifestations. (a) and (c) in point 2 above could be interpreted as if he assumed an entity "below" or "behind" individual human consciousness and ontological material objects, a dynamic "essence" which manifested itself in the different modi: human consciousness and ontological material objects. In this case Maslow's ontology should transcend the dualism in an ontological realism.

Our opinion is: it is *not* a contextual reasonable interpretation to assert that Maslow assumed any such a dynamic essence "behind" or "below" individual human consciousness and ontological material objects. Compare the following quotation:

"The B-realm must be seen through the D-realm. I would add that it can be seen in no other way since there isn't any B-realm in the geographical sense of being on the other shore someplace, or being quite different from the world, being something other than it, something not-world in the Aristotelian sense. There is only the world, only one world and the business of fusing 'B' and 'D' is really a matter of being able to retain both the 'D' and 'B' attitudes towards the one world. If we say anything else, then we fall into the trap of the other-world-liness which finally winds up in fables of a heaven above the clouds, some place which is like another house, or another room, which we can see and feel and touch, and in which religion becomes otherwordly and supernatural rather than this-worldly and humanistic and naturalistic".[87]

S. Grof, in his descriptions of various transcendent experiences in LSD-sessions, interprets Maslow's descriptions of peak-experience (actually, in our interpretation of Maslow's term "peak-experience", peak-experience of the type Cosmic consciousness) as follows:

" . . . experience of *cosmic unity*. Its basic characteristics are transcendence of the subject-object dichotomy, exceptionally strong positive affect (peace, tranquillity, joy, serenity, and bliss), a special feeling of sacredness, transcendence of time and space, an experience of pure being, and a richness of insights of cosmic relevence. Subjects frequently talk about timelessness of the present moment and say that they are in touch with infinity . . . "[88]

The key terms in this quotation, for our problem, are "cosmic unity" and "pure being". In the contexts where Maslow describes Cosmic consciousness, he uses interchangably the terms "unity" or "wholeness" (never "oneness") when he describes the character of the cosmos experienced in Cosmic consciousness. In a short conversation which the author of this dissertation had with Grof, after a lecture in february 1979, Grof stated his opinion that Maslow did not hold the existence of something "behind" the homogeneous whole in a Pan-en-hen-istic interpretation of Cosmic consciousness.[89] Our reasonable contextual interpretation is therefore: the wholeness is an addition-Gestalt and some or all ontological objects have disposition-bases of a certain kind, and in B-process, the subject$_k$ experiences this wholeness in the universe. (This ontological opinion will be precizated in chapter 4.)

D. The Values of Beings (B-values)

In Maslow's sources, there are also descriptions of CTR in non-moral terms. Maslow states that from the descriptions in his sources, the following B-values can be abstracted: "truth, wholeness, dichotomy-transcendence, order, aliveness-process, uniqueness, perfection, goodness, necessity, completion, justice, simplicity, richness, effortlessness, playfullness, self-efficiency, and beauty".[90] These B-values are not distinct from or separated from each other, they can be defined in terms of each other. "It looks as if any intrinsic or B-values is fully defined by most or all of the other B-values. Perhaps they form a unity of some sort, with each specific B-value being simply the whole seen from another angle".[91]

Maslow characterizes these as both facts about CTR and non-moral values in CTR. A contextual reasonable interpretation is: Maslow assumes an *intuitionistic value objectivism* in it's value-ontological sense. This view states that there exist certain axiological properties in CTR and that we can apprehend these axiological properties by an intuitive cognitive faculty.

> "Now we make our big jump: This same list of described characteristics of reality, of the world, seen at certain times, is just about the same as what have been called the external values, the eternal verities. We see here the old familiar trinity of truth, beauty, and goodness. That is to say, this list of described characteristics is also simultaneously a list of values".[92]

> "But B-values seen to be the same as B-facts. Reality then is ultimately fact-values or value-facts. The traditional dichotomizing of is and ought turns out to be characteristic of lower levels of living, and is transcended at the higher level of living, where fact and value fuse. For obvious reasons those words which are simultaneously descriptive and normative can we called 'fusion words'."[93]

> "The descriptive B-values, seen as aspects of reality, should be distinguished from the attitudes or emotions of the B-cognizer toward this cognized reality and it's attributes, . . . "[94]

A contextual reasonable interpretation of Maslow's intuitionistic value objectivism is: one must interpret B-values as addition-Gestalts. As we have stated above, Maslow assumes that when human beings have B-processes, other aspects of CTR open up than can be experienced in D-cognition. In this type of peak-experience, the aspects which open up are partly changed experiences of facts about CTR, such as "order, aliveness-process and necessity" and partly experiences of non-moral values in CTR, for example "justice, goodness and perfection". These non-moral values do not exist in CTR independent of human cognition. They are not primary properties. A reasonable interpretation is: there exist disposition-bases in CTR and when human beings have B-process, human beings can apprehend these non-moral values. (Maslow's ontological view will be analysed, at length, in chapter 4.)

E. Changed experiences of Space and Time

In peak-experiences there are changed experiences of Space and Time. Maslow's descriptions of these changes are very fragmentary, and he does not explicitly connect these descriptions with any of the named types of peak-experience A—D above.

Changed experience of Space

"Phenomenal Space" designates human beings' experiences of CTR with their five systems of cognitive faculties — perception, hearing, smell, feeling and tast. This phenomenal space will be distinguished from the physical space, in which ontological objects are localized.[95]

During peak-experience, P's judgement of P's localization in the phenomenal space is uncertain and P has little interest in the surrounding environment and becomes disorientated.[96]

When the attention, in suchness, is focused on one single object of knowledge, self-consciousness is dissolved and reflection over the content of consciousness disappears. The subject$_k$'s activity of localizing intentional objects and the subject$_k$'s own experienced body in the phenomenal space disappear (compare also Cosmic consciousness).

Changed experience of Time

During peak-experience the subject$_k$'s experiences of time, the so called phenomenal time, is changed.[97] P finds it difficult to make correct judgements concerning quantitative passages of time.

In suchness and Cosmic consciousness the experience of time disappear. This can be explained by the view that the experience of time is dependent on experiences of changes, and when no changes are experienced as in suchness or Cosmic consciousness, no time is experienced.

The contents of consciousness in peak-experience are also timeless in the sense that P does not relate these contents to any future course of events or any retrospective course of events. P only experiences the now-moment, and the contents are not a means to anything in the future and P does not relate the contents to P's earlier life, for example, why P is in this situation of experience.[98]

The contents of consciousness are also timeless in the sense that P judges these contents as universal. The contents of consciousness in peak-experience are timeless in the sense that they can be experienced by all human beings universally, independent of people's geographic localization or time. (Compare, Cosmic consciousness, B-values and the symbolic aspect in Unitive consciousness.)

3.3. Descriptions of How the Person Experiences Himself/Herself During Peak-Experience

These experiences are described in the same unstructured way in the writings of Maslow as his descriptions of processes of cognition and descriptions of experiences of CTR during peak-experience. Our account of how the person experiences himself/herself during peak-experience will be very brief. The reason for this is: the main object of investigation in this study is descriptions of CTR during peak-experience and their claims of being knowledge.

The person experiences of himself/herself during peak-experience are partly dependent on the situation in which peak-experience arise. Maslow states that the situations in which peak-experience are most frequent are situations associated with love-, parental-, childbirth-, nature-, music-, aesthetic- and erotic experiences, experiences associated with bodily activities, for example, dance and sport, experiences of creativity and insights in therapeutic or intellectual situations.[99]

The situations in which peak-experience arise are only one condition for peak-experience to arise. Peak-experience cannot, by volition, be forced to arise (except Unitive consciousness, see 3.6.). They arise spontaneously and primarily in the situations described above.[100]

The descriptions below of how the person experiences himself/herself during peak-experience are not distinct from or separated from each other. They are different components in the person's experiences of himself/herself during peak-experiences. Maslow calls these experiences "acute identity-experiences".[101]

The person has an *experience of identity*. This gives P, inter alia, a feeling of strong presence in the activities which P is engaged in. This experience of identity is explained by Maslow as: P is actualizing P's potentials and in connection with this activity the experiences of identity arise. P feels that P reaches the perfectibility of P's "inner nature". This experience of identity is sometimes extended to an expansion of identity. Maslow often illustrates this with two lovers' strong sense of community in which the experience of identity is extended beyond one's own content of consciousness and body to include the loving partner in one's identity. Another example of this expansion of identity is to be found in the relation between parent-child and between the artist and his/her work of art. Sometimes this expansion of identity concerns the whole universe (compare, Cosmic consciousness): the expansion of identity is extended, self-consciousness is dissolved and the experiencing-self is merged into the wholeness of the cosmos.[102]

The person can experience himself/herself as an *integrated whole* which means that there is an integration between the different functions of the body, both physiological and mental. The body's physiological and mental functions co-operate in an optimal way, i.e., a balanced harmonious and goal-directed co-operation takes place (Maslow refers in these contexts to Roger's term "full function").

The person *P does not experience any blockings*. P's activity takes place with

86

ease and naturalness, and is pointed in an unequivocal way towards an intended goal. The person P experiences himself/herself as being free from inhibitions, dread, self-criticism, fear and doubts and this leads to spontaneity and creativity in P's actions. Maslow explains this by stating that no energy is used for inhibitions and the like, P can make use of all of P's energy in P's mental or somatic activities. "He becomes like a river without dams". In these experiences the reflective consciousness disappears and P experiences the content in an unreflective way.[103]

The person experiences himself/herself as an *agent,* as a self-determined subject, as the "creative center of his activites" and this gives him a feeling of responsibility, self-confidence and high self-esteem.

3.4. Descriptions of Emotional Contents Which the Subject$_k$ Feels During Peak-Experience

Maslow is very short in his descriptions concerning the emotional content which the subject$_k$ feels during peak-experience.

He does not connect specific emotional content with certain descriptions of how the subject$_k$ experiences CTR during peak-experience or with descriptions of how the person experiences himself/herself during peak-experience.

Maslow asserts that the most common emotional contents during peak-experience are feelings of happiness, joy, grace, and a feeling of gratitude to the entity which the subject$_k$ thinks is the cause for the emergence of peak-experience, for instance, God, Nature, or some close person. Other emotional contents are: "ease", "effortlessness", "surrender", "awe, wonder, amazement, humility, reverence, exaltation and piety".[104]

3.5. Analyses of the Relations Between the Terms "Peak-Experience", "Nadir-Experience", "Plateau-Experience" and "Mystical Experience" in the Writings of Maslow

In order to clarify the term "peak-experience" further, we shall analyse the meanings of the terms which are closely related to "peak-experience" in the writings of Maslow.

Maslow contrasts peak-experience with nadir-experience. (The term "nadir" designates the point contrary to the point of zenith.)

"... the nadir experience e.g. the (to some) painful and crushing insights into the inevitability of aging and death, of ultimate aloneness and responsibility of the individual, of the impersonality of nature, of the unconscious, etc."[105]

A contextual reasonable interpretation is: descriptions of experiences embraced in the term "nadir-experience" are experiences of emotional reaction to certain existential conditions in the life of human beings, as, for instance, experiences of death, guilt, loneliness and forsakeness. These descriptions of experiences are contrary to the descriptions of experiences embraced in "peak-experience" and are not included in the term "peak-experience".

Maslow introduced the term "plateau-experience" late in his writings. This term appears for the first time in 1969.[106] Maslow discusses this term most explicitly in an article written down after a tape recorded discussion 16/4 1970.[107] In this article, Maslow distinguishes between peak-experience and plateau-experience and he identifies plateau-experience with what we in 3.2. named Unitive consciousness. He illustrates the contents of plateau-experience with his own experience in the parade, and he also gives his own experience of the surf as an illustrating example.

"With the surf, you sense a contrast between your own temporary nature and the surf's eternity—the fact it will be there always was there always, and that you are witnessing something that's a million years old and will be there a million years from now. I pass, and my own reaction to that is one of sadness on the one hand of great appreciation on the other hand. It seems to me that the surf is more beautiful to me now than it used to be, and more touching."[108]

Peak-experience and plateau-experiences are different in the following ways:

(1) Experiences embraced in "plateau-experience" can be rather perpetual and are emotionally "calm". Experiences embraced in "peak-experience" are momentary and have a strong emotional intensity. Maslow compares the latter with the sexual orgasm.

(2) Experiences which Maslow embraces in "plateau-experience" can be learnt and these experiences can be evoked by volition. Experiences embraced in "peak-experience" emerge spontaneously and cannot be evoked by volition. "Peak-experience come unexpectedly, suddenly they *happen* to us."[109]

(3) Experiences embraced in "plateau-experience" always have a cognitive content.

"The important point that emerges from these plateau experiences is that they're essentially cognitive. As a matter of fact almost by definition, they represent a witnessing of the world."[110]

Experiences embraced in "peak-experience" do not need to have cognitive content, sometimes they have only an emotional content.

He also mentions very briefly, that plateau-experiences can be of different degrees, "high or low plateau-experiences". However, he never discusses the meaning of these different degrees.

Before he introduces the term "plateau-experience", he embraces experiences of the type Unitive consciousness in "peak-experience". In 1970 he does not discuss whether plateau-experiences can be embraced in "peak-experience" or not. He only states that they have some emotional content in common. A reasonable interpretation is: he embraces plateau-experience as a specific subset within "peak-experience". We shall discuss this further in chapter 5 when we analyse what kind of term the term "peak-experience" itself is.

The relation between peak-experience and mystical-experience is very hard to clarify in Maslow's writings. One reason is that he does not define the meaning of "mystical-experience".

In some texts, he states rather briefly that peak-experience and mystical experience are two distinct experiences.[111] In these contexts Maslow argues with the help of W. James' characteristics of mystical experience. His interpretation of James' opinion is: it is necessary for the mystic to go through "the dark night of the soul" in order to have a mystical experience. This is, according to Maslow, not necessary in the case of peak-experience. Maslow does not give any other distinguishing characteristics. He only notes:

> "What their true relationship is I do not know. My best guess is that they are different in degree but not in kind. The total mystical experience, as classically described, is more or less approached by greater or lesser peak-experience."[112]

According to the quotation, Maslow asserts that there are certain "degrees" between the experiences which he embraces in "peak-experience". However, he does not give any criteria or characteristics for distinguishing between these different "degrees" of peak-experience.

In other texts, Maslow uses the terms "peak-experience" and "mystical experience" as synonyms or closely related in their meanings. A contextual reasonable interpretation is: in most texts he embraces mystical experiences in "peak-experience". Our reasons for this interpretation are: he thinks that they are "different in degree but not in kind" and he often uses these terms synonymously or very closely related.

> "Peak-experiences as I have defined them for this analysis are secularized religious or mystical or transcendent experience . . . [113]

> "And may I also emphasize that such after effects of esthetic experience, creative experience, love experience, mystic experience, insight experience, and other peak-experience . . . "[114]

3.6. A Second Precization of Argument A

After our clarification of the different cognitive faculties B-cognition and D-cognition and our clarification of the content in Maslow's term "peak-experience", we can precizate Argument A further.

In 2.3. we formulated Argument A_3 as:

(1) If a person P has P's deficiency-needs gratified and P's actions are directed towards gratifying P's self-actualizing needs, P will actualize some characteristics X, Y, Z . . ., and if P actualizes the characteristics X, Y, Z . . ., P will have B-cognition
(2) If a person P has B-cognition, P will have knowledge of Y
(3) There are persons Ps whose deficiency-needs are gratified and whose actions are directed towards gratifying their self-actualizing needs and who have the characteristics X, Y, Z . . .

(4) There are persons Ps who have knowledge of Y

After our analysis in 3.0.—3.5. we can interpret the Argument as:

Argument A_4

(1) If a person P has P's deficiency-needs gratified and P's actions are directed towards gratifying P's self-actualizing needs, P will actualize some characteristics X, Y, Z . . ., and if P actualizes the characteristics X, Y, Z . . ., P will have a process of cognition which is characterized by (a) specific changes in attention and (b) passive forms of cognizing
(2) If a person P has a process of cognition which is characterized by (a) specific changes in attention and (b) passive forms of cognizing, P will have experiences of type suchness, Unitive consciousness, Cosmic consciousness and B-values, and P has knowledge that P's descriptions of these experiences have referents in CTR
(3) There are persons Ps who have their deficiency-needs gratified and whose actions are directed towards gratifying their self-actualizing needs and who have the characteristics X, Y, Z . . .

(4) There are persons Ps who have knowledge that their descriptions of their experiences of type suchness, Unitive consciousness, Cosmic consciousness and B-values have referents in CTR.

As we noted in 2.3. there is a vagueness regarding how we shall interpret the different implications in the argument. We shall discuss this problem in 4.5.
Another difficulty is premiss (2). Maslow's connection between the genesis

and justification of knowledge can be clearly seen if we separate the two conjunctions in premiss (2):

(2') If a person P has a process of cognition which is characterized by (a) specific changes in attention and (b) passive forms of cognizing, *P will have experiences* of type suchness, Unitive consciousness, Cosmic consciousness and B-values

(2") If a person P has a process of cognition which is characterized by (a) specific changes in attention and (b) passive forms of cognizing, *P has knowledge that P's descriptions* of the content of consciousness of the types suchness, Unitive consciousness, Cosmic consciousness and B-values have referents in CTR.

In (2') we have the *genesis* of peak-experience and in (2") we have the *justification* for P knowing P's descriptions of peak-experience to have referents in CTR. In chapter 4 we shall precizate premiss (2") even further and analyse Maslow's arguments in favour of this premiss.

Chapter 4: Maslow's Theory of Knowledge

4.0. Introduction

In this chapter, we shall clarify further premiss (2) in Argument A. We shall also reconstruct Maslow's argument in favour of the reasonableness of holding premiss (2). In section 4.5., we shall discuss the tenability of the complete Argument A. A reasonable interpretation of Maslow's ontology as an intermediary between a supernaturalistic ontology and a purely materialistic ontology will also be presented in this chapter.

In chapter 1, we formulated premiss (2) in Argument A as follows:

(2) If P has B-cognition, P will have knowledge of Y

After our clarification of B-cognition and peak-experience in chapter 3, we made two interpretations of premiss 2, one concerning the genesis of peak-experiences (2') and the other concerning the epistemological justification of peak-experiences (2"). We shall discuss (2") in this section.

(2") If P has a process of cognition which is characterized by (a) specific changes in attention and (b) passive forms of cognizing, P has knowledge that P's description of the contents of consciousness of the types suchness, Unitive consciousness, Cosmic consciousness and B-values have referents in CTR.

Descriptions of contents of consciousness of the types suchness, Unitive consciousness, Cosmic consciousness and B-values are in our terminology descriptions of B-percepts. In chapter 1, we made the distinction between the following two opinions of Maslow:

1. Some B-percepts are more complete than D-percepts with regard to the parts of CTR which can be experienced in both D-cognition and B-cognition, and P has knowledge that P's descriptions of these B-percepts have referents in CTR.
2. Some B-percepts also contain aspects of CTR which cannot be experienced in D-cognition, and P has knowledge that P's descriptions of these aspects (addition-Gestalts) in B-percepts have referents in CTR.

We shall name 1 above, *Maslow's epistemological thesis 1*, and 2 above *Maslow's epistemological thesis 2*. Theses 1 and 2 are two lines of precization of premiss (2") in Argument A. The difference between thesis 1 and thesis 2 is: thesis 1 concerns contents of consciousness which attribute ontological objects properties which can be apprehended in "normal" perception, i.e., sensible properties, for example, colour, size, solidity, form, taste and temperature. With a term borrowed from G. E. Moore, we shall name these properties — *natural properties.*[1] Thesis 2 concerns contents of consciousness which attribute ontological objects properties which transcend sensible properties, that is, the addition-Gestalts which we described in 3.3. We shall name these properties — *non-natural properties.*

Theses 1 and 2 concern different descriptions of contents of consciousness in peak-experience. For our further analysis we shall make the following distinctions concerning these descriptions:

(a) contents of consciousness which can be characterized as experiences of material objects
(b) contents of consciousness which can be characterized as experiences of human beings
(c) contents of consciousness which can be characterized as experiences of symbolic aspects of material objects and human beings (Unitive consciousness)
(d) contents of consciousness which can be characterized as experiences of all that exists as interrelated (Cosmic consciousness)
(e) contents of consciousness which can be charaterized as non-moral values (B-values)

Thesis 1 concerns (a) above, that is, perceptions of material objects which do not contain any addition-Gestalts. Thesis 2 concerns the addition-Gestalts under (c), (d) and (e) above. (b) above concerns particular person's characterustics and these descriptions of contents of consciousness will not be discussed until section (6.3.). The reason being: Maslow mainly discusses these descriptions in connection with methods in personality investigations and psychotherapy.

Maslow's argumentation in favour of theses 1 and 2 is based on his theory of cognition.

> "B-cognition, because it makes human-irrelevance more possible, enables us thereby to see more truly the nature of the object in itself."[2]

> "The word and the concept 'contemplation' can, then, be understood as a form of nonactive, noninterfering witnessing and savoring. That is, it can be assimilated to Taoistic, nonintruding, receptivity to the experience. In such a moment the experience happens instead of being made to happen. Since this permits it to be itself, minimally distorted by the observer, it is in certain instances a path to more reliable and more veridical cognition."[3]

93

Maslow assumes, in his argumentation, that the process of cognition is relevant in his judgements concerning the claims of knowledge of these descriptions of contents of consciousness and therefore we have to emphasize the distinction which we put forward in 3.1., that is, (a) percept *qua* percept, that is, percept on the level of consciousness (b) descriptions of percept, that is, percept on the semantic level. Maslow oscillates between these two levels in his argumentation. In our analyses, we shall state which level is under consideration.

This chapter will be outlined as follows: we shall first clarify thesis 1 and reconstruct Maslow's argument in favour of this thesis. The reason for this being: the results of our analysis of thesis 1 can be used in a fruitful way when we clarify thesis 2 and when we reconstruct and discuss Maslow's arguments in favour of thesis 2.

When we clarify thesis 1, we shall clarify the formal differences between B-percept and D-percept (4.1.0.). This analysis will be followed by a clarification of Maslow's ontological realism (4.1.1.) and an account of Maslow's view of the relation between contents of consciousness and ontological objects (4.1.2.). These stages will lead up to a precization of thesis 1. In section 4.2., we shall reconstruct Maslow's argument in favour of thesis 1. In section 4.3., we shall precizate thesis 2 and in 4.4. we shall reconstruct Maslow's arguments in favour of thesis 2. The chapter will finish with a critical discussion of Maslow's arguments in favour of theses 1 and 2 and a discussion of the tenability of the complete Argument A 4.5.

4.1. Precization of Maslow's Epistemological Thesis 1

4.1.0. The formal differences between B-percept and D-percept

These differences concern, primarily, differences on the level of consciousness, and in order to clarify these differences we shall use the distinction between numerical, qualitative and abstract differences.[4] If the persons P and Q perceive a numerical identical ontological object (which they in our example identify as a car), their percepts are *numerically different.*

Their percepts can also be *qualitatively different*, for example, P perceives a blue car while Q perceives a grey car.[5]

These percepts can also be *abstractly different.* P identifies proximal stimuli as, for example, a small car while Q identifies proximal stimuli as a light-blue Volvo 343, of the year 1978, with sliding roof and extra headlights. In abstract difference, the percepts do not have to be logically inconsistent, but as we can see from our example, Q's percept contains more determinables-determinates than P's percept (see the analysis concerning innocent cognition, 3.3.).

Logically, P's and Q's percepts can be qualitatively different concerning some attributes and abstractly different concerning some other attributes. We can now formulate the formal differences between B-percept and D-percept:

Case a. B-percept is qualitatively different from D-percept, that is, at least one attribute in B-percept is logically inconsistent with an attribute in D-percept

Case b. Concerning at least one attribute, B-percept is abstractly different from D-percept but this or these attributes are *not* logically inconsistent with some attributes in D-percept

Case c. Concerning at least one attribute, B-percept is abstractly different from D-percept and this or these attributes are logically inconsistent with some attributes in D-percept

The logical possibilities b and c precizate in which sense B-percepts are *more complete* than D-percept (c logically implies a). Accordingly, the expression "more complete" designates a relation between B-percepts and D-percepts.

When Maslow also assumes that a person's descriptions of B-percepts are knowledge, he relates B-percepts (and D-percepts) to CTR. Therefore, when B-percepts are different from D-percepts, according to a, b and c, we shall, in the following, state that B-percept *correspond more correctly* with CTR than D-percepts.

The expression "B-percepts correspond more correctly with CTR than D-percepts" designates a relationship between B-percepts and D-percepts in relation to CTR.

The expression "correctly correspond" is vague. We shall first precizate the term "correspond" and then precizate the expression "correctly correspond".

4.1.1. Maslow's ontological realism

We have in 3.1. classified Maslow's ontological view as an ontological realism. The term "correspond" states a certain relation between percepts and ontological objects. This relation can be precizated in different ways, and below, we shall give a contextual reasonable interpretation of Maslow's view concerning this relation. However, we have first to clarify Maslow's ontological realism.

A contextual reasonable interpretation of Maslow's ontological realism is: it is in agreement with the common-sense-view which G. E. Moore formulates in *Some Main Problems of Philosophy.*[6] According to Moore, common-sense characterizes ontological material objects as:

(1) They do not have any acts of consciousness
(2) They exist even if human beings are not conscious of them

(3) They have extension in space, that is, the ontological material object x has a distance to other material objects and this distance can be specified in some direction from x
(4) They have temporal duration
(5) They are intersubjective
(6) They have the properties which human beings perceive in sense-experience.

Common-sense also assumes that human beings have acts of consciousness of different kinds, for example, perceptions, memories, dreams, wants and expectations. Moore also distinguishes between acts of consciousness, for instance, sensing, and contents of consciousness (sense-data).

4.1.2. The relation between intentional objects and ontological objects

Point 6 in the common-sense view above concerns the relation between intentional objects and their attributes and ontological objects' properties. It is very hard to find a contextual reasonble interpretation of Maslow's view on this relationship because he never discusses this problem in any explicit manner. His statements are very general as is exemplified by the following quotations.

> "To know this reality as it is rather than as we should like it to be ... Kant was certainly correct in claiming that we never fully know nonhuman reality, yet it is possible to get closer to it, to know it more truly or less truly."[7]

> "What is the best way of perceiving something as it is, least contaminated by our hopes, fears, wishes, goals? ... Is there another path to 'objectivety' that is, to seeing things as they really are."[8]

Maslow rejects the view that this relation should be analysed in terms of isomorphy. He also rejects the claim that ontological objects should be described in terms of "physical qualities". A contextual resonable interpretation is that this relation will be interpreted in terms of "picture"-correspondence, and in the ideal case, a qualitative identity can be at hand between the attributes of intentional objects and ontological objects' properties. Maslow's view can therefore be classified as *a version of representative realism.*[9]

Maslow argues against the different theories about CTR which take their basis from sense-experiences, but with regard to CTR reject the correctness of the reality which human beings experience through their senses.

> "Is the abstract world of the physicist more 'real' than the world of the phenomenologist? Why need we think so? If anything the contradiction of this statement is easier to defend. What exists here and now and what we actually experience is certainly more immediatly real than the formula, the symbol, the sign, the blueprint, the word, the name, the schema, the model, the equation, etc. What exists now is in this same sense more real than its origins, its putative constituents or causes or precursors; it is

experientially more real than anything it can be reduced to. At least we must reject the definition of reality as being only the abstractions of science."[10]

We shall make below some distinctions which will serve as our analytical conceptual framework in our attempt to establish a reasonable interpretation of Maslow's epistemological theses 1 and 2. We shall follow N. Goodman's analysis of ontological material objects. He states that they can be analysed as spatial and temporal states of series. The ontological material object is identical with the sum of the spatial and temporal states which it passes. These states of series in CTR, during time t_1-t_n, will be distinguished from the ontological material objects' presentations (phenomenological events), that is, an ontological material object's different presentations (or representations) for the persons P, Q, Z . . ., during time t_1-t_n, or in other words, how P, Q, Z . . . experience the ontological material object during time t_1-t_n. Naturally, P, Q, Z . . . only experience certain temporally different cross-sections of the ontological material object's total states of series.[11]

We shall also make a distinction which is influenced by E. Kaila. *Ontological material objects' properties* during its states of series will be named *f-properties*. The ontological objects' have these f-properties independent of human acts of consciousness.

The properties which we attribute *intentional objects*, that is, ontological objects' presentations, will be named *φ-properties*.[12]

We have in 4.0. also distinguished between *natural and non-natural-properties*. It is hard, in our attempt to state a reasonable interpretation of Maslow's view concerning the relation between intentional objects' φ-properties and ontological objects' f-properties, to judge whether or not all of intentional objects' natural φ-properties can be qualitatively identical with ontological objects' f-properties. This problem concerns the old problem between primary and secondary properties. Maslow does not discuss this problem in connection with intentional objects' natural φ-properties and in the following analysis we shall presuppose the logical possibility that all of intentional objects' natural φ-properties can be qualitatively identical with ontological objects' f-properties. We shall illustrate our distinction with a sketch which we have developed from an idea found in A. Wedberg's *Filosofins historia, del II* (The history of philosophy, vol. II).[13]

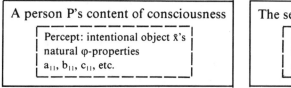
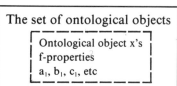

Fig. 1.

A person P's percept is a part (subset) of P's content of consciousness. An ontological object x is part (subset) of the set of ontological objects. At time t_1 the ontological object x has the f-properties a_1, b_1, c_1 etc. At time t_1 P has an act of consciousness with a content containing, inter alia, an intentional object x̄ with the natural φ-properties a_{11}, b_{11}, c_{11}, etc.

Concerning ontological material objects, we can now clarify the sentence "B-percepts correspond more correctly with CTR than D-percepts". The in B-percepts included intentional objects' natural φ-properties have always more cases of qualitative identity with ontological material objects' f-properties than the in D-percepts included intentional objects' natural φ-properties.

We can now clarify Maslow's epistemological thesis 1. This thesis can, on the level of consciousness (to be distinguished from the semantic level), be formulated as:

Epistemological thesis 1: B-percept is more complete and corresponds more correctly with ontological material objects than D-percept, that is,

(a) B-process gives a B-percept in which the included intentional objects' φ-properties are qualitatively *or* abstractly different from the in D-percept included intentional objects' φ-properties

and

(b) the in B-percept included intentional objects' natural φ-properties contains more cases of qualitative identity with the ontological material objects' f-properties than the in D-percept included intentional objects' natural φ-properties.

The disjunction in (a) is to be interpreted as non-exclusive. The conjunction between (a) and (b) is to be interpreted collectively, that is, both (a) and (b) must be at hand. In (a), we determine in which sense B-percept is more complete than D-percept. In (b), we determine in which sense B-percept corresponds more correctly with ontological material objects than D-percept, that is, concerning intentional objects' natural φ-properties. Concerning intentional objects' non-natural φ-properties and their relation to ontological objects' f-properties, see 4.2.

Maslow's argument, in favour of that P knows that P's description of the B-percepts, precizated above, have referents in CTR, will be reported in the next section.

4.2. Maslow's Argument in Favour of the Epistemological Thesis 1

Maslow does not in his argumentation distinguish between the following two different opinions:

I. B-percept A is more complete than D-percept B, and

II. B-percept A corresponds more correctly with CTR than D-percept B.

The statements I and II are logically independent of each other. B-percept A can be more complete than D-percept B, but this does not logically imply that B-percept A corresponds more correctly with CTR than D-percept B. The reversed relation between statements I and II does not follow of logical necessity either. In the following sections, we shall reconstruct Maslow's argument in favour of I simultaneously with II because his argument in favour of I is implicit in his argument in favour of II.

4.2.0. The classical account of knowledge

In this section we shall reconstruct Maslow's view of knowledge. We shall use the so called principle of generosity which states that when we interpret an author's statements we should attempt to make them as rational or as consistent as possible. In accordance with the so called classical account of knowledge the following necessary and sufficient criteria have to be satisfied.[14] Person P knows that p if, and only if:

1. The Belief-criterion is satisfied: P believes that p (p is a proposition)
2. The Truth-criterion is satisfied: p is true
3. The Evidence-criterion is satisfied: P has good and sufficient reason for believing that p

(The particular reasons r or q can be good reasons as individual reason, but not sufficient reasons as individual reason. Reasons r and q together can be a good and sufficient reason in the evidence-criterion. Accordingly, a reason has to be both good and sufficient, if the evidence-criterion shall be satisfied.)

p is in the *belief-criterion* related to a person P and P believes p because it is self-contradictory to state that "P knows p" is true and simultaneously assert that "P does not believe p" ("P knows p" implies "P believes p")

A serious problem emerges since Maslow is not clear about the distinction between content of consciousness on the level of consciousness and content of consciousness on the semantic level (that is, the descriptions of contents of consciousness, see 3.1.) and since he does not state any hypotheses concerning the relations between content of consciousness and language or between language and CTR. (However, in 3.0. we reported his opinion that contents of consciousness are more differentiated than language and therefore cannot be completely described in language.)

When we clarify *the truth-criterion* we have to reconstruct Maslow's theory of truth. By our clarification of the expression "more correctly correspond" in 4.1.1., we can make the contextual reasonable interpretation that Maslow's view can be classified as a version of the *correspondence theory of truth.* According to this theory, truth is a correspondence between statements p, q, r, etc. and CTR. (When we clarified the expression "more correctly correspond" in 4.1.2. this relation was between percept on the level of consciousness and ontological objects. In our clarification of Maslow's theory of truth we apply the principle of generosity.)

One difficulty with the correspondence theory of truth which is relevant in our analysis and which we can illustrate with our earlier car-example, is: if P identifies proximal stimuli as a car and states "This is a car", this statement in our example is true according to the correspondence theory of truth.

Q states, "This is a light-blue Volvo 343, of the year 1979, with sliding roof and extra headlight of the brand Hella". This statement is false according to the correspondence theory of truth. (In our example, we assume that one single statement in the conjunction is false, for instance, the car is from 1978.) The relation between P's statement (true) and Q's statement (false) and the car in our example, depends on the relation between a description's degree of precization and the risk of falsification, that is, there is a relationship of proportionality between a description's degree of precization (it contains more or less information) and the degree of possibility of it being a false description.

One solution to this difficulty with the correspondence theory of truth is to break down Q's statement (a conjunction) into simple statements and analyse the logical hierarchy of determinables-determinates, for example:

Volvo — model: Volvo 343
        age: 1979
        colour: a_1 blue, a_{11} light-blue
        details: b_1 headlight, b_{11} headlights of the brand Hella
           c_1 sliding roof

In our example, every single statement, excluding the description of the age of the car, is true. Q's conjunction of statements is more differentiated which means, inter alia, that it can answer more questions about the ontological object than P's descriptions. A description of D-percept can accordingly be true, but a description of B-percept includes a more complete description with more precizations and with the possibility of containing more true descriptions. We shall in section 6.5. discuss if Maslow thinks truth is a necessary criterion for knowledge.

As we mentioned in 3.1., Maslow has an empiristic tendency in his epistemology.

"Perhaps it is better to say that all of life must first be known experientially. There is no substitute for experience, none at all. All the other paraphernalia of communication and of knowledge — words, labels, concepts, symbols, theories, formulas, sciences — all are useful only because people already know experientially. The basic coin in the realm of knowing is direct, intimate, experiental knowing. Everything else can be likened to banks and bankers, to accounting systems and checks and paper money, which are useless unless there is real wealth to exchange, to manipulate, to accumulate, and to order."[15]

When we interpret Maslow's opinion concerning good reason in the evidence-criterion, sense-experience, is such a reason. Maslow does not discuss other types of reasons which in different ways can be related to sense-experience, as for instance, memory, deductive or inductive conclusions and theoretical elements in scientific theories.

He makes certain claims concerning the process of cognition when he discusses sense-experience as a good reason. In order to clarify these claims, we shall use the following illustrative example: the persons R, S, T . . . perceive one ontological material object x and they have D-percepts while person P perceives x and P has B-percept. Maslow argues in favour of P's B-percept corresponding more correctly with x than R's, S's, T's . . . D-percepts. By following his argumentation, we shall clarify his argument in favour of his epistemological thesis 1.

4.2.1. Maslow's argument in favour of the epistemological thesis 1

When Maslow argues in favour of P's B-percept corresponding more correctly with x than R's, S's, T's . . . D-percepts he does not discuss the problem concerning the existence of ontological objects, but rather what determinables-determinates (f-properties) ontological material objects have, for example, what kind of colour or form the ontological objects really have. Maslow also argues in favour of: P's B-percept can be qualitatively identical with the ontological objects. He asserts that if certain optimal conditions are at hand, P's B-percept can correspond correctly with the ontological objects.

We can express this in the following formal way: the intentional objects' natural φ-properties can, when the optimal conditions $y_1 - y_n$ are at hand, correspond correctly with the ontological material objects' f-properties.

Maslow advocates an *optimal theory* which will be distinguished from a *pattern theory* and a *standard theory* (see further below). The question is: which are these optimal conditions? Maslow only discusses conditions in relation to the subject$_k$ and *not*, for example, conditions concerning the medium between the percept and the ontological objects, for instance, smoke and fog, or conditions of light, or certain f-properties of the ontological objects', for example, transparency. Maslow focuses only on the conditions concerning the subject$_k$ and especially the different forms of cognizing which we analysed in 3.2. Maslow sets forth a view of isomorphy between the subject$_k$ and the correctness of the percept.

> "There seems to be a kind of dynamic parallelism or isomorphism here between the inner and the outer. This is to say that as the essential Being of the world is perceived by the person, so also does he concurrently come closer to his own Being (to his own perfection, of being more perfectly himself). This interaction effect seems to be in both directions, for as he comes closer to his own Being or perfection for any reason, this thereby enables him more easily to see the B-values in the world. As he becomes more unified, he tends to be able to see more unity in the world ..."[16]

Maslow's argument in favour of B-percept corresponding more correctly with ontological objects' f-properties than D-percept can be reconstructed as follows:

(1) D-percept is more worked at than B-percept
(2) The more a percept is worked at, the more incorrect will the percept be in relation to the ontological material objects

---

(3$_1$') The in B-percept included intentional objects' natural φ-properties correspond more correctly with the ontological objects' f-properties than the in D-percept included intentional objects' natural φ-properties.

The term "correct" designates percept on the level of consciousness, and concerning percept on the semantic level, we shall formulate the conclusion in the following way:

(3$_2$') Descriptions of the in B-percept included intentional objects' natural φ-properties contain more true descriptions of the ontological material objects' f-properties than descriptions of the in D-percept included intentional objects' natural φ-properties.

Maslow's argument in favour of B-percept being more complete than D-percept is a variant of the argument above:

(1) D-percept is more worked at than B-percept
(2) The more a percept is worked at, the more incomplete will the percept be in relation to CTR

(3$_1$") The in B-percept included intentional objects' natural φ-properties are more complete than the in D-percept included intentional objects' natural φ-properties.

On the semantic level, the conclusion can be formulated:

(3$_2$") Descriptions of the in B-percept included intentional objects' natural φ-properties contain more precizated descriptions than descriptions of the in D-percept included intentional objects' natural φ-properties.

Premiss (1) in the arguments follows from our account in 3.1. The conclusions are shorten formulations of Maslow's epistemological thesis 1. Premiss (2) in the arguments is Maslow's main argument and is in the arguments above formulated very generally. In a first attempt to clarify premiss (2), we shall distinguish between two lines of thoughts in Maslow's writings.

A. Maslow's assumption that the subject$_k$ does not work at the proximal stimuli. We shall name this kind of cognition *intuitive cognition*. Maslow does not explicitly use the term "intuitive cognition", but a reasonable interpretation of his term "innocent cognition" enables us to compare it with our precization of intuitive cognition in A below.

B. Maslow's assumption that the subject$_k$ works at proximal stimuli in different degrees and forms. We shall name this kind of cognition *discursive cognition*.

A. Intuitive cognition

When the subject$_k$ works at proximal stimuli, Maslow asserts the forms of cognizing which we reported in 3.1., that is, projection, selection, organization and identification. Maslow states that in intuitive cognition there is a more direct and unworked process of cognition. With direct cognition we shall in one possible interpretation (I 1 below) mean that P directly apprehends the ontological objects (compare suchness and Cosmic consciousness in 3.3.)

> "... that in the peak-experience we may even speak of identification of the perceiver and the perceived, a fusion of what was two into a new and larger whole, a superordinate unit."[17]

We shall make the following analysis in order to clarify intuitive cognition:

I 1: At time t_1 P has a percept with a content x:
  (a) P has a content of consciousness in which x is a part (subset)
  (b) the perceived ontological material object is a part (subset) of the set of ontological objects
      and
  (c) (1) x is part of P's content of consciousness and
      (2) x is simultaneously part of the perceived ontological material object

We shall illustrate this in the following way:

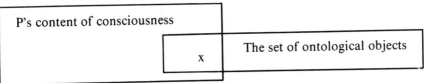

Fig. 2

x is simultaneously part of P's content of consciousness and part of the ontological material object. I 1 emphasizes the expressions "fusion" and "identification of the perceiver and the perceived" which Maslow uses in his descriptions of the relation between the content of consciousness and ontological objects in innocent cognition.

I 1 is not an unreasonable interpretation of Maslow's view on intuitive cognition. Maslow states that he is influenced by H. Bergson. When Bergson describes his view on intuitive cognition he assumes the in I 1 reported connection between the subject$_k$'s content of consciousness and the object of knowledge. Bergson names this extreme case of intuition "pure perception". B. Russell characterizes Bergson's view as *ultra-realism* : " 'In pure perception' he [Bergson] says, 'we are actually placed outside ourselves, we touch the reality of the object in an immediate intuition'. So completely does he identify perception with its object that he almost refuses to call it mental at all. 'Pure perception is really part of matter, as we understand matter' ".[18]

The Swedish philosopher A. Phalén asserts that Bergson in this view is influenced by and is in agreement with "post-Kantian speculation" which states that absolute knowledge of a (from the subject$_k$'s content of consciousness independent) reality is only possible if the subject$_k$ (or at least the content of consciousness) fuses with this reality. "I, in knowledge or in intuition, is this reality itself." However, Phalén thinks that Bergson, in disagreement with the philosophers of the post-Kantian line of thought, shows a tendency towards realism because the subject$_k$ is passive in this fusion with this independent reality. "... in Bergson's thinking the subject in knowledge or intuition, has to adjust, fuse and become merged into this independent reality." According to the post-Kantian philosophers on the other hand, it is "the subject who makes itself into an object for itself".[19]

One possible interpretation as an alternative to I 1 (I 2 below) is: Maslow does not assert that the content of consciousness x is a part of the ontological material object. We can interpret Maslow as saying:

I 2: Conditions (a) and (b) as in I 1

    (c) x̄ is an intentional object and its natural φ-properties are qualitatively identical with the ontological object's f-properties.

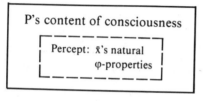
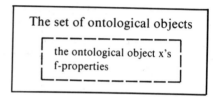

Fig. 3

I 2 designates the passive element in the process of cognition. We can also compare I 2 with Bergson's view.

Bergson thinks that in order to get knowledge of the true reality, the intellect has to be passive. During the process of cognition the intellect uses concepts which distinguish separate entities in the experienced reality. Intuition in the process of cognition, on the other hand, is immediate and passive and gives contents of consciousness which correspond more correctly with the true reality. Intelligence and intuition are completely different epistemological faculties and intelligence is only a means for practical purposes, for example, gratification of needs and survival. It cannot give correct knowledge of the true reality. Instead, intuition gives this knowledge. Bergson's opinion as to how we get knowledge of the true reality takes its basis from his ontology (his theory abour "la dureé réelle") and his theory about the nature of the cognitive faculties intellect and intuition.[20]

Maslow states that D-cognition is a means in order to get gratification of the basic needs and especially of the deficiency-needs and in D-cognition there are different forms of cognizing (see 3.1.). B-cognition does not have this aim, and in the extreme case, it can be characterized as a direct and passive process of cognition. In this kind of B-process there is no distorting of the ontological objects because proximal stimuli are minimally worked at. There is an organization in figure-ground but no projection. According to Maslow, rubricizing is the kind of form of cognizing which mostly distorts the percept. In innocent cognition, P perceives the ontological object with no rubricizing, that is, the subject$_k$ does not identify the object through concepts and the in B-percept included intentional object's natural φ-properties have qualitative identity with the ontological material object's f-properties. The subject$_k$ *discovers* the "intrinsic nature" or the "suchness meaning" of the object of knowledge.[21]

Maslow's reason for this is: in this direct process of cognition there are no forms of cognizing and therefore the subject$_k$ apprehends proximal stimuli passively and the ontological objects are perceived more completely and more correctly than in other kinds of processes of cognition.

A presupposition in Maslow's argumentation is: *all forms of cognizing distort the percept.* Proximal stimuli *cannot* be described as "raw materials" which are formed in the process of cognition. Instead, Maslow has to assume that in proximal stimuli the ontological object is presented in such a way that the subject$_k$ does not need to work on proximal stimuli in order to perceive the ontological object completely and correctly.

We shall discuss these assumptions in more detail, in 4.4. and 4.5., and in the latter section we shall also discuss Maslow's assumption: the process of cognition is relevant in judgements concerning justification of knowledge.

In summing up, we have interpreted Maslow's opinion of intuitive cognition as follows:

I.   a direct cognition according to I 1 and a passive process of cognition according to I 2

or

II. there is a passive process of cognition, but the subject$_k$'s content of consciousness is separated from the object of knowledge according to I 2.

B. Discursive cognition

In discursive cognition the direct process of cognition according to I 1 above is not at hand. Instead, the relation between the subject$_k$'s content of consciousness and the object of knowledge can be described as I 2 above. In discursive cognition there are degrees of forms of cognizing, for example, more or less organization, projection, selection or rubricizing. Maslow argues in favour of the assumption: the greater the degree of the forms of cognizing, the more incorrect and incomplete the percept. He does not make clear the relationship between incomplete and incorrect percept with regard to the different forms of cognizing, for instance: does projection distort the percept more than selection? Maslow only states that rubricizing is the form of cognizing which distorts the percept most of all.

Maslow's theory for determining which properties an ontological object really has, has been classified above as an *optimal theory*.[22] Maslow asserts that we can know which properties ontological objects really have and in his optimal theory he describes the conditions for arriving at such knowledge. According to our analysis above, these optimal conditions are focused on the subject$_k$, and importance is given to the subject$_k$'s gratification of the basic needs, the subject$_k$'s attitude and the different forms of cognizing in the process of cognition. In the extreme case, it is possible for the subject$_k$ to perceive the object of knowledge in a passive and direct way. In a formal way, we shall express this as follows: the ontological object x is attributed the f-properties a_1 because, when the optimal conditions are at hand, that is, when the subject$_k$ has the deficiency-needs gratified and has a positive attitude towards x, the forms of cognizing in the process of cognition are minimal and the subject$_k$ can experience the natural φ-property a_{11} which is assumed to have a qualitative identity with the ontological object's f-property a_1.

In intuitive cognition, according to I 1 above, a further condition in his optimal theory can be added: there is a "fusion" between the subject$_k$'s content of consciousness and the object of knowledge.

This optimal theory can be compared with the so called *pattern-theory*.[23]

One advocate of this theory is C. I. Lewis. He asserts that we can attribute an ontological object x the f-property a_1 when we can describe the complete pattern of a φ-property which x presents during all kinds of conditions. A criticism of this view is: common-sense attributes x the property red even if x during special conditions, which can be specified, presents the φ-property — purple.

A third theory, the so called *standard-theory* which N. Goodman thinks is reasonable, states that we can attribute the ontological object x the f-property a_1 because x presents φ-property a_{11} during certain standard conditions. These conditions do not logically have to be in agreement with the optimal conditions.[24]

The question which we shall discuss below is: are the optimal conditions which we have clarified in B-process necessary, sufficient or necessary and sufficient logical criteria in order for a reason to be good and sufficient in the evidence-criterion.

A contextual reasonable interpretation concerning natural φ-properties is that these optimal conditions are not suffcient logical criteria. Maslow adds the criterion of intersubjectivity:

> "As a matter of fact, the concept of objectivity itself (in the sense of the need to make knowledge public and to share it and not to trust it completely until it has been shared by at least several people) may be seen as a more complex derivative of a primary empirical rule, i.e., to check by one's own experience. This is so because public knowledge constititues an experiential check by several people on your report of your private experience. If you go into the desert and discover some unexpected mine or some improbable animal, your experiential knowledge may be certain and valid but you can hardly expect others to believe you entirely and on faith. They also have a right to see for themselves, that is, to acquire the ultimate validity of their own experiential knowledge. And that is just what objective public checking is i.e., an extension of 'see for yourself'."[25]

We shall use the following illustrative example in order to clarify Maslow's view: the persons R, S, T ... perceive an ontological object x and have D-percepts while person P perceives x and has B-percept. According to Maslow's optimal theory, P's B-percept corresponds more correctly with CTR and is more complete than R's, S's, T's ... D-percepts. For example, R, S, T ... perceive and describe x as a "red rose" while P perceives x as a unique flower. In P's description, P differentiates between the rose's different petals and each petal's unique form and colour, the rose's green stem with its unique form and colour, the forms of the spines, etc. Accordingly, P perceives the rose as a complex of attributes with more richness of details and a greater nuance concerning the determinables-determinates than do R, S, T ...

A contextual reasonable interpretation is: Maslow does *not* assume that P's optimal process of cognition (B-process) is a sufficient logical criterion for a reason to be good and sufficient in the evidence-criterion in our reconstruction of Maslow's theory of knowledge. Independent of whether or not R, S, T . . . have B-percepts, R, S, T . . . are able to perceive the natural φ-properties which P perceives and these natural φ-properties are then intersubjectively testable independent of any assumption of a special cognitive faculty.

In this section, we have discussed three criteria for a reason to be good in the evidence-criterion in our reconstruction of Maslow's view on knowledge:

1. there shall be no forms of cognizing or minimal forms of cognizing in the process of cognition
2. there shall be a "fusion" between the subject$_k$'s contents of consciousness and the object of knowledge according to I 1 above
3. descriptions of B-percept shall be intersubjectively testable and intersubjectively confirmed.

Which one or ones of these criteria does Maslow think is a necessary or a sufficient logical criteria in order for a reason to be good and sufficient in the evidence-criterion when Maslow discusses if P is justified in knowing that P's descriptions of intentional objects' *natural φ-properties* have referents in CTR? A contextual reasonable interpretation is the following: a sufficient logical criterion in order for a reason to be good and sufficient, in this context, is that these descriptions are intersubjectively testable and intersubjectively confirmed. The other two criteria above are in this context not necessary or sufficient logical criteria in order for a reason to be good and sufficient in the evidence-criterion.

4.3. Precization of Maslow's Epistemological Thesis 2

In our attempt to precizate Maslow's epistemological thesis 2, we shall make a resonable interpretation of his ontology as an intermediary between a supernaturalistic ontology, that is, an ontology which assume an ontological entity different from human consciousness and material objects, *and* a purely materialistic ontology.

In 4.0., we formulated thesis 2 as: some B-percepts contain aspects of CTR which cannot be experienced in D-cognition, and P has knowledge that P's descriptions of these aspects (addition-Gestalts) have referents in CTR.

In 4.1.1., we introduced the distinction between natural and non-natural φ-properties. We interpreted addition-Gestalts as non-natural φ-properties. In order to precizate thesis 2 further, we shall use the in 3.2. introduced distinction between primary and secondary f-properties.

"*Primary f-property*" designates property A of the ontological object which P perceives and names "A", for instance, form and solidity. Primary f-properties and natural φ-properties can in principle be qualitatively identical.

"*Secondary f-property*" designates a disposition-base, for example, disposition-base b of the ontological object, and when the condition V is added (B-process), P gets an experience of a property which P names "B". Secondary f-properties can therefore not in principle be qualitatively identical with φ-properties.

Secondary f-properties can be of two types:

(a) the disposition-base, for example, disposition-base b can be an inner property of an ontological object x, that is, x has f-property b. We shall hereafter name this type of secondary f-property — *inner disposition-base*. An illustrative example of inner disposition-base from another sphere (the aesthetic sphere) is the following: a certain picture x has an inner disposition-base b and when P perceives x P experiences a φ-property which P names "beautiful". In this example, one attributes picture x an inner disposition-base b and "beautiful" is not only a subjective experience in P's content of consciousness.

(b) the disposition-base, for example, disposition-base s can be a property of relation between two or more ontological objects. We shall hereafter name this type of secondary f-property — *relation disposition-base*. An illustrative example of relation disposition-base is the similarity between two faces (see Wittgenstein's example in 3.2.). Face A has a relation disposition-base s and face B has a relation disposition-base s and when P perceives faces A and B, P experiences a φ-property which P names "similarity". In this example one attributes face A and face B relation disposition-base s and "the similarity" between face A and B is not only a subjective experience in P's content of consciousness.

We shall clarify these various distinctions in our language of analysis with the help of the following sketch:

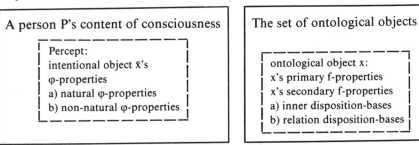

Fig. 4

In 4.1., we assumed that all intentional objects' natural φ-properties can correspond to primary f-properties. The addition-Gestalts are non-natural φ-properties and correspond in various ways (see below) to secondary f-properties.

We have introduced these distinctions in order to interpret Maslow's ontology.

> "The B-realm must be seen through the D-realm. I would add that it can be seen in no other way since there isn't any B-realm in the geographical sense of being on the other shore someplace, or being quite different from the world, being something other than it, something not-world in the Aristotelian sense. There is only the world, only one world and the business of fusing 'B' och 'D' is really a matter of being able to retain both the 'D' och 'B' attitudes toward the one world. If we say anything else, then we fall into the trap of the otherworldliness which finally winds up in fables of a heaven above the clouds, some place which is like another house, or another room, which we can see and feel and touch, and in which religion becomes otherwordly and supernatural rather than this-worldly and humanistic and naturalistic."[26]

Maslow rejects the existence of ontological objects other than ontological material objects and individual human beings' consciousness, but he is positive towards P's claim of knowledge that P's descriptions of the contents in peak-experience have referents in CTR.

We shall present below a resonable interpretation of Maslow's epistimological thesis 2 with regard to the ontology stated in the quotation above and his claims that P is justified in knowing that P's descriptions of contents in peak-experiences have referents in CTR.

Thesis 2₁: Descriptions of the in B-percept experienced content of the type Unitive consciousness have referents in CTR.

    Precization: Descriptions of Unitive consciousness include description of intentional objects' natural φ-properties and descriptions of a symbolic aspect (non-natural φ-property). The latter descriptions refer to ontological material objects' inner disposition-bases of a type a' and relation disposition-bases of a type a''.

The contents in the symbolic aspect vary with different intentional objects. The examples which Maslow gives are, for instance: a concrete woman can be experienced as Mother Earth or The Life-Giver, or a concrete man can be experienced as The Teacher. The contents in these symbolic aspects are a role or function which has been hypostatized and this role or function is experienced as eternal and sacred.

Concerning experiences of material objects, the contents of these symbolic aspects can be interpreted as follows: these objects manifest a general category which is attributed eternity and sacredness.

110

In some contexts Maslow compares this type of Unitive consciousness with Plato's theory of essence.

> "... the difference between reduced-to-the-concrete realism & the portrait which is of a particular person, like the head of Ellen [Maslow's daughter] & yet is also universal, & of a universal, of a B-symbol, i.e., of the Young Girl, any young girl seen Platonically, as in the B-analysis of male & female. Jeannie [Maslow's grand-daughter] is a particular baby, but she is also Babyhood, the representative of a whole class, of a Platonic idea."[27]

One possible interpretation of Plato's theory is: particular intentional objects are parts of eternal and unchangeable essences which exist in another onto-logical "place" than the particular intentional objects. In order to get knowl-edge of these essences, human beings must have a special cognitive faculty (noesis/dianoia). One important difference between Plato's and Maslow's view is that Maslow does not attribute the contents in the symbolic aspect any independent ontological existence. In fact Maslow's view has in this respect greater similarity with Aristotles' view than Plato's.

In the other type of Unitive consciousness there are particular human beings' potentials which are apprehended in the symbolic aspect. The type of contents in these aspects is an experience of the ideal development of the potentials of particular individuals.

The ontological claims of the contents in the symbolic aspects in Unitive consciousness are, according to a reasonable interpretation: some ontological objects have inner disposition-bases of the type a' and relation disposition-bases of the type a'' and when P has B-process P apprehends non-natural φ-properties, that is, the symbolic aspect in Unitive consciousness.

Thesis 2_2: Descriptions of the in B-percept experienced content of conscious-ness of the type Cosmic consciousness have referents in CTR.
Precization: Descriptions of Cosmic consciousness include de-scriptions of intentional objects' natural φ-properties and descrip-tions of all ontological objects and individual human beings' con-sciousness interrelatedness in a homogeneous whole. The latter descriptions refer to ontological material objects' and human be-ings consciousness' relation disposition-base of a type b''.

When P has B-process, the ontological objects' and human beings conscious-ness' relation disposition-base of a type b'' enables P to experience all entities in the universe as interrelated in a homogeneous whole. Person P experiences that he/she belongs to this whole and sometimes the differences between the experiencing-self and this whole are experienced as abolished and the experi-encing-self is merged into this whole.

The ontological claims are: all ontological material objects and all human beings' consciousness have relation disposition base of the type b". This type of disposition-base is different from the in thesis 2_1 named types of disposition-bases.

Thesis 2_3: Descriptions of the in B-percept experienced contents of consciousness of the type B-values have referents in CTR.
  Precization: Descriptions of B-values include descriptions of intentional objects' natural φ-properties and descriptions of non-natural φ-properties, that is, certain non-moral values, for example, truth, goodness and justice. The latter descriptions refer to ontological material objects' and some of human beings actions' inner disposition-bases of a type c' and relation disposition-bases of a type c".

Maslow advocates a version of intuitionistic value-objectivism in its value-ontological sense (see section 3.2.). When P has B-process some or all ontological material objects and some of human beings' actions have inner disposition-bases of the type c' or relation disposition-bases of the type c" and these disposition-bases enable P to experience B-values. The in 2_3 named types of disposition-bases are different from the ones in theses 2_1 and 2_2 named types of disposition-bases.

Thesis 2_4: Descriptions of the in B-percept experienced contents of consciousness of the type suchness have referents in CTR.
  Precization: Descriptions of suchness refer to (a) the unique organization of the material ontological object's f-properties and (b) the material ontological object's, in a strict sense, non-comparable f-properties.

In the type of peak-experience which we named suchness in 3.2. Maslow states that P apprehends a unique organization of the object's f-properties.
  We can compare Maslow's view concerning suchness with Bergson's view. Bergson states that in intuition the subject$_k$ merges into or fuses with the object of knowledge. In intuition the subject$_k$ gets what E. Kaila, in his interpretation of Bergson's view, calls a *knowledge of the essence* of the object of knowledge.[28] In the intellectual cognitive faculty the subject$_k$ can only apprehend parts of the object of knowledge. In intuition on the other hand the subject$_k$ can apprehend the uniqueness of the object of knowledge, that which cannot be compared with other objects of knowledge, the inner nature of the object of knowledge. Bergson calls this the essence or the absolute of the object of knowledge.

112

"Est relative la connaisance symbolique par concépts preexistants qui va du fixe au mouvant, mais non pas la connaissance intuitive qui s'installe dans le mouvant et adopte la vie même des choses. Cette intuition atteint un absolu."[29]

"Autant les idées abstraites peuvent rendre service à l'analyse, c'est-à-dire à une étude scientifique de l'object dans ses relations avec tous les autres, autant elles sont incapables de remplacer l'intuition, c'est-à-dire l'investigation métaphysique de l'object dans ce qu'il a d'essentiel et de propre."[30]

A possible interpretation of Bergson's opinion of the essence is: this essence is a substance which is "a carrier" of different properties of the object of knowledge. With the help of the intellect the subject$_k$ can only apprehend the natural properties of the object of knowledge, but not its substance "behind" the different properties.

We do not interpret Maslow's descriptions of the unique organization of the object of knowledge in suchness as an apprehension of a substance "behind" the different parts of the object of knowledge. The content of consciousness in suchness does not, in this interpretation, contain any non-natural φ-properties. Instead, a contextual reasonable interpretation is the following: the description of the uniqueness of an object of knowledge in suchness refers to an unique organization of the material ontological object's f-properties and these f-properties are, in a strict sense, unique or non-comparable.

4.4. Maslow's Arguments in Favour of the Epistemological thesis 2

The arguments to be analysed in this section are Maslow's own arguments and not arguments which Maslow only reports from his sources.

The ontological claims which he states are in a reasonable interpretation the following: (a) the existence of the inner disposition-bases of the types a', and c' and (b) relation disposition-bases of the types a'', b'' and c''. In order to clarify Maslow's ontological view, we have to complete the in section 4.1.1. described common-sense realism. In point 6 we have to add:

6. Ontological material objects have (1) primary f-properties, and (2) secondary f-properties of two kinds: (a) inner disposition-bases of the types a' and c' and (b) relation disposition-bases of the types a'', b'' and c''.

In his ontology Maslow *does not deny* the existence of primary f-properties. Addition-Gestalts only *add* the above mentioned (secondary) f-properties to CTR, that is, experiences of these addition-Gestalts in peak-experiences do not deny the reality experienced in D-cognition, *they merely supplement them.*

Natural φ-properties in D-percepts can in principle still be qualitatively identical with primary f-properties.

Maslow writes concerning B-cognition:

> "Partly I suppose the answer is that this kind of revelation-knowledge does not make four apples visible where there were only three before, nor do the apples change into bananas. No! it is more a shift in attention, in the organization of perception, in noticing or realizing that occurs."[31]

This view is in disagreement with the view of many mystics' own statements and the statements of many interpreters of transcendent experience. They state that the content in these experiences are veridical and that the reality experienced by ordinary senses is illusory. They state that the subject$_k$ in these transcendent experiences apprehends the *true* reality "behind" the ordinary experienced reality. Maslow's argument in favour of the existence of the disposition-bases above can be reconstructed as follows:

(1) The more a percept is worked at, the more incomplete and incorrect the percept will be in relation to the ontological objects

(2) In B-process there is minimal forms of cognizing from which there emerge contents of consciousness which can be described as Unitive consciousness, Cosmic consciousness, B-values and suchness.

From (1) and (2) Maslow concludes

(3) Descriptions of contents of consciousness named Unitive consciousness, Cosmic consciousness, B-values and suchness have referents in CTR.

Premiss (2) follows from our account in 3.1. and 3.2. The conclusion (3) is a shorten formulation of Maslow's epistemological thesis 2 and which sets forth the ontological claims in the theses 2_1, 2_2, 2_3 and 2_4.

In 4.2. we tried to clarify premiss 1. This premiss expresses Maslow's optimal theory. We shall illustrate Maslow's argument in favour of premiss 1 with an example: the persons R, S, T . . . have D-percepts and P has contents of consciousness which we can describe as Unitive consciousness or Cosmic consciousness or B-values or suchness. Certain aspects of CTR open up for P in these experiences while R, S, T . . . are unable to experience these aspects. In CTR there exist disposition-bases of the types a', a'', b'', c' and c'' which make it possible for P, in B-cognition, to experience the above named addition-Gestalts.

The question is: does Maslow think that B-process is a necessary, or sufficient, or necessary and sufficient logical criterion for a reason to be good and sufficient in the evidence-criterion when he discusses addition-Gestalts? In order to answer this question, we shall distinguish between three contexts: (a) *context of value*, (b) *context of discovery* and (c) *context of justification*.[32]

(a) *context of value* concerns the question: are contents of consciousness valuable? This question is epistemologically irrelevant because the question is about characteristics of the contents of consciousness in themselves. Maslow's answer to this question is: the contents of consciousness which are included in "peak-experience" are valuable. One reason for this is a question in Maslow's questionnarie: "I would like you to think of the most wonderful experience or experiences of your life ...?[33] They can be characterized as *intrinsic values*, that is, they are valuable because the experiences in themselves are valuable.[34] They are also *instrumental values*, that is, they can be means to ends which Maslow thinks are intrinsically valuable, for instance, P does not commit suicide, P stops using drugs or these experiences get P to feel more physically and mentally healthy.[35] They are also *contributory values*, that is, they are elements in the intrinsically good life.

(b) *context of discovery* concerns different methods for arriving at a knowledge of CTR. B-process is one such method, and B-process is even a unique cognitive faculty which reveals otherwise not knowable aspects of CTR.

> "If our hope is to describe the world fully, a place is necessary for preverbal, ineffable, metaphorical, primary process, concrete-experience, intuitive and estethic types of cognition, for there are certain aspects of reality which can be cognized in no other way."[36]

(c) *Context of justification* concerns the epistemological justification for a person P to hold P's statements to have referents in CTR. It is in this context that our question above belongs: does Maslow think that B-process is a necessary, or sufficient, or necessary and sufficient logical criterion for a reason to be good and sufficient in the evidence-criterion when he discusses addition-Gestalts?

Maslow has two lines of thoughts in answering this question.

A. According to one line of thought, B-process is a necessary and sufficient logical criterion for a reason to be good and sufficient in the evidence-criterion when he discusses evidence-criteria concerning descriptions of addition-Gestalts.

B. According to another line of thought, Maslow states other necessary logical criteria for a reason to be good and sufficient in the evidence-criterion when he discusses evidence-criteria concerning descriptions of addition-Gestalts.

We shall first analyse A.

In his argumentation in favour of this line of thought, Maslow takes his argument from his theory of cognition. His argument can be reconstructed as follows: if, and only if, the contents of consciousness have not been worked

115

at, P gets a more complete and more correct percept in relation to CTR than in processes of cognition where the contents have been worked at. A presupposition for this argument is the assumption: *all kinds and all degrees* of forms of cognizing distort the percept. In one of his journals, Maslow makes the following reflection in connection with Polanyi's book *Science, Faith and Society:*

> "It's as if he didn't understand the Taoistic attitude of yielding & surrender to the facts. 'I believe it' or 'I am the ultimate judger' is true, but not in the dichotomous sense of setting my will over against the world of nature. No, if I yield to the harmony of & with nature & 'gork' it, fuse with it, live it by being possessed by it, then I become it & the phrases 'I judge' and 'I believe' are no longer arbitary & Willfull, but are cognitive & veridical. 'Not my will, but Thine be done' is a good motto for the scientist too. Then, if he is a good, receptive, yielding Taoistic knower, he won't interfere with the knowledge he is getting & it will be less mixed up with his will & wishes & hopes. He must be a good receptacle, a noninterfering, humble 'camera' (of a peculiar kind) or it might be better said, a reporter of what is happening to him, as nature wreaks itself upon him."[37]

C. I. Lewis distinguishes between two separate lines of thoughts within epistemology:

(I)   the line of thought which emphasizes (over-emphasizes, according to Lewis) the subject's or consciousness' passive role in the process of cognition. Lewis names the following as advocates of this line of thought: different mystics, Bergson and American New Realists.

(II) the line of thought which emphasizes (over-emphasizes, according to Lewis) the subject's or consciousness' active role in the process of cognition. Lewis names the following as advocates of this line of thought: Plato, Fichte and the neo-Kantians.[38]

The former line of thought "identifies knowledge with some state of pure immediacy".[39] Lewis characterizes Bergson's criteria for knowledge as: "identification of knowledge with intuitive apprehension of the immediate". [40] Maslow's line of thought A places him in this epistemological line of thought which has the presuppositions: (1) if, and only if, the subject$_k$ does not work at proximal stimuli, the true reality is apprehended (and discovered) *or* in a weaker sense if, and only if, the subject$_k$ does not work at proximal stimuli, the subject$_k$ gets an experience of CTR which is more complete and more correct than in any other kind of process of cognition. This assumption is implicit in premiss 1 in the argument above and in Maslow's optimal theory and hence in premiss 2" in argument A_4.

Maslow can be regarded as an advocate of a theory which R. Ornstein analyses and which can be named a *filter-theory*.[41] This theory states that the subject$_k$ in *all* the different forms of cognizing takes away information from CTR. In his argumentation, Maslow makes the following generalization: some degrees and some kind of forms of cognizing distort the percept, hence *all* degrees and *all kinds* of forms of cognizing distort the percept. Maslow assumes that the true CTR reveals itself when P has taken away the *filter* in the process of cognition.

In agreement with Bergson, he assumes that a person P experiences the object of knowledge O and P has knowledge of O without identifying O through concepts (non-propositional knowledge).

The criterion for a reason to be good and sufficient in the evidence-criterion is the following: the character of the process of cognizing, that is, a process of cognition which has no forms of cognizing, or has minimal forms of cognizing. Bergson's and Maslow's argument is that concepts are inadequate in order to apprehend the true reality or certain aspects of CTR.

However, concerning identification of proximal stimuli, the primary instigator of Maslow's view, namely, Bergson, is very ambiguous on this topic. In some contexts, Bergson states that all concepts distort the percept, and in other contexts, only "static", "stable" or "immobile" concepts distort the percept.[42] The same ambiguity can be found in Maslow's writings. In some contexts, he states that an identification of proximal stimuli through concepts is a necessary causal condition in the process of cognition.

> "... words and concepts are absolutely necessary for organizing and ordering the welter of experiences and the ultraexperiential world of which they apprise us."[43]

Another argument which Maslow gives in his argumentation in favour of the line of thought A is: when the subject$_k$'s content of consciousness and the object of knowledge are integrated into a "fusion", the object of knowledge is apprehended more completely, and more correctly than in other types of processes of cognition. This argumentation hints at a kind of epistemological idealism in which the objects of knowledge (ontological material objects or relations between them) — in some way — are immanent in consciousness simultaneously as these objects of knowledge are attributed existence in CTR. We shall give some criticism of Maslow's line A in section 4.5.

Maslow's line of thought B

According to this line of thought, Maslow states other necessary logical criteria than B-process in order for a reason to be good and sufficient in the evidence-criterion when he discusses description of addition-Gestalts.

> "This problem of the veridicality of mystic illuminations is certainly an old problem. The very roots and origins of religion are involved, but we must be very careful not

to be seduced by the absolute subjective certainty of the mystics and of the peak-experiencer. To them, truth has been revealed. Most of us have experienced this same certitude in our moments of revelation. However, one thing that mankind has learned during three thousand years of recorded history is that this subjective certainty is not enough; there must also be external validation. There must be some way of checking the truth of the claim, some measure of the fruits, some pragmatic test; we must approach these claims with some reserve, some caution, some soberness. Too many visionaries, seers, and prophets have turned out to be incorrect after *feeling* absolutely certain."[44]

Maslow's reason for stating "external validation" is the rejection of psychological self-evidence as a sufficient logical criterion for a reason to be good and sufficient in the evidence-criterion. The question is: what does Maslow mean by "external validation"?

One necessary logical criterion is: intersubjective testability.

"Psychologists are only too aware of the shortcomings and even impossibility of a pure and sole introspectionism. We know too much of hallucinations, delusions, illusions, denials, repressions, and other defenses against knowing reality. Since you don't have my repressions or my illusions, comparing my subjective experience with your subjective experience is an easy and obvious way of filtering out the distorting power of my intrapsychic defensive forces. One might call this the easiest kind of reality-testing. It is a first step toward checking knowledge by making sure it is shared, i.e., that it is not a hallucination."[45]

This logical criterion is also connected with other logical criteria which Maslow names "routine skeptical and cautious procedures of science".[46] In order to clarify these criteria, Maslow's claims regarding objective scientific results have to be clarified. This clarification claims a rather extensive analysis of Maslow's philosophy of science. We shall do this in chapter 6. However, we can already hint that Maslow, in his philosophy of science, is somewhat influenced by the pragmatic line in epistemology and philosophy of science.

In some of Maslow's writings this pragmatism can be found in other contexts than in philosophy of science, for example, when Maslow states good reason in the evidence-criterion in connection with addition-Gestalts, he in some contexts states the valuableness of these experiences. They are instrumentally valuable, for example, they contribute to P's physical and mental health or they are means to fight against the culture-crises which Maslow thinks the Western-world is in today. These addition-Gestalts have an instrumental value and this value is a good reason in the evidence-criterion. In this case, Maslow thinks that *context of value* is relevant for *context of justification*. In Maslow's line of thought A above, we could notice how Maslow's argumentation presupposes that *context of discovery* is relevant for *context of justification*.

118

4.5. Discussion of the Complete Argument A

We shall analyse and discuss below the complete argument A. In 3.5., we formulated argument A_4 as follows:

Argument A_4

(1) If a person P has P's deficiency-needs gratified and P's actions are directed towards gratifying P's self-actualizing needs, P will actualize some characteristics X, Y, Z ... *and* if P actualizes the characteristics X, Y, Z ..., P will have a process of cognition which is charaterized by (a) specific changes in attention and (b) passive forms of cognizing

(2') If P has a process of cognition which is characterized by (a) specific changes in attention and (b) passive forms of cognizing, *P will have experiences* of type, suchness, Unitive consciousness, Cosmic consciousness and B-values

(2") If P has a process of cognition which is characterized by (a) specific changes in attention and (b) passive forms of cognizing P *has knowledge that P's descriptions of* the content of consciousness of the types suchness, Unitive consciousness, Cosmic consciousness and B-values have referents in CTR.

(3) There are persons P's who have their deficiency-needs gratified and whose actions are directed towards gratifying P's self-actualizing needs and P has the characteristics X, Y, Z ...

---

(4) There are persons Ps who have knowledge that their descriptions of their experiences of suchness, Cosmic consciousness, Unitive consciousness and B-values have referents in CTR.

Premiss (2') expresses the genesis of the content in peak-experience and sets forth a *causal* relation between B-process and the contents in peak-experience. This means that (2') can be excluded from argument A_4.

Premiss (2") expresses the epistemological justification for P to know that P's descriptions of the contents in peak-experience have referents in CTR.

We shall begin the discussion with some interpretations of the constants in the argument.

I. The logical form of premiss (1) can be interpreted as follows:

(1) $\forall x [(Sx \land Tx \rightarrow Px) \land (Px \rightarrow Ux \land Vx)]$

In premiss (1) Maslow sets forth, in our interpretation of argument A_4, certain sufficient conditions in order for P to have B-process: P should have

P's deficiency-needs gratified and P's actions should be directed towards gratifying P's self-actualizing needs and P should actualize some characteristics X, Y, Z ...

We have first to answer questions:

I.a.: is the gratification of the deficiency-needs and the self-actualizing needs necessary, sufficient or both necessary and sufficient conditions in order for P to actualize the characteristics X, Y, Z ...? and

I.b.: are these conditions of a causal or a logical character?

The answer to I.b. in a contextual reasonable interpretation is: these conditions are *causal*. Maslow sets forth an empirical generalization between the gratification of person P's deficiency-needs and self-actualizing needs *and* the actualization of the characteristics X, Y, Z ... It is harder to establish any unequivocal answer to I.a. In some contexts, a contextual reasonable interpretation is that the gratification of the deficiency- and self-actualizing needs are the necessary causal condition and in other context a contextual reasonable intrepretation is that these are the sufficient causal condition for the actualization of the characteristics X, Y, Z ... As we mentioned in section 2.2., Maslow does not set forth any specific relationship between gratification of specific deficiency- or self-actualizing needs and the actualizing of any specific characteristics X, Y, Z ...

In premiss (1) we have also to answer the questions:

II.a.: is the actualization of the characteristics X, Y, Z ... necessary, or sufficient, or necessary and sufficient conditions in order for P to have B-process? and

II.b.: are these conditions of a causal or a logical character?

The answer to II.b. is parallell with the answer to I.b. Maslow sets forth an empirical generalization between a person P's characteristics X, Y, Z ... and the capability to have B-process.

Concerning question II.a., Maslow often expresses himself as if these causal conditions are sufficient. This is the case in Maslow's descriptions of isomorphy between the health of the subject and the correctness of the percept.

> "In effect what I am implying is that honest knowing of oneself is logically and psychologically prior to knowing the extrapsychic world. Experiential knowledge is prior to spectator knowledge. If you want to see the world, it is obviously sensible to be as good a seer as you can make yourself. The injunction might read, then: make yourself into a good instrument of knowledge. Become as fearless as you can, as honest, authentic and ego-transcending as you can. Just as most people (or scientists) are not as fearless, ego-transcending, honest unselfish or dedicated as they could be, so most people are not as efficient cognizers as they are capable of becoming."[47]

In other contexts, however, Maslow states that these conditions are not necessary, or sufficient, or necessary and sufficient.

"Self-actualizing people tend more to this kind of perceiving [B-cognition]. But I have been able to get reports of this kind of perception in practically *all* the people I have questioned, in the highest, happiest, most perfect moments of their lives (peak-experiences)."[48]

One further problem is that Maslow does not specify which or how many of the characteristics which he attributes self-actualizing people (section 2.2.1.) are needed in order to develop the capability to have B-process.

A reasonable contextual interpretation in answering II.a. is: in most contexts some of the characteristics which Maslow attributes to self-actualizing people are necessary causal conditions for P to have B-process. However, Maslow is ambiguous on this point. In some contexts these characteristics only express a tendency, i.e., they give P a greater possibility to have B-process.

The conclusion is: the conditions in premiss (1) in argument A_4 are *causal*. Concerning the conditions in questions I.a. and II.a. it is very hard to state any unequivocal interpretation. In *one possible interpretation* the conditions in I.a. and II.a. are not together a necessary or a sufficient causal condition in order for P to have B-process. A consequence of this interpretation and the opinion that these conditions are only causal conditions is: *we can give up premiss (1) in Argument A_4*, that is, if the conjunction of the conditions I.a. and II.a. is not a necessary or a sufficient logical criterion in order for P to have B-process, premiss (1) can be excluded from Argument A_4.

An *alternative* interpretation of the conditions in I.a. and II.a. as necessary, *or* sufficient *logical* criteria in order for P to have B-process gives serious difficulties because, in our analysis in chapter 2, we found that the presuppositions and theories behind these criteria can be seriously questioned with regard to crucial points, see 2.1.1. and 2.2.4. Furthermore, it is hard to understand how the obvious casual conditions in premiss (1) can also be logical criteria.

II. Premiss (2') states certain conditions in order for P to have experiences of the types, suchness, Unitive consciousness, Cosmic consciousness and B-values (the context of discovery). These conditions are *causal* relations and hence can be excluded from argument A_4.

But we can ask the question: is B-process a necessary or sufficient causal condition in order for P to experience these types of contents of consciousness? A contextual reasonable interpretation is: Maslow states that B-process is a necessary causal condition in order for P to have these types of contents of consciousness. A reasonable interpretation is also: both (a) specific changes in attention and (b) passive forms of cognizing are necessary in order for P to get experiences of the types, suchness, Cosmic consciousness, Unitive consciousness and B-values. One reason is: we interpret Maslow as stating that (a) and (b) go together psychologically.

One critical remark against premiss (2') is that Maslow does not explain or in any other ways describe why B-process gives different B-percepts, that is, some times P experiences suchness, other times, Cosmic consciousness, etc. Other factors than B-process have to determinate the content of consciousness in peak-experience. Maybe the special situation P is in, for instance, a love-situation or insight-situation, is such a factor or some factor concerning the object of knowledge. Maslow does not discuss this problem at all.

III. Premiss (2") states criteria in order for P to be justified in holding P's descriptions of suchness, Unitive consciousness, Cosmic consciousness and B-values to have referents in CTR. In sections 4.2. and 4.4. we have discussed whether or not the logical criterion in premiss (2) (B-process) is a necessary, or sufficient or both necessary and sufficient criterion in order for P to be justified in holding these descriptions to have referents in CTR. In our analysis in 4.4. we found that Maslow has at least two separate lines concerning this question.

In *line A*, Maslow thinks that B-process is a necessary and sufficient criterion for a reason to be good and sufficient in the evidence-criterion.

In *line B*, Maslow thinks that B-process is perhaps a necessary but *not* a sufficient criterion in order for a reason to be good and sufficient in the evidence-criterion. Our discussion of line B will be put off until chapter 6 where Maslow's criteria on objective scientific results are discussed. By our interpretation, the conditions in I.a. and II.a. in premiss (1) are not necessary or sufficient logical criteria in order for B-process to take place, hence *premiss (1) in Argument A_4 can be excluded.*

Maslow's argument, in *line A*, in favour of that P is justified in knowing that P's descriptions of peak-experience have referents in CTR, can then be formulated as follows (we shall name this type of argument, argument B):

Argument B

(1) If a person P has B-process, P knows that P's descriptions of the contents of consciousness of the types, suchness, Unitive consciousness, Cosmic consciousness and B-values have referents in CTR

(2) There are persons Ps who have B-process

_____

(3) There are persons Ps who are justified in knowing that their descriptions of suchness, Unitive consciousness, Cosmic consciousness and B-values have referents in CTR.

122

The process of cognition is, in Maslow's line A, a necessary and sufficient logical criterion for the epistemological justification for P holding all the descriptions of the four types to have referents in CTR. We shall make the following remarks with regard to argument B.

1. In our interpretation of Maslow's line A, we have set forth that Maslow's argument takes it basis from his theory of cognition and especially from his assumption of B-process as a special cognitive faculty.

According to our view, there is a difference between the assumptions:

(1) In D-process there is a "filtering" of information from CTR
(2) If this "filtering" ceases or is reduced, CTR reveals itself in human beings' content of consciousness. (And in Maslow's view with regard to some aspects of CTR, CTR reveals itself in a "picture-like" way.)

In (1) there can be disagreement among advocates of various versions of a *filter-theory* about (a) the nature of the *filter*, (b) the causes of the *filter's* presence (c) the origin of the *filter* (genetic or learnt) (d) the means in order to take the *filter* away and (e) the criteria which determine when the *whole filter* is taken away.

In (2) there can be disagreements about the *content* of consciousness which becomes the result when the *filter* is taken away, that is, about the nature of CTR which the subject$_k$ *discovers*. For example, Maslow's, W. James', Stace's and Zaehner's opinion of this content are different, only to mention some of the most famous interpreters of transcendent experiences. Various mystics' descriptions of this content are also in disagreement with each other.

A. Ayer discusses the problem of a special cognitive faculty and he sets forth the following claims for the reasonableness in holding that a cognitive faculty brings knowledge: (a) the use of this faculty should bring "similar" content of consciousness to the various subjects$_k$ who use this kind of cognitive faculty and (b) the subject$_k$ should be able to use this cognitive faculty by volition.[49]

A counter argument against claim (a) which is often set forth goes as follows: the descriptions of these contents are shaped by culture-dependent language and this is the reason for the disagreement. If these culture-dependent descriptions are taken away, there is an agreement between various mystics and various interpreters of these experiences about the nature of CTR which the subject$_k$ discovers when the *filter* is taken away.

One version of this counter argument is James' over-belief-theory. Maslow applies this theory in his interpretation of transcendent experiences. In chapter 5, we shall discuss James' theory at length.

One weakness, according to our opinion, in Maslow's assumption (2), that is, if this "filtering" is ceased or is reduced, CTR reveals itself in human beings' content of consciousness, is the following: Maslow only talks about ceasing the psychological and the conceptual elements in this *filter*. There is also, according to our view, reasons for assuming physiological elements in this *filter*, for instance, the human eye can only receive lightwaves of a limited wavelength. These important physiological limits are not taken into consideration by Maslow in his assumption (2) and this is a weakness. Human beings' *visual* experiences of CTR are always shaped and limited by our visual senses' physiological conditions.

Ayer's claim (b) is in our view a reasonable claim. Otherwise this cognitive faculty is at work arbitrarily and it is very hard to state conditions in order for a statement to be intersubjectively testable. The only experience in peak-experience which Maslow thinks the subject$_k$ can bring forth by volition is Unitive consciousness. The other types of experiences in peak-experience arise spontaneously and cannot be experienced by the help of volition.

Maslow writes:

> "Can you bring about these experiences at will? No! Or almost entirely no! In general we are "Surprised by Joy", to use the title of C. S. Lewis' book on just this question. Peaks come unexpectedly, suddenly they *happen* to us. You can't count on them. And, hunting them is little like hunting happiness."[50]

One weakness, according to our opinion, in Maslow's assumption concerning a specific cognitive faculty, is that it cannot be influenced by the subject$_k$'s volition.

2. When Maslow in line A states that B-process is a necessary and sufficient criterion in order for a reason to be good and sufficient in the evidence-criterion, this necessary and sufficient criterion is dependent on a given theory of cognition. The question one ask is: how can Maslow justify the reasonableness concerning the assumptions in this theory of cognition, in its turn? For example: are the forms of cognizing which Maslow assumes reasonable? are these forms of cognizing the only forms of cognizing? are Maslow's hypotheses concerning when these forms of work are at hand reasonable?

If one transforms the epistemological justification of a statement of contents of consciousness to its process of cognition (to conditions concerning its genesis), the following problem emerges: how does one justify the theory of this process of cognition, in its turn? There is a *clash* between Maslow's assumptions which are proposed in his theory of knowledge (his theory of cognition) and the assumption which can, in principle, be possible to justify or falsify by his theory of knowledge.

This clash is inescapable because "you cannot measure, the measuring-rod you measure with". This is one version of *the problem of self-reference*. None the less it is a weakness in a theory of knowledge to transform the ultimate logical criterion for knowledge to an, in principle, *empirical* theory of cognition. Instead, this ultimate logical criterion should be of non-empirical matter, for instance, logical consistency, according to our opinion.

In section 6.5. we shall discuss *the problem of self-reference* in connection with the so called *problem of the infinite regress of reasons.*[51] This problem can be formulated as follows: P states that a necessary and sufficient logical criterion for a reason to be good and sufficient in the evidence-criterion is, for instance, a certain process of cognition q or intersubjective confirmation s, how does P know that when a reason r satisfies q or s and the evidence-criterion is satisfied, P has knowledge that p (the belief- and truth-criterion are also satisfied)? P has to know that when q or s are satisfied and the belief- and truth-criteria are also satisfied, P know that p. *How does P know that?* Does not P have to have (1), a good reason t for holding that, when q or s are satisfied, the evidence-criterion is satisfied, and (2) criteria for holding reason t to be a good and sufficient reason in favour of that, when q or s are satisfied, the evidence-criterion is satisfied? An infinite regress of reasons starts out. We shall in 6.5. discuss various answers to this problem.

3. We shall discuss below whether or not Maslow's descriptions of the four types of content of consciousness are logically consistent descriptions of CTR. Descriptions of suchness, Unitive consciousness and some of the B-values are descriptions of individual objects. According to our view, there is no logical inconsistency between descriptions of these types of contents of consciousness on the semantic level, that is, the descriptions of (a) a unique organization of an object's properties, (b) a symbolic aspect and (c) certain non-moral values. Neither is there any logical inconsistency in our reasonable interpretation of their ontological claims, that is, the existence of inner disposition-bases of types a', c' and relation disposition-bases of types a" and c".

The descriptions of Cosmic consciousness concern descriptions of relations between ontological objects. These descriptions are not logically inconsistent with the descriptions of suchness, Unitive consciousness and B-values. Nor are the ontological claims of the existence of relation disposition-bases of type b" inconsistent with inner disposition-bases of types a' and c' or relation disposition-bases of types a" and c".

The descriptions of B-values which concern human beings' actions are also logically consistent with descriptions of suchness, Unitive consciousness and Cosmic consciousness.

Our conclusion is: the descriptions of the four types of content of consciousness are not logically inconsistent, either on their semantic level or concerning their ontological claims.

If there had been any logical inconsistency in their ontological claims, some of these claims would have to be changed.

4. In line A, Maslow states a view of non-propositional knowledge.
We have first to distinguish between
(a) is non-propositional apprehension possible?
(b) can non-propositional contents of consciousness be knowledge?

Even if the case in (a) is possible (many mystics claim this) we reject the reasonableness of (b).
Our reasons are:

C 1: The content of consciousness, which claims to state the existence of something in CTR, has to be expressible in language in order to set forth the claim of being knowledge. This is the *problem of communication*, which we mentioned in section 3.1. Knowledge of CTR is, according to our opinion, a matter of intersubjectivity, and a necessary criterion is: knowledge-claims, that is, concerning *knowledge that*, should be expressible in statements.
We have to complete this claim of ours by the distinction
(1) content of consciousness of type X, Y . . . is in principle not expressible in language
(2) content of consciousness of type X, Y . . . cannot by person P be expressed in language, that is, P has not the capability to express X, Y . . ., but Q has this capability.

Our rejection concerns (1), where contents of consciousness are, in principle, not expressible in language.

C 2: We reject the view in epistemology which "identify knowledge with some state of intuitive apprehension of the immediate".[52] Our reason is that the psychological feeling of self-evidence is not a sufficient logical criterion in order for a reason to be good and sufficient in the evidence-criterion. There are too many examples of logical inconsistent ontological claims which various people have set forth against each other and they have argued in favour of their different views with reasons which have been justified by this psychological self-evidence criterion.
Furthermore, in his view that B-process is a sufficient logical criterion for a reason to be good and sufficient in the evidence-criterion, we think Maslow makes a mistake when he makes the following generalization: from stating that *some* degrees and *some* forms of cognizing distort the percept, he generalizes to *all* degrees and *all* forms of cognizing distort the percept. Contrary to Maslow we think it is necessary in the reflexion on the content of consciousness to identify the intentional object through concepts.

126

Our criticism in C 1 and C 2 takes its basis from our view of intersubjective testability as a necessary criterion for a reason to be good and sufficient in the evidence-criterion, and when the knowledge-claims concern the content of consciousness which Maslow embraces in his term "peak-experience".

The criterion of intersubjective testability is discussed a great deal within epistemology and philosophy of science. Questions discussed are, for instance: how many people shall test statement p ; some, most or all people? What competence should these people have? Should statement p be intersubjective testable in principle or in fact? Which method may these people use in order to test statement p ? In our case statement p is the statement which expresses the ontological claims Maslow sets forth in his interpretation of peak-experience. The problem of intersubjective testability in this context will be discussed in section 6.5. after our analysis of Maslow's use of James' over-belief-theory in chapter 5 and Maslow's criteria for objective scientific results in 6.4. In section 6.5. we shall also summarize our critical remarks on arguments A and B above.

Chapter 5: Maslow's Theory of Religion

5.0. Introduction

The main aim of this chapter is to explicate some basic theses in Maslow's theory of Religion and discuss the tenability of some of his arguments in favour of these theses. In this analysis, we shall make use of some of our results in chapters 2, 3 and 4.

Maslow's theory of Religion contains, inter alia, hypotheses which try to explain the genesis of Religions, assumptions of what is essential in Religions and hypotheses concerning the basic functions of religious ceremonies, myths and symbols.

With "Religion", Maslow means the established world-Religions which he also calls "organized Religions" or "orthodox Religions". There are two sides to these Religions, namely, (a) Religion as an official institution and (b) various individual's inner or private religious faith. Maslow designates the former with a capital R (Religion) and the latter with a small r (religion).[1]

We shall begin our analysis with the following central quotations:

> "The very beginning, the intrinsic core, the essence, the universal nucleus of every known high religion (unless Confucianism is also called a religion) has been the private, lonely, personal illumination, revelation, or ecstasy of some acutely sensitive prophet or seer. The high religions call themselves revealed religions and each of them tends to rest its validity, its function, and its right to exist on the codification and the communication of this original mystic experience or revelation from the lonely prophet to the mass of human beings in general.
>
> But it has recently begun to appear that these 'revelations' or mystical illuminations can be subsumed under the head of the 'peak-experiences' or 'ecstasies' or 'transcendent' experiences which are now being eagerly investigated by many psychologists. That is to say, it is very likely, indeed almost certain, that these older reports, phrased in terms of supernatural revelation, were, in fact, perfectly natural, human peak-experiences of the kind that can easily be examined today, which, however, were phrased in terms of whatever conceptual, cultural, and linguistic framework the particular seer had available in his time (Laski).
>
> In a word, we can study today what happened in the past and was then explainable in supernatural terms only. By so doing, we are enabled to examine religion in all its facets and in all its meanings in a way that makes it a part of science rather than something outside and exclusive of it.
>
> Also this kind of study leads us to another very plausible hypothesis: to the extent that all mystical or peak-experiences are the same in their essence and have always been the same, all religions are the same in their essence and always have been the

same. They should, therefore, come to agree in principle on teaching that which is common to all of them, i.e., whatever it is that peak-experiences teach in common (whatever is *different* about these illuminations can fairly be taken to be localisms both in time and space, and are, therefore, peripheral, expendable, not essential). This something common, this something which is left over after we peel away all the localisms, all the accidents of particular languages or particular philosophies, all the ethnocentric phrasings, all those elements which are *not* common, we may call the 'core-religious experience' or the 'transcendent experience'."[2]

"To summarize, it looks probable that the peak-experience may be the model of the religious revelation or the religious illumination or conversion which has played so great a role in the history of religions. But because peak-experiences are in the natural world and because we can research with them and investigate them, and because our knowledge of such experiences is growing and may be confidently expected to grow in the future, we may now fairly hope to understand more about the big revelations, conversions, and illuminations upon which the high religions were founded."[3]

In these quotations, and from other contexts in Maslow's writings, we can reconstruct the following basic theses in Maslow's theory of Religion.

Thesis 1: "Religious experiences of a certain type" can be found in every Religion.

Thesis 2: "Religious experiences of a certain type" are the essential element in every Religion.

Thesis 3: "Religious experiences of a certain type" can be subsumed under the term "peak-experience".

From 1—3 Maslow seems to make the conclusion:

Thesis 4: Peak-experiences are the essential element in every Religion.

Maslow develops his line of thought in conjunction with the following theses:

Thesis 5: It is possible to construct one for all human beings common Religion because the various differences between Religions with regard to dogmas, ethics, rituals, etc., are only secondary in relation to "religious experiences of a certain type".

Thesis 6: "Religious experiences of a certain type" which have been interpreted in supernaturalistic terms need not be interpreted in these terms, and accordingly, an ontology containing supernaturalistic entities need not be assumed.

From 5 and 6 Maslow concludes:

Thesis 7: One, for all human beings, common constructed Religion or *Weltanschauung* does not need to assume the existence of ontological entities besides individual human beings consciousness and matter.

Maslow also states the following normative thesis:

Thesis 8: This common constructed Religion or *Weltanschauung* ought to be developed.

In section 5.1., we shall clarify and discuss these theses further.

Maslow also criticises the orthodox Religions (see 5.2. below), but as can be seen from the theses 5—8 above, he also states a constructive alternative "religion-surrogate", that is, his own *Weltanschauung.*[4] His alternative *Weltanschauung* claims, inter alia, to be able to replace orthodox Religions.

5.1. Maslow's Naturalistic Theory of Religion

Thesis 1: "Religious experiences of a certain type" can be found in every Religion.

In the quotations in 5.0., Maslow uses the term "religious experience". This term is very vague. The task here is to clarify this term and a contextual reasonable interpretation is: Maslow does not think that all the experiences which are named religious experiences can be found in every Religion.

A contextual reasonable interpretation of some of the limitations Maslow makes is: some of the experiences which W. James calls "religious experiences", for instance, experiences of being granted, experiences of remission of sins and experiences of a supervised Providence[5] are not included in Maslow's term "religious experience". The reason for this is: Maslow uses the terms "illumination", "ecstacy", "revelation", "great awaking", "original mystical experience" and "transcendent experiences" as closely related to or as synonyms for the term "religious experiences".

Unfortunately, he does not clarify the meaning of these terms, and the most he does is to count such experiences as arising in "religious contexts", or if the contents of consciousness have been interpreted in supernaturalistic terms, as "religious experiences". With "supernaturalism" Maslow means: a view about a personal entity outside the material world who can direct events in this world (theism).

Maslow sometimes takes the religious context in which the experiences have emerged as an explanation for the experiences being interpreted in supernaturalistic terms. Unfortunately, he does not clarify the meaning of the term "religious context" either. An experience can be "religious" even if it is not interpreted in supernaturalistic terms. Maslow includes experiences which he names "nirvana" or "satori" in his term "religious experience".[6]

Since Maslow restricts the religious experiences which he thinks can be found in every Religion to a certain type of religious experience, these restricted religious experiences will be named "religious experiences of a certain type" in this dissertation. The meaning of this central expression in Maslow's theory of Religion is very vague as can be understood from the above.

Thesis 2: "Religious experiences of a certain type" are the essential element in every Religion.

"Religion" is also a vague term, but as was mentioned in 5.0., a contextual reasonable interpretation of this term in Maslow's writings is: it designates the existing world-Religions.

Maslow assumes that all these Religions have had founders who themselves had "religious experiences of a certain type". From these experiences, these founders have formulated the contents of the various dogmas in the Religions. A contextual reasonable interpretation of thesis 2 is: "religious experiences of a certain type" are the essential element in a given Religion because

(a) they are the genesis of Religions. Maslow states that from these experiences the founders have formulated the dogmas which are contained in a given Religion, for instance, dogmas concerning God, the world, man and ethics.[7] "Religious experiences of a certain type" are a necessary causal condition for the genesis of the dogmas in a certain Religion to be formulated. If the founders did not have these experiences, these dogmas could not have been formulated (context of discovery)

(b) these experiences are the epistemological justification for these dogmas (context of justification)

(c) a very important function for the officials of a given Religion is to teach the followers to experience "religious experiences of a certain type".[8]

(d) these experiences are a neccessary causal condition in order for the religious ceremonies, rituals, myths and symbols to function as intermediaries of the religious message.
    If these ceremonies, rituals, etc., are not related to "religious experiences of a certain type", these ceremonies, rituals, etc., are hypostasized and the religious messages are thereby distorted.[9]

Thesis 3: "Religious experiences of a certain type" can be subsumed under the term "peak-experience".

In sections 3.1.—3.4., we have analysed the content of the term "peak-experience". In thesis 3, Maslow makes a reductive interpretation of "religious experiences of a certain type" and in this approach he is certainly influenced by the methods and the results which W. James puts forth in *The Varities of Religious Experiences* (1902).[10] In this book, James uses the term "over-belief" and in order to clarify the meaning of this term, we shall give a brief account of James' opinion concerning his methods and his results in the above

131

mentioned book. This account aims at giving a basis to our analysis of Maslow's argument in favour of thesis 3 and a clarification of his reductive approach.

James states that particular individual's religious experiences are the primary object of investigation for "Science of Religions". James is very critical of "religious rationalist" who assert that it is possible to construct theological systems merely on the basis of rational thought. According to James, theology must always have its genesis and epistemological justification in particular individual's religious experiences.[11] This view expresses James' opinion that a theology can be constructed with the help of Science of Religions.

James asserts that human beings can never express the true reality in words alone.[12] In the case of religious experiences, the descriptions of the content of consciousness are only secondary in relation to the "pure" experiences. The concepts used in the interpretation of these contents of consciousness are culture-dependent.[13] However, scientists in Science of Religions can, by comparative investigations, eliminate what is culture-dependent in the descriptions and establish the common "nucleus". This can be done by comparing particular individual's different descriptions of their religious experiences, and by comparing the, in relation to the religious experiences, secondary dogmas and cults in various Religions. The dogmas are secondary in the sense that the religious experiences are a necessary causal condition in order to formulate the dogmas.[14]

James does not make explicit the distinction between the content of consciousness on the psychological level and the content of consciousness on the semantic level. A contextual reasonable interpretation is: he tries to find the common element in the content of consciousness on the psychological level by identifying the common element in the various descriptions of the content of consciousness in religious experiences (on the semantic level). The common element ("nucleus") is accordingly on the psychological level.

The results of this comparative method, that is, the common element in the contents of consciousness, will, in a second phase in James' recommended method for Science of Religions, be compared with the results from "natural science" in order to further remove the, in comparison with these results, unreasonable element in the common "nucleus". The remaining elements of the descriptions of religious experiences and dogmas—the "common nucleus" of Religions—will be taken as hypotheses which should be constantly tested against the results of human and natural sciences and various individual's descriptions of their religious experiences.

The contents which are added to the established "common nucleus" in the various descriptions of religious experiences and which are secondary dogmas are what James names—over-beliefs.

Scientists in Science of Religions can in this way construct, in relation to various interpretations of the content of consciousness in religious experiences and the secondary dogmas, an intermediary interpretation. This interpretation can be taken as a basis for fruitful dialogues between scholars from different religious communities and Religions.[15]

James presents his own results of investigations of the various religious experiences in his sources in three steps. (A) Firstly, he tries to formulate the content in the "common nucleus", (B) secondly, he puts forth a hypothesis of interpretation of this "common nucleus" from the point of view of Science of Religions. In addition to (A) and (B) he makes (C) thirdly, his own over-belief-interpretation of this "common nucleus".

(A) He finds that the basic element in various religious experiences is "feeling":

> "I do believe that feeling is the deeper source of religion, and that philosophic and theological formulas are secondary products, like translations of a text into another tongue".[16]
>
> " ... the feelings on the one hand and the conduct on the other are almost always the same, for Stoic, Christian, and Buddhists saints are practically indistinguishable in their lives. The theories which Religion generates, being thus variable, are secondary; and if you wish to grasp her essence, you must look to the feelings and the conduct as being the more constant elements."[17]

He characterizes the common quality of feeling in various religious experiences as " ... what Kant calls a 'sthenic' affection, an excitement of the cheerful, expansive, 'dynamogenic' order ... "[18]

He also tries to find the "common nucleus" in the *cognitive* content in various religious experiences. The cognitive content is the intellect's interpretation of the quality of feeling. According to James, a Religion could in principle exist without this secondary cognitive content.[19] His description of the common cognitive content in various religious experiences is: the individual experiences within himself/herself a "better" and "higher part" which is in relation to a MORE of the same qualitative ontological status as this "better" and "higher part".

> "He becomes conscious that this higher part is conterminous and continuous with a MORE of the same quality which is operative in the universe outside of him, and which he can keep in working touch with, and in a fashion get on board of and save himself when all his lower being has gone to pieces in the wreck."[20]

When different Religions try to answer, inter alia, the following questions concerning this MORE their over-beliefs emerge: "Does this MORE exist?" "If so, in what shape does it exist?" "Does this MORE act?" "How should we understand the experiences of 'union' with this MORE which some individuals claims to experience?"

(B) James asserts that scientists in Science of Religions are able to formulate, in relation to the existing Religions, an intermediary interpretation of this "common nucleus" which can be tested against other results in science. The content in this hypothesis is formulated by James himself with the help of a particular theory of consciousness. In this hypothesis, the term "subconscious self" has a basic function. James is influenced by the psychologist Myer in clarifying the meaning of this term.[21] James names our conscious content of consciousness our "low self" or "consciousness of everyday life". He also thinks that human beings have a "higher self" or "subconscious self". He sets forth the hypothesis that in religious experiences the individual experiences (a) a 'union' with her/his "higher self" which James also names the "hither side" of this MORE (b) a connection with a "mystical region" or "supernatural region" which he names the "farther side" of this MORE.[22]

(C) From the point of view of "Science of Religions", James makes the choice *not* to name this "mystical region" anything more. But from his own over-belief he names this region — "God".

> "God is the natural appelation for us Christians at least, for the supreme reality, so I will call this higher part of the universe by the name of God ... 'God' is a causal agent as well as a medium of communion, and that is the aspect which I wish to emphasize."[23]

A contextual reasonable interpretation is: James assumes that this mystical region cannot be adequately described in words, and this is a reason why James is so careful when he thinks of naming this region. The quality of feeling of this region is the basic element in different individual's various religious experiences. But in their reflexion over these feelings and in their communication with other people they have to express these feelings in words.

James' hypothesis of interpretation from the point of view of Science of Religions is one type of interpretation, his own over-belief-interpretation is another type of interpretation. He is in both of these cases conscious of the concepts' limitation to adequately convey the basic quality of feeling.

The aim in this section is not to criticize James' results, for instance, his characterization of the quality of feeling, whether or not his assumption of the unity of consciousness is consistent with his distinctions, between emotional and cognitive content of consciousness, or between "the consciousness of everyday life" and "subconscious self",[24] whether or not his own over-belief-interpretation is already assumed in his hypothesis of interpretation of the "common nucleus" from the point of view of Science of Religions, and whether or not it can even be found in his description of the "common nucleus" as a quality of feeling and as an experience of something MORE.

One aim in this chapter is to set forth some agreements between James' and Maslow's analyses of religious experience. We find the following important agreements:

1. They are focusing their study on particular individual's religious experiences.
2. They try to find a common nucleus in various descriptions of religious experiences from different Religions.
3. They state that it is possible to find such a "nucleus" by scientific methods.
4. They determinate the content in this "nucleus" in such a way that this determination has a reductive tendency.
5. They assert that dogmas, rituals, ceremonies, myths and symbols in Religions are only secondary in relation to the followers' religious experiences.
6. They try to make the explicated "nucleus" the basis for dialogues between scholars from different Religions.
7. They state that the content in religious experiences cannot be adequately described in words.
8. They state that this content of consciousness can be understood by an intuitive cognitive faculty.
9. They state that various Religions have their genesis and epistemological justification in religious experiences.

Below, we shall use our results of analysis of James' *The Varities of Religious Experience* when we try to determinate Maslow's *method* in his attempt to subsume different experiences under his term "peak-experience". We shall also try to determinate the *content* in the common element in these experiences.

Maslow's argument in favour of his subsumption of "religious experiences of a certain type" under his term "peak-experience" and the *term* "peak-experience" itself will also be clarified.

We shall present three interpretations as answers to the question: *are there any common contents of consciousness in peak-experience?* The material in Maslow's writings which answers this question is very vague and scanty, and below, we make three reasonable interpretations I 1, I 2 and I 3.

I 1: All peak-experiences have some common content of consciousness, but various individual's descriptions on the semantic level are different. This can be explained in the following way: they use concepts which are at hand in their particular religious and cultural context when they try to express the content of consciousness in peak-experience.

"It has been demonstrated again and again that the transcendent experiences have occured to some people in any culture and at any time and of any religion and in any caste or class. All these experiences are described in about the same general way; the

135

language and the concrete contents may be different, indeed must be different. These experiences are essentially ineffable (in the sense that even the best verbal phrasings are not quite good enough), which is also to say that they are unstructured (like Rorschach ink-blots). Also throughout history, they have never been understood in a naturalistic way. Small wonder it is then that the mystic, trying to describe his experience, can do it only in a local, culture-bound, ignorance-bound, language-bound way, confusing his description of the experience with whatever explanation of it and phrasing of it is most readily available to him in his time and in his place.

Larski discusses the problem in detail in her chapters on 'Overbeliefs' and in other places and agrees with James in disregarding them. For instance, she points out 'To a substantial extent the people in the religious group knew the vocabulary for such experiences before they knew the experience; inevitably when the experiences are known, they tend to be recounted in the vocabulary already accepted as appropriate'.

Koestler also said it well, 'But because the experience is inarticulate, has no sensory shape, color or words, it lends itself to transcription in many forms, including visions of the cross, or of the goodness of Kali; they are like dreams of a person born blind ... Thus a genuine mystic experience may mediate a bona fide conversion to practically any creed, Cristianity, Buddhism or Fire-Worship'. In the same volume, Koestler reports in vivid detail a mystic experience of his own. Still another way of understanding this phenomenon is to liken the peak-experiences to raw materials which can be used for different styles of structures, as the same bricks and mortar and lumber would be built into different kinds of houses by a Frenchman, a Japanese, or a Tahitian.

I have, therefore, paid no attention to these localisms since they cancel one another out. I take the generalized peak-experience to be that which is common to all places and times".[25]

In order to clarify I 1 and the following I 2 and I 3, we shall make the logical distinction between the following levels:

(a) A hypothetical assumed original element, hereafter named *the given*. This can be characterized as "unstructured like Rorschach's ink-blots ... raw materials which can be used for different styles of structures ...". *The given* can be interpreted as an *ontological entity* or as *a content of consciousness on a subconscious level of consciousness*. In this stage of analysis, we do not need to make any judgement concerning this disjunction.

(b) P interprets *the given* through culture-dependent concepts at time t_1. The concepts shape P's content of consciousness, that is, the content of consciousness on the psychological level are shaped by the culture-dependent concepts at time t_1. For example, P identifies the content as an experience of God, Brahman or Allah through the concepts of "God", "Brahman" or "Allah". The culture-dependent concepts are P's over-beliefs.

The contents which are shaped by the culture-dependent concepts are on the level of *conscious consciousness*.

136

(c) At time t_{1+n} P expresses the content in (b). P has then a *memory* of the content of consciousness at t_1 and from this memory P expresses P's content in the statements *p, q,* etc.

(d) *The descriptions on the semantic level* of P's content of consciousness in b or c, that is, *p, q* etc.

The distinction between these levels needs some comments.

In (b), we assume that P at time t_{1-n}, has become acquainted with some concepts, for instance, "God", "Brahman", "Allah", "The Cosmic Unity" or "The Universal Self".

When P at time t_1 has a peak-experience, we assume that P interprets the content of consciousness in the learnt concepts and on the level of conscious consciousness, P experiences, for instance, God or that P is united with the Universal Self.

Level (c) is assumed because the verbal or written descriptions *p, q,* etc. are often not expressed simultaneously with the experiences. The levels (b) and (c) are psychological levels. (d) is the semantic level, and (a) is a hypothetically assumed level, an ontological or subconscious level.

In I 1, Maslow states that the content on the level of conscious consciousness (b) cannot be adequately described in words and that it is unstructured. Maslow compares it with Rorschach's ink-blots or "raw-materials . . .".

According to I 1, it is *first* when P expresses this content of consciousness on level (c) that the culture-dependent concepts make the descriptions in different cultures or subcultures different. According to this interpretation, the contents on level (b) are "similar" and the differences emerge when various individuals describe their content on level (c).

> "The stimuli are very different: the subjective experience tends to be similar. Or to say it in another way: our kicks are the same: we just get them from different paths, perhaps even from rock and roll, drug addiction and alcohol in less strong people. I feel more sure of this after reading in the literatures of mystic experiences, cosmic consciousness, oceanic experiences, estatic experiences, creative experiences, love experiences, parental experiences, sexual experiences and insight experiences. They all overlap; they approach similarity and even identity."[26]

From our position of analysis, we dismiss the reasonableness of I 1. The reason for this is: we assume that the conceptual interpretations are already at hand on level (b), and accordingly, we think that people not only express their content in different ways but also their content of consciousness are different since they, inter alia, shape their contents through the different concepts which they use in their interpretations.

I 2: All peak-experiences have a common element, but their content on the level of consciousness are different as well as their descriptions on the semantic level. This can be explained in the following way: they use concepts which are at hand in their particular religious and cultural context when they identify their content of consciousness as well as when they try to describe the content on the semantic level.

Maslow takes over James' over-belief theory and by using this theory, he thinks that he is justified, given the descriptions in (d), in assuming that "religious experiences of a certain type", that is, the content of consciousness in (b) and (c) have a numerical or qualitative identical *given* in (a). This *given* is assumed to be "behind" the different content of consciousness on the level of conscious consciousness, if the contents were not interpreted through culture-dependent concepts. The *given* is a construction of an assumed unmediated entity.

The *given* in (a) is in I 2 the common element in the "religious experiences of a certain type". Maslow uses Spearman's terms "g-factor" and "s-factor" in order to clarify this. The "g-factor" is the common element not only in "religious experiences of a certain type" but in all of the experiences which Maslow subsumes under "peak-experience".

> "If we were to go further with our analysis, we should find that, succeeding upon the discovery of the generality of all peak-experiences, there are also 'specific' factors in each of the peak-experiences which differentiate them from each other to some extent. This relationship of specific to general is as figure to ground. It is something like that described by Spearman for 'g' and 's' factors in intelligence.
> I do not discuss these 's' factors here because the 'g' factor is far more important for the problem at hand and at this stage in its development."[27]

The existence of the "g-factor" justifies Maslow in subsuming "religious experiences of a certain type" and other experiences under "peak-experience". They all have a common element — the g-factor — which, in I 2, can be identified as *the given* on level (a) above.

By making the logical distinctions between a − d, Maslow's statements about P's confusion in the quotation under I 1 can be clarified. The confusion can be explained in the following way: P is not clear about the differences between *the given* in (a) and the content of consciousness which is interpreted by culture-dependent concepts in (b) or (c). Therefore P attributes to *the given* properties which in fact are attributed to *the given* because of the properties which are entailed in the culture-dependent concepts.

James' opinion concerning the "common nucleus" can be interpreted in accordance with I 2. The g-factor is the "feelings" which from the point of view of Science of Religions can be interpreted as follows: the subject is in contact with its "higher self" and this in turn is in connection with a "mystical region".

When Maslow states that all the experiences he subsumes under "peak-experiences" have a common element (g-factor), he also sets himself the task of *determining the content of this common element*. In our analysis of the term "peak-experience" in 3.2.—3.4. we made the distinction between:

A. descriptions of the subject$_k$'s experiences of CTR during peak-experiences (cognitive content)
B. descriptions of the person's experiences of himself/herself during peak-experiences
C. descriptions of emotional content during peak-experiences

The question to be posed here is: does the g-factor consist of content in A, B, or C or of any conjunction between these?

Can the g-factor be sought in descriptions of the subject$_k$'s experiences of CTR during peak-experience? If this is the case, the g-factor, that is, *the given* in I 2 is an experience of an assumed ontological object. That this is the case is the claim in Maslow's sources, but Maslow also hints that this is his own view.

> "Perhaps most important of all, however, was the report in these experiences of the feeling that they had really seen the ultimate truth, the essence of things, the secret of life, as if veils had been pulled aside."[28]

> "In any case, enough knowledge is already available so that I feel I can say very confidently that these concepts [purely "religious concepts as the sacred, the eternal, heaven and hell, the good death . . .] are *not* mere hallucinations, illusions, or delusions, or rather, more accurately, that they need not be. They can and do have referents in the real world."[29]

In our analysis in 3.2. about the subject$_k$'s experiences of CTR during peak-experiences, we found four different types of experiences, namely, suchness, Cosmic consciousness, Unitive consciousness and B-values. Our conclusion is therefore: there is *no* common cognitive element in Maslow's description of the subject$_k$'s experiences of CTR during peak-experience since the four types of cognitive content do not contain any common element.

Can the g-factor be found under B: the descriptions of a person's experiences of himself/herself during peak-experiences? This question is hard to answer because Maslow does not make clear whether or not the experiences reported in 3.3. take place in every peak-experience. Furthermore, it is not possible to determinate the experiences of the transcendence of the distinction between the experiencing-self and the object of knowledge as g-factor either because this is not experienced in the types of peak-experience which we have named Unitive consciousness and B-values.

Can the g-factor be found under C, that is, in Maslow's descriptions of emotional content in peak-experiences? This is also hard to answer because

Maslow does not make clear whether the descriptions of emotional content reported in 3.4. take place in every peak-experience.

We have also to dismiss an argument which Maslow hints at in favour of I 2, namely, all the experiences he subsumes under peak-experience are ineffable and this ineffability hints at a common content on the level of consciousness. This argument is not tenable because of the fact that all experiences which are ineffable do not necessarily have a common content.[30]

Our conclusion is: it is very hard to find any common element in various peak-experiences. One possibility is that this common element can be found under B or C, but the vagueness of Maslow's descriptions do not make it possible to establish any contextual reasonable interpretation. This conclusion is relevant in our attempt to determinate which principle of subsumption Maslow uses when he embraces various experiences under his term "peak-experience" and how we can determinate the *term* "peak-experience" itself. We shall soon discuss this consequence below.

A third interpretation concerning the question: are there any common contents of consciousness in peak-experiences? is the following:

I 3: All peak-experiences can be divided into *some few types* of experiences, and these types can be found in every culture. Various individuals interpret these types of experiences through different concepts at the level of consciousness as well as in their descriptions of these experiences on the semantic level. This can be explained in the following way: they use concepts which are at hand in their particular religious and cultural context when they identify their content of consciousness on the level of consciousness and when they try to describe these contents on the semantic level.

One question in connection with I 3 is: which types of experiences can peak-experience be divided into, according to Maslow?

Given our analysis of peak-experience in 3.2. our answer is: suchness, Unitive consciousness, Cosmic consciousness and B-values.

Our next question is: how can Maslow limit the various experiences which he embraces under peak-experience to just these types and what are his arguments for this?

One of Maslow's arguments is his adoption of James over-belief-theory, and with the help of this theory he makes the claim of being able to reduce "religious experiences of a certain type" to the above reported types. However, he does not show by any comparative analysis or in any other way why "religious experiences of a certain type" and the other experiences which he

140

subsumes under "peak-experience" can be reduced to the above named types. His reduction takes place in three different forms:

(A) *Ontological reduction,* that is, "x is reducible to y if it is possible to show that x is nothing but y".[31] Maslow makes the claim that experiences of ontological entities which transcend matter and individual human beings' consciousness can be reduced to his ontology which we clarified in chapter 4. For example, descriptions of a personal God (theism) or non-personal ontological entities as can be found in, for instance, Buddhistic or Hindu ontology, can be reduced to the four types, suchness, Unitive consciousness, Cosmic consciousness and B-values, and consequently to the ontology which we clarified in chapter 4.

(B) *Epistemological reduction,* that is, "x can be explained in terms of y".[32] Maslow makes the claim that the various descriptions of content of consciousness in the experiences which he subsumes under "peak-experience" can be explained by the terms in the four suggested descriptions of suchness, Unitive consciousness, Cosmic consciousness and B-values.

(C) *Semantic reduction,* that is, x can be completely translated in terms of y. Maslow makes the claim that descriptions of the various content of consciousness in the experiences which he subsumes under "peak-experience" can be completely described by his four suggested descriptions of suchness, Unitive consciousness, Cosmic consciousness and B-values.

The relation between A, B, and C is asymetric. A implies B and C, but not the contrary. B implies C, but not the contrary.

The only argument Maslow sets forth is premiss 2' in argument A_4, that is, if P has a process of cognition which is characterized by (a) specific changes in attention and (b) passive forms of cognizing, P will have experiences of types suchness, Unitive consciousness, Cosmic consciousness and B-values. But Maslow never gives any argument why exactly these types of content of consciousness emerge when the *filter* is taken away (see 4.4. and 4.5.).

Since we cannot find any other argument in favour of his ontological, epistemological or semantic reduction, we state: Maslow has a normative and apologetic purpose in his writings. Maslow himself is aware of the lack of arguments. In his Journal 4/8 1963 he writes: "Night before last bad dreams. Finally worked out to be uneasiness over religion lecture & book [Religion, Values and Peak-Experiences] I guess I don't feel sure enough of my ground, or at least of the proofs".[33]

In the light of this, we state that Maslow uses the over-belief-theory gratuitously. He does not argue why his use of this theory leads him to the types

141

which he describes. This is an important result of analysis and one which has relevance for the judgements concerning the reasonableness of other theses in his theory of Religion.

I 3 is according to our view the most reasonable interpretation of the meaning in Maslow's thesis 3. Our reason for this is: from our analyses of peak-experience in 3.2.—3.4., we found that four types of cognitive content of consciousness could be found in the experiences which Maslow subsumes under "peak-experience". These cannot be ontologically, epistemologically or semantically reduced further, because they do not contain any common element. Our choice of I 3 as the most reasonable interpretation is relevant for determinating which principle of subsumption Maslow has used in order to embrace different experiences under "peak-experience" and what kind of term "peak-experience" itself is.

In I 1 and I 2 there is a common element in all the experiences which Maslow subsumes under "peak-experience". The term "peak-experience" can then be characterized as a general term in which the various experiences which constitute the extension of the concept have a common element (analytical specification) and which allows these experiences to be subsumed under a common general term. In I 1 the analytical specification is the unstructed, non-propositional content of consciousness or the person's experiences of himself/herself or the emotional content the subject$_k$ experiences during peak-experience.

In I 2 the analytical specification can be the hypothetical assumed *given* or the person's experiences of himself/herself or the emotional content the subject$_k$'s experiences during peak-experience.

It is possible that the analytical specification in I 3 can be found in the person's experiences of himself/herself or the emotional content during peak-experience, but this is very hard to determinate because of the vagueness of Maslow's writings. One possible interpretation is that there is no common element in all of the experiences which Maslow subsumes under "peak-experience". The term "peak-experience" can then be characterized as a *species-term,* that is, the four suggested types of cognitive content are subordinate categories in the general term "peak-experience" and the experience which can be reduced to any of these categories (given Maslow's use of James' over-belief-theory) can also be subsumed under the species-term "peak-experience".

Our opinion is that I 3 is the most reasonable interpretation of thesis 3 and therefore the term "peak-experience" itself should be understood as a species-term. A support for this interpretation is Maslow's own description of the term "peak-experience" as "generalized abstract schema or model". Concerning the cognitive content, the model could be understood as the four

142

subordinate categories. Maslow's statements about the person's experiences of himself/herself and of the emotional content during peak-experience are very vague, and this is the reason why we cannot clarify the meaning any further in this species-term or "generalized abstract schema or model".

Given the clarification of the theses 1—3, we can clarify below Maslow's thesis 4 which is a conclusion of 1—3.

Thesis 4: Peak-experiences are the essential element in every Religion.[34]

Thesis 4 follows from theses 1—3 because "religious experiences of a certain type" can be found in every Religion and these experiences are the essential element in all Religions and these experiences can be subsumed under the term "peak-experience".

From our discussions concerning theses 1—3, we can easily notice the vagueness of thesis 4. First of all, there is the uncertainty concerning the common element in "peak-experience", and, in the second place, if there is any common element, it is very hard to determinate the content of this common element.

Furthermore, Maslow does not show how his use of James' over-belief-theory leads to any of the interpretations I 1, I 2 or I 3.

Under thesis 3, we set forth our opinion that Maslow has a normative and apologetic approach in his ontological reduction. This is also in accordance with his purpose to construct an alternative *Weltanschauung* with a special ontology in exchange for the traditional Religions' ontologies and ontologies of contemporary *Weltanschauungen*. In his Journals, he formulates, quite explicitly, his aim to construct a naturalistic Religion.

> "It's possible now to make a completely coherent & comprehensive psychological & naturalistic theory of religion — far more clear & real than any theology or religion has ever been".[35]

> "Practically all the words used by the priests & by now totally identified with 'religion' I can give a naturalistic meaning and bring back into the realm of human cognition & science."[36]

Maslow's opinion that peak-experience is the essential element in Religions is naturally very controversial. The degree of controversty depends upon, inter alia, the precization of the central term "peak-experience". Other candidates for the essential element in a Religion are: holding as true some basic dogmas, living in accordance with certain rules, rituals or ceremonies, or endeavouring to act in accordance with some normative ethics.

Below, we shall very briefly analyse Maslow's constructive aim in his theory of Religion in the theses 5—8. The explication of these theses aims at further clarifying Maslow's own *Weltanschauung*.

Thesis 5: It is possible to construct one for all human beings common Religion or *Weltanschauung*, because the various differences between Religions with regard to dogmas, ethics, rituals, etc are only secondary in relation to "religious experiences of a certain type".

"As a matter of fact, they [humanistic sects] might very well become very similar to the reformed church organizations. It's quite possible that there wouldn't be much difference between them in the long run, if both groups accepted the primary importance and reality of the basic personal revelations (and their consequences) and if they could agree in regarding everything else as secondary, peripheral, and not necessary, not essentially defining characteristics of religion, they then could focus upon the examination of the personal revelations—the mystic experience, the peak-experience, the personal illumination—and of the B-cognitions which then ensue."[37]

In thesis 3, Maslow states that "religious experiences of a certain type" can be ontologically, epistemologically and semantically reduced. In thesis 2, we stated that "religious experiences of a certain type" are a necessary causal condition in order for the genesis and a necessary (or sufficient) logical criterion for the justification of dogmas in Religions.

Given Maslow's claim that "religious experiences of a certain type" can be ontologically, epistemologically and semantically reduced, the specific religious epistemological justification of the various dogmas in different Religions disappears because the content in these experiences are shaped by the culture-dependent concepts with which the experiences have been interpreted. The contents are therefore relative, and secondary in relation to the hypothetical assumed "pure" content, that is, some of the four types which Maslow suggests.

The theoretical dogmas and the normative ethics in different Religions are therefore possible to exchange. According to Maslow, they ought to be exchanged by his own constructed alternative *Weltanschauung* (see thesis 8 in 5.0.) One example of this exchange is orthodox Religions' normative ethics and their theological translation-theory in the meta-ethical sphere.

"... that the highest spiritual values appear to have naturalistic sanctions and that supernatural sanctions for these values are, therefore, not necessary—raises some questions which have not been raised before in quite this form. For instance, why were supernatural sanctions for goodness, altruism, virtue, and love necessary in the first place? ... it becomes crystal clear that any doctrine of the innate depravity of man or any maligning of his animal nature very easily leads to some extra-human interpretation of goodness, saintliness, virtue, selfsacrifice, altruism, etc. If they can't be explained from within human nature—and explained they must be—then they must be explained from outside of human nature. The worse man is, the poorer a thing he is conceived to be, the more necessary becomes a god."[38]

Thesis 6: "Religious experiences of a certain type" which have been interpreted in supernaturalistic terms, need not be interpreted in these terms, and accordingly, an ontology containing supernaturalistic entities need not be assumed.

In this thesis we can notice Maslow's ontological reductive aim. Maslow does this, as we have seen above, with the help of James' over-belief-theory.

"I shall, therefore, use these words [religious words], since I have no others to use, to refer to subjective happenings in human beings without necessarily implying any supernatural reference. I claim that it is not necessary to appeal to principles outside of nature and human nature in order to explain these experiences."[39]

Thesis 7: One, for all human beings, common constructed Religion or *Weltanschauung* does not need to assume the existence of ontological entities besides individual human beings' consciousness and matter.

"Instead of God, if the divine is within human nature, then must be 'obedient' to that naturalistic divinity, i.e. to one's own highest potentials, to one's highest aspirations, to one's highest (B-)values. One's highest transcendent experience (peak, plateau, mystic, unitive) can be translated as a "religious experience". Since one can & should sacralize the cosmos, nature, people, animals, trees & flowers (& also perceive them unitively, which is different), then that too can be treated as 'divine', & one can then talk meaningfully in all the traditional church-&-dogma language; e.g. not my will but thine be done; surrender & obediance to the divine, the sacred, the sanctified (we sanctify & sacralize by perceiving, by taking a different attitude, by permitting ourselves to B-cognize, etc.), which means cultivating ourselves so as to be envolved enough (spiritual enough? holy enough? pious enough?) to be isomorphic with the highest = one aspect of the religious path is to cultivate our own personal growth to a higher level of consciousness & of Being, i.e., to be able to not to remain ontologically stupid (spiritually blind, unable to hear the messages from the divine within us & in the world, i.e., not to remain ontologically stupid) spiritually blind, unable to sacralize, reduced, to the concrete & to the positivistic = to a Cartesian-Newtonian external world of things pushed & seen thru the camera & taperecorder senses only."[40]

In this quotation, Maslow's own ontological view can be noticed. As was clarified in chapter 4, our reasonable interpretation of his ontological claims are:

There exist (1) individual human beings' consciousness and (2) material ontological object which have primary and secondary f-properties. Secondary f-properties are of two kinds (a) inner disposition-bases, and (b) relation disposition-bases.

In his naturalistic theory of Religion, Maslow states that experiences of other ontological entities can be ontologically reduced to the ontological entities above. In his ontological position, we can notice Maslow's intermediated opinion in the discussion in Philosophy of Religion between ontologies with supernaturalistic entities or ontologies which assume some ontological entity/ies beyond matter and individual human beings' consciousness *and* purely materialistic ontologies.

In 4.4. and 4.5. we analysed and discussed Maslow's arguments in his attempts to justify these ontological claims. We rejected, from our position of analysis, the tenability in his argumentation in line A.

His mode of procedure in his reduction takes place in three steps: (a) epistemological reduction, that is, he states with the help of James' over-belief-theory that "religious experiences of a certain type" can be explained in terms of "peak-experience"; (b) ontological reduction, that is, from the epistemological reduction he states that orthodox Religions' ontologies can be reduced to the ontology set forth by the content in "peak-experience"; and (c) semantic reduction, that is, from step (a) and (b) he thinks he is justified in making the semantic reduction.

Our main criticisms of his mode of procedure have been:
(1) his determination of "religious experiences of a certain type" are very vague
(2) In spite of (1), one can question whether or not he does not leave out central religious experiences, inter alia, of intrapersonal character, for example, experiences of forgivenness or what Stace calls "introvert mysticism".[41]
(3) He does not make explicit the content in his sources and he does not show, by any comparative method, how his use of James' over-belief-theory gives the content he attributes to peak-experience
(4) It is hard to determinate whether or not there is any common content in peak-experience, and if there is any, what is the character of this content.

5.2. Maslow's Critique of Orthodox Religions

We shall end this chapter with a brief account of Maslow's critique of ortodox Religions.

1. Maslow states that orthodox Religions have separated certain "parts" of CTR as holy and other "parts" of CTR as non-holy. Certain places, things, buildings, foods and human beings are considered holy while other places, etc., are considered non-holy. Maslow assumes, inter alia, from Unitive consciousness and Cosmic consciousness that all existing things are holy, independent of time or localization in space. It is dependent on the particular individual's capability to apprehend the holiness of every entity in CTR.[42] In this context Maslow uses a quotation from Rilke: "If your life seems poor to you ... do not accuse it; accuse yourself, tell yourself you are not poet enough to summon up its riches, since for the creator there is no poverty and no poor or unimportant place."[43]

2. Priests and other officials of Religions are not sole owners of some exclusive knowledge about the content of the dogmas in Religions. Maslow's reason for this is: all human beings have the capability to experience peak-experience and consequently all people have the capability to understand the meaning of various religious dogmas[44] (and from Maslow's expectations and point of view, of the correctness of Maslow's alternative *Weltanschauung*).

3. Orthodox Religions have been too irrational and dogmatic. They have completely separated their dogmas from rational investigations. This has led to a claim on the followers to believe the dogmas in blind faith.[45]

4. The primary task for the officials of Religions is to teach the followers to experience "religious experiences of a certain type". This task has often, in the history of Religions, been offered to officials who themselves have not had any "religious experiences of a certain type" (so called "non-peakers"). A consequence of this fact has been that the officials have hypostatized both the verbal or nonverbal religious symbols, and sometimes, even fought against peakers and peak-experience.[46] Maslow thinks that a Religion has to have its basis in peak-experience, otherwise Religion is transformed to certain stereo-typed behaviour and the messages in the rituals, cermonies and symbols become distorted.[47]

5. From his ontological point of view, Maslow also criticizes orthodox Religions' opinion that "heaven" is localized in space. Instead, Maslow states that "heaven" should be understood as a content of consciousness to be experienced in this life.[48] He rejects a life after death.[49]

6. As have been noted earlier, Maslow also criticized orthodox Religions for holding a theological translation-theory in the meta-ethical sphere. In-stead, he thinks that the normative ethics can be justified from an intuitionistic or value-objectivistic naturalistic meta-ethical point of view.[50]

Chapter 6: Maslow's Philosophy of Science

6.0. Introduction

This chapter contains an account of some basic theses in Maslow's philosophy of science. With philosophy of science we mean not only studies and theories about scientific results (the products) but also studies and theories about the scientists (the producers), the process of science (the production) and different relations between these factors. Maslow's philosophy of science has been the subject matter of one dissertation (Bärmark 1976). Our account is very brief where our and Bärmark's analyses are in agreement. Our account is different from Bärmark's in two ways: (a) In our analysis of Maslow's philosophy of science we use some of our results of analysis in chapters 1—5 and (b) we take special notice of Maslow's recommended method in Psychology of Religion for studying transcendent experiences.

An important basis for Maslow's theses in his philosophy of science are the overreaching problems which he thinks human beings have to solve, that is, "to create the Good Human Being . . . and The Good Society" and his view of science's, and especially the psychological science, central position in order to solve these overreaching problems (see section 1.1.).

A very important means for becoming a Good Human Being, that is, to be a self-actualizing person, is to have self-knowledge (see 2.2.). The psychological science's goal is to give human beings knowledge of themselves because (a) this knowledge has an intrinsic value and (b) this knowledge gives human beings the possibilities for becoming self-actualizing persons and for creating the Good Society.

Behaviorism and psychoanalysis cannot give human beings this knowledge, according to Maslow. In order to get this knowledge other areas of investigation have to be open up for psychology. Research in these areas are now prevented by, inter alia, the strict criteria for scientific results which are claimed, for instance, within behaviorism. Maslow states that the need to solve the overreaching problems justifies the tendency to weaken these criteria and also to use other not established methods in the process of science.

Maslow sets forth certain problems and he finds, as an active researcher, that these problems cannot be solved by the established methods used in behaviorism and psychoanalysis.[1] He therefore questions the reasonableness of these traditions' methodological ideal and argues in favour of the reasonableness in using other methods in order to solve these problems. The conclusive criterion for deciding whether or not to use a certain method should be: the method should be fruitful for the solution of the overreaching problems. Maslow writes: "What needs doing, is worth doing even though *not* very well". "It is only the goals or ends of science that dignity and validate its methods".[2] His influence from pragmatism can be noticed in this argumentation.

In his discussions of topics in philosophy of science, Maslow often hints at the controversy about the methodological ideal of the humanistic sciences *versus* the methodological ideal of the natural sciences. Most often, he hints at this complex of problems in his criticisms of behaviorism and psychoanalysis. His aim is not to replace these schools' ideal of science, but to *complement* them.[3]

His criticisms of the ideal of science in behaviorism and psychoanalysis are extended to a critique of a general tradition in philosophy of science, which he names "orthodox science". It is hard to clarify which line of thought in the philosophy of science Maslow designates by this term. Bärmark identifies it with "Scientism", which proclaims an ontological materialism, and suggests that this reality can be studied with *one* science, with only *one* method.[4] Maslow's view of some of the contents in orthodox science will be explicated when we analyse in concrete topics his criticisms of orthodox science.

Maslow also has a constructive tendency in his philosophy of science, besides this critical approach. For example, he suggests several alternative methods in the process of science and recommends alternative less strict criteria for the reliability and validity of the scientific results. He also discusses problems in the area of psychology of science at length. Science is a product of human beings and knowledge of the *people* who produce scientific results are therefore of central importance, as well as the scientific activities, the scientific results and the various relations between these three factors, according to Maslow.[5] Maslow's emphasis on studying areas within psychology of science can also be understood against the background of his stress on the forms of cognizing's relevance in his epistemology.

In the areas of investigation for psychology of science, he includes, inter alia, creativity, the process of abstraction and the influence of personality-, theoretical- and ethical presuppositions in the process of science.[6]

Maslow's critical and constructive philosophy of science is very unstructured and very general. He uses terms such as "orthodox science", "behaviorism" and "psychoanalysis" without specifying any advocates of these "schools". In this chapter, Maslow's critical and constructive philosophy of science will be reported and analysed under the following head-lines: 6.1. non-scientific presumptions; 6.2. the goal of science; 6.3. the process of science and 6.4. the scientific results. At the end of the chapter 6.5., we shall make some final remarks on Argument A and discuss Maslow's suggested method for studying transcendent experience.

With "process of science" we mean the different activities which lead to scientific results, for example: (a) various choices of problems, methods, models and levels of ambition; (b) various activities of making observations, experiments, tests, and interviews; (c) interpretations of these observations, experiments, etc., and (d) presentations and distributions of the results.[7]

With "non-scientific presumptions" we mean very general assumptions about ontology, man, history, etc and ethical norms and values. The term "non-scientific" means that these presumptions can be conscious, or unconscious or not articulated for the scientist. They are not explicitly argued for, but they influence the process of science and the scientific results.[8]

With "scientific results" we mean, theories, hypotheses, explanations, descriptions, predictions and other propositions which express the results of the process of science.[9]

6.1. Non-Scientific Presumptions

Maslow states that both behaviorism and psychoanalysis have been unconscious of their non-scientific presumptions.[10] One task Maslow sets himself is the following: clarify in which areas of problems these presumptions have been at hand; determinate their content and show their reasonableness/ unreasonableness or truth/falsity.

It is problematic to set forth any criteria in order to make any sharp line of demarcation between non-scientific and scientific presumptions. My reasonable interpretation is that the non-scientific presumptions are of a general character, for instance, view of man, ontology and normative ethics. Maslow never discusses any criteria in order to draw this line of demarcation, but inspite of this he stresses science's influence on the creating and preservation of different assumptions of this non-scientific character.

Maslow emphasizes that non-scientific presumptions should be made explicit and discussed in philosophy of science; and this is one point where Maslow is in agreement with, inter alia, the hermeneutic-dialectic school of meta-science, and such philosophers of science as Kuhn and Polanyi.[11]

Maslow assumes that orthodox science's non-scientific presumptions are "reflections" of a *Weltanschauung*, which he names "mechanical world view". Maslow thinks that this "mechanical world view" has its origin in a limited culture during a particular time and he concludes: the non-scientific presumptions in this world view are relative and false, and therefore some of the scientific results which are produced by this orthodox science are also false.[12]

This general argument is not tenable. He has to clarify the content in these particular assumptions, show their falsity/unreasonableness, show in what way they influence the process of science and demonstrate that they logically lead to false scientific results.

He makes some of these clarifications, for example, he states that some of the assumptions in the view of man in behaviorism and the principle of determinism are such assumptions. These assumptions have been created because the behavioristic psychologists in an uncritical way have taken over a methodological ideal from the natural sciences. This has created serious problems for the behavioristic psychologist, according to Maslow. These problems have their origin in their view of man, because they have not taken into consideration the special nature of their object of investigation. Maslow states the following specific characteristics of man as an object of investigation, and these express his own non-scientific presumptions (including his view of man) in his own scientific activity and in his constructive methodological ideal for psychology.

1. Maslow is critical of an *atomistic-reductive view of man and methodological ideal,* according to which the psychologist has to begin by studying some fundamental irreducible data, for instance, "basic sensation bits, stimulus-response or associative bands, reflex or conditioned reflexes, etc", and from these "simple elements" build up theories of human beings behavior.[13] This atomistic-reductive view entails a view of man, which, in some versions of behaviorism, assumes that human beings are "an empty organism" (except for some physiological drives). Instead Maslow proclaims: *the human being is a whole.* This wholeness cannot be grasped by studying particular parts of human beings. The psychologist has, in the first phase, to apprehend human beings in their unique wholeness, and in the second phase, begin to investigate different parts or part-processes. Knowledge of P is discovered by a combination of studying P's different behaviors, P's traits and the wholeness of P, that is, the unique organization of P's traits.[14] This methodological recommendation can be seen as a version of the hermeneutic circle (or spiral), (see further 6.3. point 6).

2. The atomistic-reductive view is in orthodox science linked with a *static mechanical-causal view.* This view is, for instance, implicit in the theory of homeostasis, which entails the assumptions: human beings are bound in stimuli-response bands and react only in order to reduce tension and reach equilibrium.

Maslow argues against this view from his own view of man. He states that

151

human beings are *dynamic, striving, oriented to the future with intentions and goals,* and who experience themselves as *agents* with a *self-consciousness.*[15]

3. Scientists are able to get information about these goals, intentions and how P feels. The scientists can understand P's "Eigenwelt" by P's *verbal reports* or more indirectly by reports of dreams, projective tests, paintings, gestures, etc. But their is a risk in this. P can lie or withhold information, because people have a *resistance to give information about themselves.* One reason is that this information is a treat to their self-esteem and self-image, another reason is that they fear to leave out information about themselves to another person and because human beings have *unconscious and preconscious aims, thoughts, feelings and processes.* These circumstances make, according to Maslow, the claim of a special relation between the subject of knowledge (the scientists) and the object of knowledge (human beings) and this relation has been overlooked by orthodox science and in particular behaviorism.[16]

(In our description of Maslow's *taoistic* method for studying human beings, some of these specific factors in studying human beings will be clarified further, see 6.3. point 6.)

6.2. The Goal of Science

Maslow is critical of orthodox science and in particular behaviorism, but also of psychoanalysis for their proclaimed goal of science, which he identifies as follows: to create nomothetic knowledge in order to control, predict and classify human behavior.

Maslow states that the goal of science and in particular the goal of psychology is to make particular human beings less controllable by outer factors and give them self-knowledge as a means for actualizing their potentials and to be self-actualizing persons, which contribute to the other overreaching goal, that is, to create "the Good Human Society".[17] Maslow does not neglect the significance of nomothetic knowledge (his motivation- and personality theories are examples of this kind of knowledge), but in his constructive scientific ideal for psychology and especially for clinical psychology, he emphasizes idiographic understanding as a goal.[18]

6.3. The Process of Science

Maslow's criticisms of orthodox science's, behaviorism's and psychoanalysis' view on the process of science can be summarized under the following points:

152

1. Maslow states that orthodox science and within psychology, behaviorism, have yielded to what he names *"means-centering" or "method-centering"*.[19] This means, inter alia, that the process of science is concentrated on following the established methods which are regarded to be the only methods that bring knowledge. This has as one of its consequences that the problems in psychology have been elected on the *criterion of settlement,* that is, they are possible to solve with the established methods. The problems are not elected from the *criterion of interest,* that is, they are judged to be important to solve. A consequence of this means-centering is: very little knowledge of human beings have been discovered. The researchs in psychology have instead been a drill in applying methods, according to Maslow.

As an alternative, Maslow proclaims: *problem-centering,* that is, psychologists have first to elect which problem they think are important to solve and then they have to look for and develop methods which can bring knowledge and which are as correct as possible. His argumentation in favour of problem-centering are, besides his view of the overreaching problems of mankind, the following:

P 1: He thinks that *knowledge grows in a cumulative way.*

> "And so it is also possible for all of them to accept in principle the empirical spirit and empirical methods and to humbly admit that knowledge is not complete, that it must grow, that it is in time and space, in history and in culture, and that, though it is relative to man's powers and to his limits, it can yet come closer and closer to 'the Truth' that is not dependent on man."[20]

Therefore, it is, in an area of problem, legitimate to begin with an idea, which successively can be formulated in hypotheses, and which, in the first phase, can only be tested with uncertain methods. Gradually these hypotheses can be further precizated and tested; be made more reliable and be linked with more established theories. Maslow states that his own research concerning self-actualizing persons is one example of this mode of procedure. A contextual reasonable interpretation is: the growth of knowledge takes place both in a quantitative and a qualitative way, that is, Maslow thinks that the stock of information about human beings are growing *and* the degree of correctness of these informations are becoming greater and greater.[21] It is uncertain whether or not Maslow has (a) *a teleological cumulative opinion,* that is, there is a goal of Absolute knowledge and that our knowledge comes, successively, nearer and nearer to this Absolute knowledge, *or* (b) if he has *a non-teleological cumulative opinion,* that is, our theories become more and more coherent, but that this coherent-net of theories can be exchanged with another coherent-net of theories (Kuhn). This latter opinion can also imply a relativism in the sphere of justification of knowledge. A reasonable interpretation of Maslow's opinion from his other opinions, for example, his ontological realism, representative realism, and correspondence theory of truth, is that he adopts (a).

P 2: Maslow does not specify any definite limit between knowledge and non-knowledge. He thinks that their are *degrees of knowledge*. He uses this view in his argumentation in favour of problem-centering, because this vague borderline between knowledge and non-knowledge justifies the use of non-established methods.

> "Knowledge is a matter of degree. Any increment of knowledge or of reliability is better than nothing. One case is better than none, and two are better then one. Neither knowledge in general nor reliability in particular is an all-or-none matter. There is no sharp shoreline which marks off the land of knowledge from the ocean of not-knowledge.[22]

We shall discuss his opinion of degrees of knowledge in 6.4.

P 3: He also thinks that *psychology is in its beginning as a science;* that there are few established methods; very little accumulated knowledge and few established and well-tested theories to take as basis and to develop further. Therefore, he thinks that it is legitimate to search in every direction, for example, in literature and art in order to find fruitful information in the areas of problems which are important to solve, in order to overcome the overreaching problems.

> "Too many psychologists have sought their philosophy in the physical science concepts of the 19th century, apparently merely because these sciences were successful. But psychology is in its infancy as a science and must work out its own philosophy and its own methodology, suitable to its own nature, problems and goals."[23]

2. The concentration on methods in orthodox science has led to a "*normal science*" which is done by rational scientists who are very skilled with the methods while the creative "revolutionary" scientists are locked out. The activities of science become very rigid, and science becomes a closed system, an enclosed paradigm. No creation of methods take place. Maslow thinks that this closed paradigm can be broken up by growing knowledge in the area of psychology of science and by a growing insight into the importance of solving the overreaching urgent problems. These two factors contribute to the justification of questioning the fruitfulness of means-centering in orthodox science's paradigm.[24] Other alternatives, to Maslow's opinion of central factors which can change a paradigm, are illustrated by the different positions in the debate concerning Kuhn's book *The Structure of Scientific Revolution*. For example, the paradigm can be changed because of anomalies within the paradigm, or by non-scientific factors, for instance, political decisions and technological developments.

Futhermore, Maslow thinks that "normal science" is maintained because many scientists use science as a "safety-science", that is, to give them gratifi-

154

cation of their safety-needs. A consequence of this is that these scientists have not the courage to question the basic assumptions in the established paradigm. Only self-actualizing scientists have this courage and are open to the "unknown".[25]

3. The area of investigations within psychology have been limited by the methods and by the strict criteria for objective scientific results. Parts of reality have therefore been left unaccessible for scientific inquiries. A sharp line of demarcation is created between the part of reality which can be studied with scientific methods and that part of reality which cannot be studied with scientific methods. Areas such as, religious experiences and non-moral values have been omitted. Maslow emphasizes the importance of psychology to study human content of consciousness *qua* content of consciousness. These contents are part of reality (in a wider sense of "reality") and are therefore legitimate to study.[26] The line of demarcation between non-scientific and scientific presumptions which we discussed in 6.2. are relevant here. According to Maslow, orthodox science's non-scientific presumptions have determinated the line of demarcation between the part of reality which can be studied and the part of reality which cannot be studied with scientific methods. Sometimes this line of demarcation has also been used as a criterion in an ontological reduction as, for instance, in ontological behaviorism and in some versions of logical positivism.

A serious consequence of this line of demarcation, is: the scientific results within the areas which can be investigated get an illusive objectivity in relation to the areas which are unaccessible for scientific investigations. The part of reality which cannot be investigated with scientific methods are left open to speculation and irrationalism, according to Maslow. Maslow refers to his thesis of different degrees of knowledge as an argument against the view of this sharp line of demarcation between these two parts of reality. There are no such sharp lines of demarcation because there is no sharp or absolute borderline between knowledge and non-knowledge. Furthermore, this sharp line of demarcation creates difficulties for co-operation between scientists and non-scientists, as well as difficulties for interdisciplinary co-operations because of the tendency toward hierarchies within different scientific disciplines. The most strict sciences as, for instance, physics cannot co-operate with the humanities and the reasons are: different methods and different criteria for reliability and validity concerning the scientific results are being used.[27]

Maslow gives his alternative and states methodological and personality pluralism in science.

Personality pluralism means that in the process of science there ought to be a co-operation between scientists of different personalities. Different scientists are in their work driven by many various motives, for instance, some try to solve the problem of mankind, others look for elegance, knowledge itself, safety, respect or curiosity. These different personalities complement each other in the various activities in the process of science. Maslow makes an analogy between the process of science and an orchestra, and states: it is impossible to play a symphony, if everybody played the oboe.[28]

Maslow also proclaims *methodological pluralism,* which means that it is legitimate to use different methods in the process of science. Maslow justifies this view by referring to the importance of solving the overreaching problems, his opinions on the cumulative growth of knowledge, the different degrees of knowledge and his view of psychology as being in its beginning as a science.[29] He exemplifies his view on methodological pluralism by his recommendation that the taoistic method should also be used in the process of science (the taoistic method is described in point 6 below) and his view of the complementarity between human and natural sciences' methodology. An argument which Maslow hints at in favour of both personality and methodological pluralism is that these two types of pluralism counter-balance individual personalities' and a specific method's influence on a particular object of investigation.

4. When Maslow dismisses the sharp line of demarcation between science and non-science, he also criticizes orthodox science's claim to be *norm- and value-free or neutral.*[30] He argues that orthodox science is not norm- and value-free or neutral. His example of norms and values within orthodox science is: orthodox science is looking for truth, and have certain criteria for acceptable methods and certain norms on what counts as sufficient evidence for a hypothesis to be confirmed. He does not make explicit the distinction between internal and external scientific norms and values. But this distinction follows from our distinction between non-scientific and scientific presumptions in 6.1. Even if this distinction is not very sharp it is fruitful, and a contextual reasonable interpretation is: that Maslow's examples of values and norms can be classified as internal scientific norms and values.[31]

That different lines of thought in the philosophy of science have different internal scientific norms and values is a truism. Maslow is, however, right when he ascribes to orthodox scientists *non-moral values* which influence their choices of problems, and claims that scientific results imply values and norms.

Maslow states that a value-neutral science (in the sense of non-moral values) is not only impossible, it is even dangerous. He illustrates this with the nazi-scientists who did not ask for the goal of their research and in some cases did not take ethical problems into consideration in their experiments with human beings.[32]

Maslow proclaims his own view: the process of science and scientific results ought to be normative.

156

"In principle, at least, science should be capable of generating normative psychologies of psychotherapy, of personal development, of eupsychian or utopan social psychology, of religion, of work, play, and leisure, of esthetics, of economics, and politics, and who knows what else?"[33]

Science ought to be an important means in order to solve the overreaching problems. Furthermore the scientific results, and especially the results from psychology, can justify a naturalistic normative ethics. If the value-questions are outside the realm of science, they are only a matter for speculation and anti-intellectualism.

In summing up, Maslow thinks that the results from science (and particular from psychology) ought to *contain* and *express* norms and values.

5. Maslow criticizes the behavioristic approach of creating theories about human beings from their studies of animal behaviour. These generalizations are very uncertain, according to Maslow, because human beings are, in important respects, very different from animals.[34] He also criticizes psychoanalysis for their focus on "psychic sick" people. Maslow states that psychology should also use data from "normal" and self-actualizing persons in their search for knowledge about human beings.[35]

6. Maslow sets forth a special method for studying human beings and he names this method — *the taoistic method*. This method can also be used in other sciences in their studies of various objects. Maslow used the taoistic method himself in his research about dominance and sexual behaviour in women (1939), self-actualizing people (1945—1949) and peak-experiences (1956).

Maslow introduces this method as a change in perspective, he wants the scientists to set out from the study of human beings instead of the natural sciences' objects of investigation.

"Let us try to take knowledge of the person as the model case from which to create paradigms or models of methodology, conceptualization, and Weltanschauung, of philosophy and epistemology. What are the consequences (for the moment) of taking as the ultimate bit of knowledge that which occurs in the I-Thou, interpersonal, Agapean-love relationship between two people. Let us think of this knowledge as 'normal', 'basic', 'routine' as our basic measuring stick to judge how 'knowledgy' any bit of knowledge is."[36]

When he describes the taoistic method, he takes the psychoterapeutic situation as the paradigmatic example.

He also stresses that the taoistic method is only a *complement* to other methods in science, it cannot replace them.[37]

Kluckhorn, Murray and Schneider make the following distinctions:
"Every man is in certain respects
a. like all other men
b. like some other men
c. like no other men."[38]

Nomothetic methods are applicable in a and b. Maslow's taoistic method is applicable in a and b, but especially in c.

Maslow distinguishes between two phases in the taoistic method.[39]

Phase 1: In the first phase, the aim is to get knowledge of the unique organization of P's personality traits, P's *suchness*.

The method to get this knowledge is: the scientist (hereafter S) should take a taoistic attitude, that is, in a passive way and without presuppositions, concepts, models, theories or earlier knowledge about P, let "the experiences rush in without hindrance", that is, have B-process. S should not ask questions or in other ways direct his/her dialogue only let P's spontaneous behaviour and speech give impressions to S. By this taoistic attitude, S gets more complete and more correct informations about P. S can apprehend and discover the unique organization of P's personality traits. This would not have been the case if S had started by questioning P, analysing and clarifying P with the help of nomothetic concepts and theories.

One ideal in this first phase is: S should try to become congenial with P and by empathy try to grasp P's "Eigenwelt". In so called "fusion knowledge" this empathy is driven to its ideal limit: S experiences an identity with P.

> "The ultimate limit, the completion toward which this kind of interpersonal knowledge moves, is through intimacy to the mystical fusion in which the two people become one in a phenomenological way that has been best described by mystics, Zen Buddhists, peak experiencers, lovers, estheticians, etc. In this experience of fusion a knowing of the other comes about through *becoming* the other, i.e., it becomes experiential knowledge from within. I know it because I know myself, and it has now become part of myself. Fusion with the object of knowledge permits experiential knowledge. And since experiential knowledge is the best kind of knowledge for many human purposes, a good mode of cognizing an object is to move toward fusion with is."[40]

In its first phase, the taoistic method sets certain claims on S and on the relation between S and P. In this relation S's personality is very important. The personality properties which Maslow thinks are most important for S to have are influenced by his ideal view of a psychotherapist and these are:

(a) S should be a self-actualizing person

(b) S should have a ability to empathise, theory-independent distancing and a passive judgement-free attitude. It is an advantage if S has had varied experiences of living. Futhermore, it is desirable if S has had similar experiences as P, in order to understand the information which P gives and which P often gives in indirect forms as, for instance, in metaphoric language, dream reports and hidden message.

(c) S should show P a feeling of care, and intermediate, an attitude of respect and acceptance. P should feel that P is a unique individual. In the

158

unique relation between S and P, and because of S's attitudes towards P, P react in certain ways to S, that is, P feels confident and trusts S. P feels S's respect and acceptance and gives S informations of P which are a treat to P's self-esteem and self-image. The relation between S and P, between the subject and object of knowledge is unique; S cannot be ex-changed and this makes S propositions about P less reliable.[41]

In Maslow's description of this first phase of the taoistic method, we can notice how he applies his assumptions of:

(I)   the existence of an ontological object's unique organization of its properties, its suchness

(II)   the importance of first grasping this suchness in order to study the different parts of the objects of knowledge

(III)   a unique cognitive faculty, that is, B-cognition

(IV)   the subject's characteristics' influence in the process of cognition

He connects his view on B-cognition with his view of suchness, that is, B-cognition is the *only* way to apprehend and to *discover* the suchness of the object of knowledge.

He uses his assumption of the need to first grasp the suchness in order to study the different parts of the object of knowledge. This can be seen as a version of the hermeneutic circle, that is, in order to understand the different parts of P, S has to have an adequate *Vorverstandnis*—P's suchness. But note the differences between Maslow's view and that of the hermeneutics. In the latters' view, there is an alternation between the whole and the parts. In Maslow's taoistic method the whole is *first* apprehended and then the different parts are related to this whole. Another difference is that this whole has an ontological character in Maslow's taoistic method, this is not the case in the hermeneutic-dialectics' view of the whole.

The discovery of the wholeness (suchness) and the parts are also related to the subject$_k$'s ability or *know how*. Different subjects$_k$ have different *degrees of know how* and accordingly different ability to get knowledge of P's suchness and different parts of P. (Different degrees of know how is one meaning in Polanyi's term "tacit knowledge").

We can also notice how Maslow thinks that it is possible for S to become congenial with P, namely, by becoming "identical" with P. One interpretation of "identical" is in accordance with our analysis of B-process in terms of intuitive cognition, where the subject$_k$'s content of consciousness becomes numerically identical with the object of knowledge (see 4.2.). An alternative interpretation, and according to our opinion, a more reasonable interpretation, is: S does not become numerically identical with P, S does not come into P or P's "Eigenwelt", *but* S can, through B-process, grasp *what* P's

159

"Eigenwelt" *is about,* S becomes congenial with P in the sense that S grasps the *content* in P's "Eigenwelt".

Phase 2: In this second phase S begins to ask P questions and S is more directing. In this phase, Maslow himself used different tests, for example, S-I-test (a test created by Maslow), TAT and Rorschach. S directs his/her observation to the special topics which S is interested in studying. This phase can be characterized as more active and experimental in comparison to the passive, understanding and receptive phase 1. A contextual reasonable interpretation is that the relation between phase 1 and phase 2 is not continuously changing, but that S first, in phase 1, grasps P's suchness and from the basis of this insight, in phase 2, begins to study P's different personality traits experimentally.

In phase 1, S does not use any theories, but a contextual reasonable interpretation is that S, in phase 2, uses certain nomothetic theories, for instance, Maslow's own motivation- and personality theories. In this taoistic method we can also notice how Maslow applies his opinion that different cognitive faculties give us knowledge of different aspects of reality.

> "This is, I maintain, a method [the receptive phase 1] a particular path to certain kinds of truth, which are better approached and achieved by this path. I do not maintain that it is the only path, or that all truths are obtainable in this way ... I would maintain only that in the full armamentarium of scientific methods, that love knowledge or "Taoistic objectivity" has its particular advantages in particular situations for particular purposes."[42]

B-cognition gives us knowledge of suchness, and the experimental methods, in phase 2, give us information of P's different personality traits, motives, etc.; from the basis of P's suchness. This methodological innovation is one example of Maslow's methodological pluralism. A contextual reasonable interpretation of his methodological pluralism is: he is in agreement with, inter alia, the hermeneutic-dialectic philosophers of science who proclaim *complementarity* as a methodological ideal, that is, both human and natural scientific methods should be used in the humanistic as well as the naturalistic areas of investigation.

6.4. Scientific Results

We shall, in this section, distinguish between: (a) Maslow's criteria for scientific results' objectivity and (b) Maslow's preference-criteria for scientific theories. We shall begin with (a).

In the sphere of objective scientific results, concerning individual hypotheses, Maslow distinguishes between:

(i) *classic objectivity* which has its origin in the studies in the natural sciences of things, vegetables and animals. The scientific results which emerge from the application of the methods in orthodox science has classic objectivity. The scientist arranges experiments and manipulates the object of knowledge in many ways, and the scientist is emotionally distant from the object of knowledge. The propositions which express the results are "clear, lucid, unequivocally defined, unmistakable, demonstrable, repeatable, communicable, logical, rational, verbalizable, conscious".[43] We make the following contextual reasonable interpretation: a scientific result should fulfil the following criteria in order to be objective in the "classic" sense of objectivity; (1) unequivocally formulated, (2) intersubjectively testable and (3) have a "high level" of reliability. 1, 2 and 3 are together sufficient logical criteria.

(ii) *taoistic objectivity* which has its primary origin in the study of human beings and emerges when a scientist applies the taoistic method. As we mentioned in 6.3., this method is a unique method which gives, inter alia information about otherwise inaccessible parts of reality. The propositions which express these results have a low reliability, *but* nevertheless, as we have reported above, Maslow argues in favour of the reasonableness in producing scientific results with this taoistic objectivity. In this argumentation he uses his thesis about degrees of knowledge, and we shall, below, try to precizate this thesis. In his taoistic method, he talks about *degrees of knowledge how,* that is, different subject$_k$s have different ability to apply B-process in phase 1 in the taoistic method. In our actual context, we shall relate his thesis of degrees of knowledge to *knowledge that* and make the following contextual reasonable interpretation: a hypothesis h is confirmed by information i at time t_n to the degree d. The confirmation of h to the degree d is related to a set of statement S, for instance, to a general theory T including other relevant hypotheses (confirmed to varied degrees) at time t_n. Hence, degrees of knowledge are interpreted in terms of positive confirmation/verification.

This interpretation can be connected with Maslow's thesis that knowledge grows cumulatively, partly quantitatively (that is, new information of parts of reality are discovered) and partly qualitatively (that is, the degrees of knowledge in the various hypotheses in the stock of information are growing). In this interpretation, various facts, hypotheses and theories form a coherent whole and the degrees of knowledge of a given fact, hypothesis and theory are related to the other facts, hypotheses and theories in this coherent whole. In 6.3., we interpreted Maslow as *not* stating a non-teleological cumulative opinion or a relativism in the sphere of justification of knowledge (because of his ontological realism, representative realism and correspondence theory of truth). A reasonable interpretation is therefore that the degrees of knowledge are not only related to the coherent net of facts, hypotheses and theories, but this coherent net and the hypothesis in question are also related to CTR.

Maslow justifies his view on degrees of knowledge by his view on psychology being in its beginning as science and the urgent need to solve the overreaching problems. He sees problem-solving as a process proceeding at the following levels. At the first level, the scientist has some "hunches, guesses, intuitions, ... vague 'prethoughts' not yet verbalized" concerning a certain problem. At the second level, the scientist tries to formulate a hypothesis and tests it with the "best method available". As a result of the activities on this second level the scientist is more able to formulate the hypothesis in a more unequivocal way and use more established and intersubjective methods in order to test the hypothesis. This hypothesis can perhaps also be related to other hypotheses and even a general theory. When these other hypotheses and the hypothesis in question are tested and united, the degrees of knowledge grow concering the hypothesis in question.

> "It is both useful and correct to consider as falling within the definition of knowledge all 'protoknowledge', so long as its probability of being correct is greater than chance. This usage would imply then a hierarchy of stages or levels or degrees of knowledge, ranging downward in degree of reliability to expert guesses, hunches and intuitions, tentative conclusions based on insufficient cases or upon crude methods, etc. Knowledge is then seen as more reliable or less reliable but still knowledge so long as its probability is greater than chance."[44]

We shall make some critical remarks of Maslow's view on classic and taoistic objectivity in section 6.5.

Maslow also sets forth *certain preference-criteria for scientific theories* which we shall try to reconstruct below.

Maslow has a hypothetical view of scientific theories. He emphasizes that the basic propositions and the deduced hypotheses and testimplications have to be tested by (1) experiments (2) controllable experiences and (3) introspective data. (Maslow names the latter sometimes "experiential data" or "subjective experience"). The most important claims on a scientific theory is (his focus is on *psychological* theories): the theory has to be testable by 1 − 3.

> "In contrast the empirical theory or empirical system remains connected with the experiential facts that it organizes into a manageable, graspable unity and in close parallel with these facts. As a consequence it can shift and change and easily modify itself as new information becomes available. That is, if it purports to interpret and organize our knowledge of reality, then it must of necessity be a changing thing, since our knowledge of reality keeps on changing, and it must be adaptable and flexible in the sense of adapting itself to this foundation of changing and increasing knowledge. There is a kind of mutual feedback involved here between theory and facts, a feedback which can be totally lacking in the functionally autonomous abstract theory or system which has become self-borne."[45]

The theory which gets most support from the conjunction of 1 − 3 is to be preferred.

162

The second preference-criterion is: the theory should have a *great exten-sion*, that is, the theory which explains most phenomena ought to be prefer-red.[46] By"phenomena" Maslow also means introspective data which can be classified and whose meanings can be understood. One reason for Maslow to state this preference-criterion is to include introspective data in the area of investigation which also explains his claim 3 above. Maslow is very critical of theories with an axiomatic-deductive structure in which the axioms are based only on rational thinking. He is also very critical of preference-criteria which he thinks are of system-character, for instance, simplicity and logical consis-tence.[47] Simplicity can be interpreted as (a) simplest net of relations between the different factors in a theory and (b) least number of existence-assumption among the factors.

Maslow's arguments against these preference-criteria are: (1) These criteria have limited the areas of reality which can be investigated with scentific methods and (2) theories which have been preferred by these criteria contain theoretical models which are characterized as more real than the experienced, that is, he argues against a "model platonism". "Model platonism" means that the theoretical models are more real than the experienced. Maslow states that the experiential data are, epistemologically primary and cannot be reduced or dismissed by any theoretical models.

> "If the empirical attitude means anything at all, it means at least this. First comes 'knowing' in the experiential sense: then come the checks on the fallibilities of the senses and of experiential knowledge; then come the abstractions, the theories, i.e. orthodox science".[48]
> "Facts must become before theories."[49]
> "The world of experience exists and comprehends all experiences, i.e. the experi-ential, phenomenological, or esthetically experienced world. The other, the world of the physicists, mathematicians, and chemists, of abstractions, 'laws', and formulas, of systems of postulates, is a world that is not directly experienced but rather rests *upon* the experiential world, is inferred from it, and is an effort to comprehend it and to make sense of it, to see behind its contradictions, to order it and structure it."[50]

Maslow discusses, inter alia, the well-known example of Eddington, that is: which of the following two descriptions of a table corresponds most accura-tely with the ontological object x?: (a) the physical description of the table or (b) the description of a person's percept of the table?

Maslow makes his judgement and states that the description of the percept is more correct in relation to the ontological material object x than the physical description of the table. His main argument is: the percept is, epis-temologically primary, with regard to both (i) the genesis of our experiences of CTR and (ii) our justification of our statements of CTR. Maslow is an ontological realist and he thinks that one aim for science is to formulate theories about CTR. This takes the form of a construction where the episte-mologically primary is the experiential data. The most correct and complete percepts are B-percept. These can be regarded as "brute facts" or theory-independent basic percepts and the constructions ought to start out from these data in the attempt to construct theories about CTR. The theories and models which are constructed from these data can never question the correctness of the contents of B-percept.[51]

Maslow's view on simplicity and logical consistency as logically leading to a model-platonism is not tenable. There are other alternatives, for example, instrumentalism or critical realism, which are reasonable to hold, in the problem of the epistemological status of theoretical models in science.[52] We can compare Maslow's view on the epistemological status of theoretical models in scientific theories with Hempel's view.[53] Hempel states: the two descriptions of the table are from two different perspectives. The description of the percept (macroscopic characteristics) have to be at hand, as "bridge-principle" to make the physical description (in terms of microstructures and microproces-ses) meaningful. The description of the table in physical terms does not deny the correctness of the description of the percept, only to describe the material object x (the table) from another perspective.

6.5. Final remarks on Argument A

In this final section, we shall use our account of Maslow's theory of science in 6.1.—6.4. to complete and summarize our discussions about Argument A.

In 1.0., we made the first formulation of Argument A, and successively, we have precizated this argument. In 4.5., we formulated it as follows:

Argument A_4

(1) If a person P has P's deficiency needs gratified and P's actions are directed towards gratifying P's self-actualizing needs, P will actualize some characte-ristics X, Y, Z . . . *and* if P actualizes the characteristics X, Y, Z . . ., P will have a process of cognition which is characterized by (a) specific changes in attention and (b) passive forms of cognizing

(2') If P has a process of cognition which is characterized by (a) specific changes in attention and (b) passive forms of cognizing, *P will have experien-ces* of types, suchness, Unitive consciousness, Cosmic consciousness and B-values.

(2'') If P has a process of cognition which is characterized by (a) specific changes in attention and (b) passive forms of cognizing *P has knowledge that*

164

P's descriptions of the content of consciousness of the types suchness, Unitive consciousness, Cosmic consciousness and B-values have referents in CTR.

(3) There are persons Ps who have their deficiency-needs gratified and whose actions are directed towards gratifying P's self-actualizing needs and P has the characteristics X, Y, Z ...

---

(4) There are persons Ps who have knowledge that their descriptions of their experiences of suchness, Cosmic consciousness, Unitive consciousness and B-values have referents in CTR.

In 4.5., we made two interpretations of *premiss 1*.

I 1: The basic conjunction in premiss 1 is *not* a necessary or sufficient logical criterion in order for B-cognition to take place. A consequence of I 1 is that premiss 1 can be excluded from Argument A_4.

I 2: The basic conjunction in premiss 1 is a necessary or a sufficient logical criterion in order for B-cognition to take place. Premiss 1 can then be criticized in accordance with the criticism which we made of Maslow's motivation and personality theories in sections 2.1.1. and 2.2.4.

We interpreted *premiss 2'* in section 4.5. as a causal condition in order to get B-percept. As such, premiss 2' is irrelevant for the context of justification and can be excluded from Argument A_4.

In our interpretation of *premiss 2''* we have first to distinguish between Maslow's epistemological theses 1 and 2. In thesis 1 he states: some B-percepts are more complete than D-percepts with regard to the parts of CTR which can be experienced in both D-cognition and B-cognition, and P has knowledge that P's descriptions of these B-percepts have referents in CTR. In thesis 2 he states: some B-percepts contain aspects of CTR which cannot be experienced in D-cognition and P has knowledge that P's description of these aspects (addition-Gestalts) have referents in CTR.

In our analysis of theses 1 and 2 we used as an analytical conceptual framework the so called classical account of knowledge, which states: P know that *p* if, and only if:
1. The Belief-criterion is satisfied: P believes that *p*
2. The Truth-criterion is satisfied: *p* is true
3. The Evidence-criterion is satisfied: P has good and sufficient reason for believing that *p*

In Maslow's epistemological thesis 2 we distinguished between two lines. In *line A* we have interpreted Maslow as stating: B-process is a necessary and sufficient logical criterion in order for a reason to be good and sufficient in

165

the evidence-criterion. In *line B* we have interpreted Maslow as stating: B-process is not a sufficient logical criterion for a reason to be good and sufficient in the evidence-criterion. Instead, Maslow sets forth "external validation" and "routine skeptical and cautious procedures of science". In section 6.4. we have tried to reconstruct these sufficient logical criteria and we interpreted these criteria as being the following: an objective scientific result should fulfil the following claims: it should be (1) unequivocally formulated (2) intersubjectively testable and (3) have a "high" level of reliability.

We shall summarize below our discussion of *line A*. Maslow "identifies knowledge with intuitive apprehension of the immediate" and he has the presupposition: if, and only if, the subject does not work at proximal stimuli, the true reality is apprehended (and discovered) *or* in a weaker sense if, and only if, the subject$_k$ does not work at proximal stimuli, the subject$_k$ gets an experience of CTR which is more complete and more correct than in any other kind of process of cognition. Maslow generalizes from *some* kinds and *some* forms of cognition distort the percept to *all* kinds and *all* forms of cognition distort the percept. He thinks it is possible to have a self-evident non-propositional knowledge of CTR and that concepts are inadequate in order to apprehend certain aspects of CTR. Contrary to Maslow, we hold that there is a conceptual interpretation in all apprehension of CTR. Furthermore, he is ambiguous on the point of non-propositional self-evident knowledge because in some contexts he state: human beings have to interpret proximal stimuli through concepts in order to make the percepts meaningful.

Another problematic point in line A is: there is a disagreement between different interpreters of transcendent experiences and even between different mystics about the content of consciousness which the subject$_k$ experiences when the subject$_k$ has reduced the forms of cognizing to a minimum. Maslow meets these difficulties by using James' over-belief-theory. In chapter 5 we have tried to reconstruct this theory and Maslow's opinion of the common content in "peak-experience". Our conclusion was the following: Maslow used James' over-belief-theory gratuitously and it is very difficult to make the common content in "peak-experience" explicit.

Another argument he sets forth in favour of line A is: there is in B-cognition a "fusion" between the subject$_k$'s content of consciousness and the object of knowledge. We have to distinguish between a *psychological "fusion"*, that is, the person experiences that the subject-object distinction is transcended and an *ontological "fusion"*, that is, the subject$_k$'s content of consciousness and the object of knowledge are forming a unit in an ontological sense. We have in 4.2., tried to interpret this unit in accordance with Bergson's *ultra-realism*, but it is hard to clarify this view. Furthermore, the ontological "fusion" is not in

166

agreement with Maslow's ontological realism in which the basic ontological categories are individual human consciousness and matter.

In his argumentation in favour of self-evident non-propositional knowledge of the addition-Gestalts he excludes the criterion of intersubjective testability. He states that B-percept is only communicable if, and only if, the receivers have had B-percepts themselves. This is *the problem of communication* which we discussed in section 3.1. P's content of consciousness has first to be communicable before other persons can test P's knowledge-claims about the contents because others have first to know what to test. In line A Maslow does not think that intersubjective testability is a necessary logical criterion for a reason to be good and sufficient in the evidence-criterion. Since we hold intersubjective testability as a necessary logical criterion for a reason to be good in the evidence-criterion, we also think that Ayer's claim (b) on the ability for the subject$_k$ to bring forth the content of consciousness by volition is an argument against Maslow's argumentation in favour of line A. Furthermore, we think that concerning the problem of communication it is not reasonable to hold that the receivers should have had experiences of B-percepts themselves in order to understand the descriptions of B-percept.

Another argument against Maslow's line A is that he in his epistemology assumes an empirical theory of cognition which within this epistemology cannot be justified because this empirical theory of cognition is logically prior to his evidence-criteria for knowledge. This actualizes what we have called *the problem of the infinite regress of reasons* and which will be discussed at the end of this section.

We now pass to Maslow's *line B.*

He distinguishes between classic and taoistic objectivity. In classic objectivity he thinks that scientific results are considered objective if they are (1) unequivocally formulated (2) intersubjectively testable and (3) have a "high" level of reliability. A reasonable interpretation is the following: Maslow holds the conjunction of 1−3 as a sufficient logical criterion in order for a reason to be good and sufficient in the evidence-criterion.

In his discussion of taoistic objectivity he sets forth the idea of degrees of *knowledge that.* The question is: has he by his introduction of degrees of *knowledge that* and methodological pluralism added something to his evidence-criterion in line A? Is non-propositional apprehension in B-cognition still knowledge, but at a low level of reliability? The ideal is that knowledge at a low level of reliability should be pressed to knowledge at a high level of reliability by becoming verified by the established methods in orthodox science. In the case of addition-Gestalts, in line B, a contextual reasonable interpretation is the following: the descriptions of addition-

Gestalts are knowledge at a low level of reliability, but they should be pressed to become tested by the established methods in orthodox science and (if confirmed) get a high level of reliability. In this interpretation we have presupposed that the methods in orthodox science can falsify the "proto-knowledge" found in B-cognition. A consequence of this opinion is that *truth cannot be a necessary criterion for knowledge* because protoknowledge can at a later level be falsified.

In line A we have interpreted Maslow's opinion as follows: he thinks that B-cognition and the methods in orthodox science are qualitative different sources of knowledge and the results of orthodox science can never question B-results. In our proposed interpretation of line B above, the relationship between orthodox science's results and B-cognition is the following: B-cognition is one way to discover and state certain hypotheses about CTR. B-results are regarded as embryos to more valid knowledge. B-results put forth certain views on different states of affairs and brings these into the sphere of science. As a consequence they can also bring some presumptions into the open regarding orthodox science's view on a certain state of affair. In this interpretation the addition-Gestalts can in principle be falsified by the results of orthodox science. We shall compare below this principle view of the relationship between orthodox science's claims on scientific results and Maslow's own scientific investigation concerning peak-experience.

Maslow recommends in his constructive philosophy of science the following methodological procedure in studying peak-experience (compare section 3.1.):

a) the scientist (S) should interview the examinee (E) about his/her peak-experiences. If E has problems to describe or remember such experiences S should give E descriptions of such experiences in order to "help" E to remember or describe his/her experiences.

b) These descriptions and descriptions found in various literature can be interpreted with the help of James' over-belief-theory. By using this theory it is possible to make ontological, epistemological and semantic reductions of the descriptions in the sources, according to our analysis in section 5.1.

We can make the following *critical remarks* of this recommended method in studying transcendent experiences in the Psychology of Religion:
1. Maslow's results are not intersubjectively testable because
    a. he does not give a description of the contents in his sources
    b. he uses the over-belief theory gratuitiously because he never shows how his use of this theory leads him to his results.
2. He has not taken sufficient attention of *the problem of communication* concerning studies about peak-experience, partly because of the problems in his interview-technique when he questions his examinees (see section

3.1.), and partly because he did not take *the problem of private language* into consideration in his investigations.

Maslow states that various individuals from different social-cultural environments have some qualitative identical contents in peak-experience (after he has interpreted them with the help of James' over-belief-theory) and he uses this consensus as an argument in favour of the ontological claims he sets forth. With the criticism in 1 and 2 above, we think that Maslow's argument against Ayer's claim (a), that is, that the use of a specific cognitive faculty should bring "similar" contents of consciousness to the various subjects$_k$ who use this cognitive faculty, is not tenable.

Maslow's investigation has not shown that descriptions of addition-Gestalts are justified in their claims of being knowledge, according to the evidence-criteria in line B. Neither can we understand how methods within orthodox science can be used to investigate the knowledge-claims in the descriptions of addition-Gestalts.

Our conclusion, *from our point of analysis, concerning both line A and line B is the following: the knowledge-claims set forth by Maslow in his interpretation of peak-experience are not justified, because, by the arguments which we have summed up above, in line A, the reasonableness in his criteria for a reason to be good and sufficient in the evidence-criterion are to be rejected. In line B, we think that Maslow's criteria in order for a reason to be good and sufficient in the evidence-criterion are reasonable, but Maslow's arguments in favour of peak-experiences having referents in CTR do not fulfil these criteria.*

In this dissertation, we have analysed central parts of Maslow's *Weltanschauung*. We think, generally speaking, that a person P's evidence-criterion for knowledge are influenced in different ways by other parts of P's *Weltanschauung*. In our reconstruction and analysis of Argument A, we have made explicit Maslow's view of man, normative ethics, ontology, philosophy of science and epistemology.

We shall speculate below a little about these factors' relationship in Maslow's *Weltanschauung* and as an end to the dissertation state our view of some connections between some factors in a *Weltanschauung* and the evidence-criterion for knowledge. By this we shall also discuss *the problem of the infinite regress of reasons.*

We think that Maslow began to question the established view of man in *behaviorism,* inter alia, the view that man is determined only by the physiological needs and the environment, and the identification between outer and inner personality, and in *psychoanalysis,* inter alia, the homoestatis-theory, the content and ontological character of the Unconscious, and the content and character of man's basic needs. This criticism had its basis in his own more and more explicit view of man and normative ethics. He also began to question the established ontologies in various orthodox Religions which he interpreted as various versions of supernaturalism, and ontologies of contemporary *Weltanschauungen,* for example, purely ontological materialism. His experience in the parade in 1941 became a turning point and his mission became: to formulate an alternative *Weltanschauung* which he wanted to be proved with scientific results. This was one reason why he started to criticize some opinions in the philosophy of orthodox science, for instance, its means-centering, the atomistic-reductive view, its limited sphere of investigation, the claim of being norm- and value-free, and disregarding of its non-scientific presumptions. Instead, he started to formulate a constructive philosophy of science, containing: method-centering, personality and methodological pluralism, degrees of knowledge, and explicit normative aims.

The relationships named above are mostly of a *causal* character, but sometimes even of an *argumentative* character, that is, F and R have an argumentative character, if opinion F is, more or less explicit, contained in the premisses in an argumentation in favour of R.[54] For instance, as our analyses have tried to show, various elements in Maslow's view of man are premisses in his criticism of (1) the view of man in behaviorism and psychoanalysis (2) orthodox science and (3) the normative ethics he finds in various versions of Christianity. Another example of relationship of an argumentative character is his ontological view, for instance, in his criticism of supernaturalism. Furthermore, his ontological view functions as a hidden presumption in his research about peak-experience.

Naturally, there are also complex argumentative relationships between elements in Maslow's own *Weltanschauung.* We have one example in our analysis of Argument A between his view of man, theory of cognition and ontology. Other examples are his view of man and normative ethics and elements in his constructive philosphy of science, for instance, his claim on method-centering, personality and methodological pluralism.

We shall end this dissertation with a discussion of *the problem of the infinite regress of reasons.* This problem is of central importance because there is a difference between:

(a) *what* one thinks, for example, one has a certain view of man or a certain ontology, and

(b) *how to justify, epistemologically,* what one thinks, that is, what kind of reasons one has for on's views in (a).

There can be conflicts between people about the content in (a), for example, between different views of man. *This is a conflict on one level.* Another (and according to our opinion, in some respect more serious) conflict is between

170

people who have different views concerning how to justify, epistemologically, the views in (a). For example, P holds that only reasons which satisfy some version of the empiricist principle of verification are good and sufficient reasons in (b), Q holds that reasons which satisfy this principle *plus* reasons justified by some intuitive cognitive faculty are good and sufficient reasons in (b). *This is a conflict on another level than conflicts in (a) above.*

It is in the context (b) that *the problem of the infinite regress of reasons* is relevant because this problem concerns what reasons one holds as good (and sufficient) when one argues in favour of what types of reasons are good (and sufficient) on level (b) above.

The problem of the infinite regress of reasons was presented in section 4.5. It emerges in the classical account of knowledge which states the following logical distinct necessary and sufficient criteria in order for P to know that *p:*

1. The Belief-criterion should be satisfied: P believes that *p*
2. The Truth-criterion should be satisfied: *p* is true
3. The Evidence-criterion should be satisfied: P has good and sufficient reasons for believing that *p*

If P believes that *p, p* is true and P has reason q in favour of *p,* the problem of the infinite regress of reasons is the following: how can P know that reason q is a good and sufficient reason in favour of *p?* does not P have to give a reason *r* in favour of that reason *q* is a good and sufficient reason in favour of *p,* and in that case how can P know that *r* is a good and sufficient reason in favour of *q?* An infinite regress begins. This problem was already noticed by Plato in Theaetetus.[55]

In the history of philosophy different solutions or reactions have been given to this problem. Below, we shall sketch very briefly some of them.[56]

1. **The sceptical reaction:** There is at least three subcategories of this reaction:
   a. *There is no end of the regress,*
   b. *We can not know if the regress is infinite or not,* and
   c. *We refrain from making any judgement whether or not the regress is finite or infinite, but we have an open mind and seek actively a solution to this problem.*

   The propositions in a. and b. have been criticized in the history of philosophy for holding at least one proposition as true, that is, the proposition in a. or b. respectively. A. Naess in *Scepticism* identifies standpoints a. and b. as Academic scepticism and standpoint c. as Pyrrhonism as depicted by Sextus Empiricus.[57]

2. **The self-evidence solution.** *There is an end to the regress and it ends with some self-evidence reasons.* One advocates of this tradition is, for instance, Descartes, who directly apprehends the truth in "Cogio ergo sum". We can

classify Bergson and Maslow in his line A in this category of solution. Above, we have summed up our arguments against Maslow's line A.

3. **The ethical solution.** *The regress cannot be ended by any theoretical reasons. Instead it ends by a judgement of ethical character.* In this solution epistemology transforms to ethics and meta-ethical problems.

4. **The pragmatic solution:** *The regress is finite.* A reason q is a good and sufficient reason in favour of p, if p in a fruitful way is related to the solution of a problem which P has set himself/herself to solve. Maslow's normative non-scientific aim, to create a *Weltanschauung* which could conteract the cultural crisis which Maslow thought the Western-world was in influences to some extent his view of the evidence-criterion in his line B. We can therefore classify him under this category.

   One critical remark against this pragmatic solution is that the evidence-criterion becomes dependent on different problems and various individuals' judgements about fruitful solutions to these problems.

5. **The existentialistic reaction:** *The regress ends by an existentialistic choice.* q is a good and sufficient reason in favour of p because I make the choice to believe that q is a good and sufficient reason, or I make the choice to believe p. Advocates of this standpoint are, for example, Kierkegaard and W. James (in his essay *The Will to Believe*).[58]

   A criticism is that one can question to what extent the choice is free. To what extent is the outcome of the choice influenced by a person's earlier experiences and beliefs?

6. **Wittgenstein's reaction:** *The regress does never start.* It is meaningful to say "P knows that p", but it is not meaningful to say that "P knows that q is a good reason in favour of p, in the evidence-criterion". This is one possible interpretation of Wittgenstein's standpoint in *Philosophical Investigations*.

   "There is *one* thing of which we can say neither that it is one metre long, nor that it is not one metre long, and that is the standard metre in Paris. — But this is, of course, not to ascribe any extraordinary property to it, but only to mark its peculiar role in the language-game of measuring with a metre-rule. — Let us imagine samples of colour being preserved in Paris like the standard metre. We define: 'sepia' means the colour of the standard sepia which is there kept hermetically sealed. Then it will make no sense to say of this sample either that it is of this colour or that it is not. We can put it like this: This sample is an instrument of the language used in ascriptions of colour. In this language-game it is not something that is represented, but is a means of representation."[59]

   In analogy to the standard metre and standard sepia, the reasons for sufficient and good reasons in the evidence-criterion have a special position in a certain language-game and therefore one cannot meaningsfully use "knowledge" in the description of P's relation to q.

7. **The immediate knowledge solution:** *The regress ends by "immediate*

knowledge". Advocates of this solution are G.E. Moore and D.M. Armstrong.[60] Moore distinguishes between *immediate knowledge* and *direct apprehension*. P has immediate knowledge of the proposition *p*, "without knowing any other proposition whatever to be true". P has immediate knowledge only of propositions. Immediate knowledge is logical independent of direct apprehension (therefore, this solution can be distinguished from the self-evidence solution above). P can have immediate knowledge of the directly apprehended proposition *p*, but also of other proposition which are not directly apprehended. Accordingly, the fact that P directly apprehends proposition *p* is not a necessary logical criterion in order for P to have immediate knowledge that *p*. P can have immediate knowledge that *p* at time t_2, without directly apprehend proposition *p*. Furthermore P can, at one and the same time, have both immediate *and* mediate knowledge that *p*. Mediate knowledge is the case when P knows that *p* because P knows some other proposition from which *p* follows. Accordingly immediate and mediate knowledge do not logically exclude each other.[61]

8. **The Holistic solution:** *The regress is finite, but it has no end. p* is supported by *q* which is supported by *r*, which is supported by ... which is supported by *p*. Different reasons stand in a (coherent) net of (logical) relations to each other. This whole can, for instance, be structured as a hypothetical-deductive system in which certain propositions have a more central position, in the sense that many of the propositions in this whole (Weltanschauung) follow from these propositions. The hypothetical component is that the system as a whole and the various propositions in this whole have to be tested by our sense-experiences and other informations we get in our process of living. Such a holistic solution can be found in Føllesdal & Walløe (1977).[62] W.V. Quine sets forth, in the article *Two Dogmas of Empiricism,* a very radical holistic view, in that he thinks logic and mathematics do not hold any exceptional position, they can also be revised by future experiences.[63]

We think the contemporary debate about paradigm and paradigm-dependent evidence-criteria can be classified under this holistic solution.

Maslow has a tendency to think that his different theories are forming a *Weltanschauung* and that his different theories and parts of theories can be judged only from this holistic perspective (see section 1.3.). An interpretation of his line B in this holistic perspective justifies that Maslow can be classified under this holistic solution.

The author's of this dissertation own sympathies lie in the existentialistic reaction and in the holistic solution and two famous ship-metaphors will be used in order to illustrate the author's own view.

"The choice itself is decisive for the content of the personality, through the choice the personality immerses itself in the thing chosen, and when it does not choose it withers away in consumption. For an instant it is so, for an instant it may seem as if the thing between which a choice is to be made lie outside of the chooser, that he stands in no relationship to it, that he can preserve a state of indifference over against it. This is the instant of deliberation, but this, like the Platonic instant, has no existence, least of all in the abstract sense in which you would hold it fast, and the longer one stares at it the less it exists. That which has to be chosen stands in the deepest relationship to the chooser, . . . Think of the captain on his ship at the instant when it has to come about. He will perhaps be able to say, 'I can either do this or that'; but in case he is not a pretty poor navigator, he will be aware at the same time that the ship is all the while making its usual headway, and that therefore it is only an instant when it is indifferent whether he does this or that. So it is with a man. If he forgets to take account of the headway, there comes at last an instant when there no longer is any question of an either/or, not because he has chosen but because he has neglected to choose, which is equivalent to saying, because others have chosen for him, because he has lost his self."[64]

The ambition is not to make any intentional interpretation of this quotation from Kierkegaard. The author of this dissertation only thinks that the quotation gives a clear illustration of one of our existential dilemmas: we have, in our process of life, all the time, to face different choice-situations and in these situations we have to act, we have to be agents. One important factor in our choices and actions is our beliefs, our values or norms, our choices and actions are "belief-impregneted".[65] We have in the process of life to act and our actions are in various ways influenced by our *Weltanschauung*. The reflexion and justification of our *Weltanschauung* is not only a theoretical matter, it is also important for our practical living. (In the quotation, Kierkegaard states that we in our choices in one sense also create our personality, earlier choices have in different ways influenced our actual personality, and our choice, here and now, influence our future personality).

The other ship-metaphor is the following:

"We are like sailors who must rebuild their ship on the open sea, never able to dismantle it in dry-dock and to reconstruct it out of the best materials."[66]

This famous qoutation from O. Neurath gives, according to the author's of this dissertation opinion, a clear illustration of how we ought, all the time, to question and test our different beliefs, norms and values in our *Weltanschauung* and that none of them are absolutely true or unquestionable. We should have an *open mind,* and this open mind even includes that we ought to have the courage and capability to accept that the problems in our *Weltanschauung* can be judge as problems only from our *Weltanschauung* or from a subclass of *Weltanschauungen.* These problems, (for instance, *the problem of the infinite regress of reasons*) can be *dissolved* as we successively transform our *Weltanschauung* or in a sudden "leap" pass to another *Weltanschauung.*

Notes

Chapter 1

1. Naess 1969.
2. Bergson, James and Dewey have different opinions with regard to other epistemological areas of problem, but, in our opinion, they can be connected with regard to the epistemological case in question. These philosophers have been chosen as advocates of the epistemological tradition in question because they have influenced Maslow in his epistemological opinions. See our analysis in chapters 4, 5 and 6.
3. For a short description of the differences between D-cognition and B-cognition, see Maslow 1968a, pp. 202−203.
4. See Ornsten 1975; Naranjo 1974: Ornstein and Naranjo 1971; Tart 1969.
5. Maslow 1968a, p. 100.
6. Ibid, p. 203. See also ibid., pp. 41, 65 and 184; Maslow 1976a, pp. 123−124 and 149−150.
7. The variables in A_2 are: Sx = P's basic needs are satisfied, Tx = P can be characterized as a self-actualizing person, Qx = P has B-cognition, and Rx = P will have knowledge of Y.
8. For a survey of this criticism, see, for example, Radnitzsky 1968, Vol. II.
9. The biographical data are taken from Lowry 1973 and Wilson 1972. These books can be regarded as reliable because the authors received their data from Maslow himself, and after his death in 1970, from Maslow's widow Bertha. See also Poelling 1971 and Saussy 1977.
10. Some of Maslow's results from these research can be found in the articles which he published during 1932−1935. See Maslow's bibliography in Maslow 1979, pp. 1313−1329.
11. Maslow 1939; Maslow 1942a.
12. See Maslow's own account in the preface Maslow 1954, or Maslow's letter to Globe, Globe 1975, pp 12−13.
13. In this research the interview took about 15 hour/examinee. They were, however, spread over several occasions. The interviews were combined with a paper-and-pencil test: Malow's S-I-test (see Maslow 1940 and Maslow 1942b), Maslow 1939, pp. 5−7. For Maslow's interviewing technique, see Maslow 1942a, pp. 262−263; Maslow 1970a, pp. 297−299; Maslow 1976a, pp. 72−73.
14. *Methodological behaviorism*, that is, the methodological opinion that only behavior is the object of investigation in psychology, should be distingushed from (a) *ontological behaviorism*, which denies the existence of human consciousness as a mental entity and (b) *logical behaviorism*, which holds that statements about "mental states" should be translated into statements about behavior or dispositions in order to be meaningful.
15. Maslow 1942a, pp. 36−38.
16. Wilson states that Maslow wrote the main part of the first edition 1941, and Mittelmann alone made the changes in the second edition 1955. Wilson 1972, p. 147.

17. Hall 1968, pp. 54—55. Compare Maslow's letter to Sutich: "This [A Theory of Meta-motivation, Maslow 1976a] is really the end of the programme that I set out for myself—secretly—about 25 or so years ago when I changed everything I was doing and devoted myself grandiosely to a Psychology for the Peace Table". Sutich 1976, p. 15. See also Maslow 1965, p. 3; Maslows 1979, pp. 93,531,868,895, 922.

18. See, for instance, Maslow 1959b, p. vii-vii; Maslow 1976b, pp. 9, 38—39. Many of the humanistic psychologists think that the Western-world is in a cultural crisis. See Bühler & Allen 1972, pp. 53—68. They assert some causes for this crisis, for instance, the First and Second World-wars, the misstrust of democracy, pollution and the violence in everyday life. See also Shaffer 1978, pp. 5—8.

19. "When the philosophy of man (his nature, his goals, his potentialities, his fulfillment) changes, then everything changes, not only the philosophy of politics, of economics, of ethics and values, of interpersonal relations and of history itself, but also the philosophy of education, of psychotherapy and of personal growth, the theory of how to help men become what they can and deeply need to become." Maslow 1968a, p. 189.

20. Maslow 1976a, p. 18.

21. Ibid.

22. Ibid., pp. 7, 19, 194 and 204. See also the section "The Theory of Social Improvement" in Maslow 1965, p. 247—265. Maslow 1979, vol II contains some material concerning Maslow's views on the organisation of community.

23. Maslow 1976a, pp. 188, 194; Maslow 1965, p. 20; Maslow 1962a, p. 60.

24. Maslow 1976a, pp. 206—207; Maslow 1970a, p. 255; Maslow 1964a, p. 58.

25. Maslow 1956, 17—18. Maslow's opinion, concerning the central position for psychology as a means to create a better society, is probably influenced by Watson's behavioristic programme. Maslow 1966a, p. 7; Maslow 1979, pp. 164, 112.

26. Lowry edited Maslow's journals 1959—1970 in two volumes covering 1309 pages. Maslow 1979, vol. I and II.

27. Maslow 1979, pp. 26—27, 292.

28. Maslow 1979, pp. 210, 345, 422, 489. See also Mackinnon's judgement of Maslow, MacKinnon 1972, p. 162.

29. Maslow 1979, pp. 767—768; see also pp. 5, 34, 43, 64, 768.

30. These different assumptions of reasonableness concern primarily a given text or article or book because Maslow often changes his opinion from article to article.

31. We are influenced by Grenholm in our attempt to distinguish between these two types of reasonable interpretation, see Grenholm 1981, pp. 55—70.

32. We disagree with "intentional interpretation" which holds that the aim of the interpretation-hypothesis is to find out the author's intention behind his/her statements. Our reasons are, inter alia, these interpretation-hypotheses are not possible to verify and you make the so called *fallacy of intention*, see Føllesdal & Walløe 1977, pp. 88—91; Halldén 1981, pp. 51—56 and Aspelin 1955, pp. 154—165.

33. Maslow 1979, p. 345; see also pp. 426—427, 713, 922.

34. Lindström, 1973, p. 28.

35. According to Sutich, Maslow took the first contacts as early as 1954. Sutich 1961, p. viii. See also Misiah & Sexton 1973, p. 111.

36. According to Misiah & Sexton, the choice of Maslow as "president of the American Psychological Association 1968" should be seen as an acknowledgement of Humanistic Psychology among American psychologists, Misiah & Sexton, 1973, p. 112.

37. See, for instance, Bühler & Allen 1972, Bärmark 1974, Bugental 1964, Globe 1975, Shaffer 1978, Litt 1977.

38. See for instance, appendix A in Maslow 1970a for examples of areas of investigation, Maslow 1970a, pp. 281—293.
39. "These new developments [Humanistic and Transpersonal Psychologies] may very well offer a tangible, usable, effective satisfaction of the'frustrated idealism' of many quietly desperate people, especially young people. These psychologies give promise of developing into the life-philosophy, the religion-surrogate, the value-system, the life-program that these people have been missing". Maslow 1968a p. iv; see also Maslow 1970a, p. 266 and Maslow 1976b, p. 4.
40. See, for example, Rogers 1975: Smedslund 1972; Maslow 1970a, pp. 241—264.
41. One example is Maslow 1966a.
42. Maslow 1968a p. iii. Maslow first named this psychology "Being-psychology", Maslow 1962a. In this article he also states its areas of investigation. In order to get a description concerning the organisation of the edition of "The Journal of Transpersonal Psychology", see Sutich 1976. Sutich was earlier editior of "Journal of Humanistic Psychology" and he was editor of "Journal of Transpersonal Psychology" to his death in 1976. He describes Maslow's influence, as: "Maslow has made a profound theoretical contribution to the new area of scientific psychological contribution ... qualify his as the prime mover not only of Humanistic Psychology but of Transpersonal Psychology as well". Sutich 1969, p. 19.
43. Sutich, 1969, p. 15.
44. Boucouvalas, 1980, p. 37—46.
45. For psychoterapeutic methods in Transpersonal Psychology, see Pelletier & Garfield 1972, p. 222—274.
46. A data search was made on 26/11 1981 in PHILOSOPHERS INDEX, PSYINFO, SOCIAL SCISEARCH and COMP DISERT ABS on A. H. Maslow/PEAK-EXPERIENCE.
47. See also Bärmark 1974.

Chapter 2

1. Madsén makes the distinction between activating and directing factors. Among the former he distinguishes between (a) inner factors, that is, physiological or mental factors, and (b) outer factors, that is, stimuli from CTR. Madsén 1976, pp. 145, 147, 150, 156.
2. We use "practical syllogism" in von Wright's meaning, see von Wright 1971, Nordenfelt 1979, p. 62. For a discussion concerning causal or logical relationships between (1)—(4), see von Wright 1971, pp. 96—131; Nordenfelt 1974, pp. 27—36; Fhanér 1979, pp. 82—86.
3. For means-goal-hierarchies, see Nordenfelt 1974, pp. 82—86.
4. For this complication, see thesis (v) in 2.1.
5. See, for example, von Wright 1971, pp. 83—84; Nordenfelt 1974, p. 22.
6. Maslow's theory of motivation can, at least concerning the so called deficiency-needs (see 2.1. thesis (vi)), be characterized as a "drive-reduction"-theory. According to MacIntyre, in these kinds of theories, needs and gratification of needs, become both causes and goal respectively. MacIntyre 1976, pp. 60—66. See also Peters, 1974, pp. 124—129.
7. This double tencency can also be found in Freud's theory of motivation, see Nilsson 1980 pp. 48—61.

8. Maslow does not make explicit the distinction between drive and source of drive because of his holistic view of man. Maslow states that he tries to avoid distinguishing between different elements in the process of motivation, see Maslow 1970a, pp. 20, 26. However, he often does this in his works, see Maslow 1970a, pp. 80–81, 91; Maslow 1976a pp. 366–368.
9. Maslow 1970a, pp. 21, 61, 90, 91, 107; Maslow 1965, p. 190; Maslow 1976a, p. 368.
10. Maslow 1970a, pp. 27, 81, 88–89, 101.
11. Ibid., pp. 27, 81–82; Maslow 1968a, p. 162. There is, according to Maslow, a difference of strength between different animals' instincts, and this is connected with the phylogenetical development of the species. For instance, rats have rather closed instincts, primates have a possibility for greater varying behavior as a response to the genetic instincts, see also Lowry 1973, p. 92.
12. Maslow 1970a, ch. 6; Maslow 1976a, appendix D; Maslow 1968a, p. 162.
13. Maslow & Mittelmann 1941, p. 602.
14. See Maslow 1970a, p. 20 "... desires that flit through consciousness are most often desires for clothes, automobiles ...". For a survey of theories concerning the psychological character of intentional ideas, see Malmgren 1978, pp. 115–128.
15. See Furberg 1975, p. 91.
16. Maslow 1949, p. 275; see also Maslow 1951a, p. 257.
17. Maslow is conscious of the theoretical model's different epistemological status: "Because psychology as yet does not have an adequate scientific vocabulary for its purposes, it often has to rely upon words that are used by analogy. Very frequently these are mechanical analogies. Therefore we shall have to speak of 'forces', of 'conflict' of 'mechanisms' and the like. This is extremely unfortunate, for there is great danger of reifying these concepts, that is, thinking of them as real palpable things that we can touch, feel and see". Maslow & Mittelman 1941, pp. 20–21.
18. Ibid., pp. 18–19.
19. Maslow and Mittelman distinguish between neuroses and more serious psychopathologies, ibid., p. 607.
20. Reprinted in Maslow 1954 and 1970a.
21. Maslow 1970a, p. 88.
22. Ibid., p. 80, Maslow 1968a, p. 162; Maslow 1968b p. 3; Maslow 1976a, p. 22.
23. Maslow 1976a, p. 22.
24. Maslow 1970a, pp. 80–81, 88–89.
25. Ibid., pp. 62–63, 90–92; Maslow 1968a p. 191; Maslow 1951, p. 260.
26. Maslow 1970a, p. 47, 55, 62. Concerning the term "canalization", see Murphy 1947, pp. 161–191.
27. Maslow 1968a, pp. 45, 48, 57, 150, 198; Maslow 1976a, pp. 13–14. In his later writings, he states some limitations for this principle, Maslow 1970a, p. 278, Concerning criticism of "wisdom of the body", see Madsén 1976, p. 155; Cofer-Appley 1968, p. 366.
28. See, for instance, Maslow 1968a, p. 33; Maslow 1970a, pp. 36–37, 80; Maslow 1951, p. 351. von Wright is critical of the theory of homeostasis. For instance, the theory does not answer the following questions: (a) why does non-equilibrium emerge? (b) why is the organism striving for homeostasis? (c) what is meant by homeostasis? and (d) how can we measure homeostasis? von Wright 1971, pp. 84, 157.
29. Maslow 1968a, p. 151; Maslow 1976a, pp. 5–9.
30. Maslow 1976a, pp. 13–15 1968a, p. 55.
31. Maslow 1976a, p. 163.
32. Maslow 1970a, pp. 22, 80, 314; Maslow 1939, p. 36.

33. Maslow 1970a, pp. 47, 55, 62, 78, 92, 106; Maslow 1968a, p. 175; Maslow 1976a, p. 370.
34. Not only basic needs can be unconscious. Emotions, attitudes, judgments and percep-
    tions can also be unconscious, Maslow 1968a, p. 192; Maslow 1970a, p. 141. Maslow
    also assumes healthy unconscious elements, Maslow 1968a, pp. 182, 196; Maslow
    1976a, pp. 157, 167; Maslow 1976b, p. 42.
35. Maslow 1970a, pp. 21−22.
36. For various meanings of the terms "unconscious" and "The Unconscious" see Broad
    1980, pp. 353−400. Our contextual reasonable interpretation of Maslow's term "un-
    conscious" is similar to one meaning which MacIntyre presents, that is, the term
    "unconscious" can refer to the case when P makes an action without being conscious
    of which goal-object P wants to attain, MacIntyre 1976, pp. 41−45; see also Marc-
    Wogau 1967a, pp. 81−144.
37. Maslow's theory of motivation is influenced by, among others, Freud's theory of
    motivation, partly through direct agreement and partly as reaction against Freud's
    theory. Some parts of Freud's theory willl be described below in order to contrast
    Maslow's theory with Freud's. To describe Freud's theory, in a brief way, is difficult for
    many reasons, for example, Freud revised his theory over and over again. My descrip-
    tion below is primarily from Freud's *Interpretation of Dreams* and *The Unconscious*.
    The following levels can be distinguished in Freud's theory of motivation:
    1. Somatic level: On this level there are the genetic physiological drives. Freud deter-
    minates these differently because of changes in his theory. In his earlier works he names
    these drives sexual drive and the drive of self-preservation, in an intermediate period
    he only assumes the sexual drive, and in his later writings sexual drive and aggressive
    drive.
    2. Psychic level: These physiological drives are transformed to psychic energy, sexual
    drive to libido and aggressive drive to destro.
    3. Psychic level: Unconscious ideas of goal or means which are the drives' represen-
    tations ("Repräsentanz") and these ideas are loaded ("Besetzung") with psychic energy.
    The stronger "Besetzung" an idea of goal has the more the individual strives to gratify
    the idea in question.
    4. Psychic level: Preconscious ideas of goal or means which are representations of
    physiological drives and are loaded with psychic energy. The difference between
    preconscious and unconscious ideas are: the former can, relatively easy, be conscious,
    the latter cannot be conscious or only be conscious through psychoanalytic therapy.
    5. Psychic level: Conscious intentional ideas of goal or means, that is, non-censured
    representations of drives or unconscious or preconscious ideas which through subli-
    mation or in other ways are channelled to non-censured intentional ideas of goal or
    means.

In *Interpretation of Dreams* and *The Unconscious* Freud assumes that the unconscious
ideas are of a psychic nature. Freud also distinguishes between unconscious in the
proper sense and unconscious in the non-proper sense. Unconscious in the proper
sense is only ideas, unconscious in the non-proper sense are emotions or drives,
because the ideas which are their representations are unconscious in the proper sense.

According to Freud, in *Interpretation of Dreams*, the human consciousness can be
described as an "inner sense-organ" which can be directed to the perceptual content,
but it can also be directed to preconscious ideas. "Durch die Qualitäten dieses Systems
wird jetzt das Bewusstsein, das vorher nur Sinnesorgan für die Wahrnehmungen war,
auch zum Sinnesorgan für einen Teil unserer Denkvorgänge. Es gibt Jetzt Gleichsam

zwei Sinnesoberflächen, die einen dem Wahrnehemen, die andre den vorbewussten Denkvorgängen zugevendet." Freud 1925, p. 491. "Welche Rolle vorbleibt in unserer Darstellung dem einst allmächtigen, alles andere verdeckenden Bewusstsein? Keine andere, als die e i n e s S i n n e s o r g a n s z u r W a h r n e h m u n g p s y c h i s - c h e r Q u a l i t ä t e n . " . Ibid., p. 532.

An idea is conscious when this idea is the object of this "inner sense-organ". An unconscious idea cannot be the object for this "inner sense-organ" or only be this through psychoanalytic therapy. MacIntyre asserts that Freud is influenced by Kant's epistemology when Freud compares the unconscious ideas with Kant's "Das Ding-an-sich". MacIntyre 1976, pp. 30—70. Compare the following quotation "Das unbewusste ist das eigentlich reale Psychische, uns nach seiner inneren Natur so unbekannt wie das Reale der Ausserwelt, und uns durch die Daten des Bewusstseins ebenso unvollständig gegeben die Ausserwelt durch die Angaben unseren Sinnesorgane." Freud 1925, p. 529.

38. Maslow 1970a, p. 22.
39. Ibid., p. 23, 55.
40. Ibid., pp. 56, 80, 106.
41. See especially the article "Criteria for Judging Needs to Be Instinctoid", reprinted in Maslow 1976a; see also Maslow 1968a, p. 153. Compare von Wright's determination of "need" in terms of what is bad or injurious for living creatures welfare to do without, von Wright 1982, pp. 1—12.
42. Maslow 1976a, pp. 22, 368.
43. Maslow 1970a, p. 48; Maslow 1968a, pp. 24—27, 32—33; Maslow 1976a, pp. 31, 317.
44. Maslow 1968a, pp. 24—26, 155; Maslow 1970a, p. 68.
45. Maslow 1970a, pp. 35—45.
46. Maslow refers to human beings instinct of flock. He thinks that this need in great degree is ungratified in the Western-world, and the most common cause of neurosis are the frustrations of this/these needs. He thinks that the growing interest in "T-groups and other personal growth-groups" are a form to get gratification of this/these needs. Ibid., 43—44.
47. Maslow distinguishes between really owned esteem and false esteem and emphasizes the danger to build one's self-esteem on the latter. Maslow 1970a, pp. 45—46; Maslow 1965, p. 45.
48. Maslow 1968a, p. 191.
49. See especially the article "A Theory of Meta-motivation: The Biological Rooting of the Value-life", reprinted in Maslow 1976a. Concerning the distinction between moral and non-moral values, see Frankena 1973, pp. 79—83.
50. Maslow 1976a, p. 176; Maslow 1968a, p. 38. Though Maslow often uses the term "Weltanschauung", he never tries to define or precizate this term. We think that Jeffner's stipulative definition of "Weltanschauung"/"Livsåskådning" can be used in order to clarify Maslow's use or the term "Weltanschauung". Jeffner thinks that the following three factors can be distinguished in a Weltanschauung: a. Central value-system, that is, a person P's values and norms, inter alia, P's normative ethics; b. Basic emotional attitude, which can be somewhere between the poles optimistic—pessimistic, and c. Theoretical beliefs, which contain, inter alia, a person P's ontology, view of man and view of history. These theoretical beliefs have to be related to the factors in a. and b. Jeffner, 1974, pp. 12ff.
51. For the distinction between the ideal of specialization and the ideal of versatility, see Furberg 1975, pp. 146—149; Ryding 1979, p. 29; Hansson 1982, pp. 6—7.

52. Maslow 1970a, p. 272; Maslow 1976a, p. 88.
53. Maslow 1970a, pp. 24, 53.
54. Some of the criteria for this dominance-hierarchy are:

    a. the lower needs are the ones which dominate if some needs are not gratified
    b. the higher needs develop later in the individual's ontogenetic development
    c. the higher a need is, the lesser it is needed in order to survive
    d. the higher a need is, the weaker drive it has and the longer it can wait for gratification.

    These criteria are most clearly described in the article "Higher and Lower Needs", reprinted in Maslow 1954, 1970a. For exceptions from this dominance-hierarchy, see Maslow 1970a, pp. 51—53.
55. Ibid., pp. xxv, 46.
56. This thesis is most exhaustively described in the article "Is Destructiveness Instinctoid", reprinted in Maslow 1954, 1970a, see also Maslow 1968a, p. 159. A criticism of the opinion concerning man's morally evil instincts, is given in the article "Our Malined Animal Nature" Maslow 1949. In some contexts Maslow even describes the basic needs as non-moral good, see Maslow 1970a, p. 103.
57. Maslow 1970a, p. 86; Maslow 1968a, pp. 3, 159; Maslow 1962b, p. 7; Maslow 1976a, pp. 167—168.
58. Maslow 1970a, pp. 101, 121; Maslow 1968a, pp. 3, 195.Concerning other causes for morally evil behavior, see Maslow 1970a, p. 117.
59. Maslow 1968a, pp. 162, 196.
60. Maslow 1976b, p. 49.
61. Maslow 1968a, pp. 4, 50, 162, 164, 191, 192, 197; Maslow 1976a, pp. 179, 367; Maslow 1951a, p. 262.
62. Besides the basic needs, Maslow, in some context, also includes "anatomical equipment, physiological or temperamental balances, prenatal and natal injuries and traumata to the neonate" in the "inner-core", Maslow 1968a, p. 190; Maslow 1976a, pp. 126, 304.
63. Maslow 1968a, p. 160f; Maslow 1976a, p. 152.
64. The term "Real Self" Maslow took over from K. Horney. Maslow 1976a, pp. 31, 62, 126, 327; Maslow 1966a, p. 124.
65. Maslow 1968a, pp. 7, 194; Maslow 1976a, p. 326; Maslow 1964, p. 131. Maslow acknowledges, concerning the term "intrinsic conscience", that he is influenced by Horney's and Fromm's criticism of Freud's term "super-ego". In this context Maslow also states the relativeness of the terms "healthy" and "sick" in relation to Freud's "superego". Sometimes a neurosis can be a "healthy" reaction against a "sick" super-ego. Maslow 1968a, pp. 5.
66. Maslow 1976a, pp. 32, 49.
67. Ibid., p. 177.
68. Maslow 1970a, p. 68; see also Maslow 1968a, pp. 35, 193; Maslow 1966a, pp. 41—43; Maslow 1976a, pp. 77, 119. Maslow is in this context critical of Sartre's concept of freedom, see Maslow 1970a, p. 178; Maslow 1968a, pp. 12—13.
69. Maslow 1970a, p. 275.
70. For a clarification of necessary and sufficient causal conditions, see Section 2.3.
71. Maslow is most explicit concerning this problem in Maslow 1976a, p. 10.
72. Wahba & Bridwell 1976.
73. Maslow 1968a, p. 21; Maslow 1970a, p. 35; Maslow 1976a, p. 365.

74. Maslow 1976a, p. 365, see also ibid., pp. 4, 21, 32, 37, 177, 193, 205 and Maslow 1970a, pp. 11, 57, 67, 109.
75. Maslow 1970a, p. 111. Maslow asserts that the main cause of psychopathologies is non-gratification of the basic needs. He mainly rejects genetic predispositions as causes of psychopathologies. Maslow 1976a, p. 30.
76. Accordingly, Maslow does not reject associative learning of personality traits. Other important factors in the development of personality traits are, for example, prefound personal experiences and attempts to copy some personal ideal. Maslow 1970a, p. 63.
77. Maslow 1970a, p. 303, see also Maslow 1939.
78. Maslow 1976a, pp. 22, 43, 315; Maslow 1968a, p. 206.
79. Reprinted in Maslow 1954, 1970a.
80. Maslow 1970a, p. 60; Maslow 1976a, pp. 290, 366.
81. Maslow 1968a, pp. 26, 44—59, 97, 115, 204, 211; Maslow 1976b, p. 97; Maslow 1976a, pp. 44, 49.
82. Maslow 1968a, p. 46.
83. Maslow 1976a, p. 44, see also Maslow 1979, p. 592.
84. The result of this investigation was published in 1951 in the article "Self-actualizing People: A Study of Psychological Health" reprinted in Maslow 1954, 1970a, see also Maslow 1976a, pp. 43—49, 270—286, Maslow 1979, pp. 481—483. Jones has constructed a personality test which tries to measure if a person P is a self-actualizing person, in Maslow's meaning of the term. Jones 1975.
85. Maslow 1976a, pp. 9, 12, 117, 177, 189.
86. Maslow has several articles about creativity, see for instance Maslow 1976a, ch. 4—7; Maslow 1968a, ch. 10; Maslow 1963a, p. 132—135. Maslow distinguishes between two phases in the creative process. The first he calls "primary creativity", that is, the genesis of the creative idea. The second he calls "secondary creativity", that is, the capability to work out the idea and here P needs patience, "know how" and a critical ability. Maslow illustrates his distinction with Tolstoy's idea of "War and Peace" (primary creativity) and his work to write down the book (secondary creativity).
87. Maslow 1976a, p. 113.
88. Ibid., p. 63, 115.
89. Maslow 1976a, pp. 20, 42, 187, 262, 267, 301; Maslow 1965, p. 88; Maslow 1970a, p. 193.
90. Maslow 1976a, pp. 42, 291, 303; Maslow 1965 p.6.
91. Maslow 1956, p. 18.
92. Maslow 1976b, p. 49; see also Maslow 1976a, p. 201; Maslow 1968a, p. 153.
93. Maslow 1968a, p. 167; see also Maslow 1970a, pp. 102, 266, 270; Maslow 1976a, pp. 26, 144, 310.
94. Maslow 1976a, pp. 75—76; Maslow 1968a, p. 5. Passmore distinguishes between the following main types of perfectibility:
    (1) Technical perfection, that is, the development of a special task, for example, to be a perfect tennis player or secretary
    (2) Obediency perfection, that is, to fulfil one's or God's or a member's of the élite given call or commission
    (3) Moral perfection, that is, to fulfil a moral ideal
    (4) Teleological perfection, that is, man should reach his "natural end". Different philosophers state different "natural ends". For example Aristotle state eudaimonia. Passmore states that advocates of this type of perfectibility presuppose that man's potentials are non-morally good

(5) Exemplary perfection, that is, to initiate the example set by a person, for example Jesus or Socrates.
Passmore 1972, pp. 11—27.

95. Maslow 1976a, pp. 75, 167—168, 178; Maslow 1965, p. 194; Maslow 1968b, pp. 1—3; Maslow 1976b, p. xvi. For a comparison between (a) Skinner and Maslow, see Underwood 1975, and (b) Maslow and Marx, see Bay 1980.
96. Maslow 1976a, p. 49; Maslow 1968a, p. 97.
97. Maslow is vague on this point. A contextual reasonable interpretation is that these degrees can only be ranked quantitatively. Maslow 1976a, p. 27; Maslow 1962a, p. 52.
98. Bühler & Allen, 1970, p 45.
99. Maslow distinguishes between two kinds of self-actualizing people (a) the ones who have peak-experiences and (b) the ones who do not have peak-experiences, Maslow 1976a, chapter 22.
100. Maslow 1976a, pp. 31—35, 107, 171, 176, 179, 318; Maslow 1966a, p. 41; Maslow 1968a, p. 165; Maslow 1970a, p. 271
101. Maslow 1976a, p. 162, 172, 177, 182. For a closer presentation of Maslow's term "intrinsic learning", see Morris 1972.
102. Maslow 1970b, p. 29; Maslow 1976b, p. 49.
103. Ryding 1979, p. 31.
104. Maslow 1968a, p. 204.
105. Maslow wrote journals about this research. These journals are published in Lowry 1973, pp. 81—105. In these journals we can read how Maslow struggles to find criteria to judge if a person has his/her deficiency needs gratified, see pp. 81, 88, 90, 95, 98, 102. He writes 6/5 1945: "It would seem that ulimately a full psychoanalysis is the only valid technique for picking. And then, since everyone would show up with some neurotic trends, what degree is necessary for inclusion as GHB (Good Human Being) ... The whole concept has to be defined operationally anyhow. Otherwise I find myself looking for some essence or Platonic idea which may not exist anywhere but in my mind". For a background to Maslow's research, see Maslow 1976a, chapter 3. There he states that he got the idea of self-actualizing people's characteristics by studying his teachers R. Benedict and M. Wertheimer.
Suassy shows, through M. Mead's biography about R. Benedict, that Benedict missed a great number of the characteristics which Maslow attributed to self-actualizing people. Saussy 1977, p. 52. B. Smith discusses some of the theoretical difficulties with Maslow's criteria, see B. Smith 1973.
106. As early as 1951, Maslow was conscious of the metodological short-comings of his research, but he justifies his results by the importance of the research and his theses of the growth of knowledge and degrees of knowledge (see further ch. 6). Maslow 1970a, pp. xxi, 149; Maslow 1965, pp. 54, 74; Maslow 1966a, p. 15; Maslow 1979, p. 113. Maslow 1976a, p. 41, Maslow 1968a, p. 25
107. Maslow 1976a, p. 42; Maslow 1968a, p. 12. See also note 76 above.
108. For a critique of Maslow's view of self-actualizing from a sociological point of view, see Geller 1982; Franck 1966; Antsyferova 1973; Buss 1979.
109. Our account is influenced by Franck in distinguishing between Maslow's three uses of the term "self-actualization", see Franck 1977.
110. Maslow 1959b, p. 242.
111. Maslow 1968a, p. 155; see also Maslow 1970a, p. 78.
112. Maslow 1970a, p. 270; Maslow 1968a, pp. 24—25.
113. Moritz 1967, pp. 103—115.

114. Compare Nielsen 1962, Franck 1977.
115. Maslow1976a, p. 128—129, Maslow 1968a, pp. 83—84.
116. Maslow does not state explicitly that he knows the distinction between normative ethics and meta-ethics. The classification is our reasonable interpretation of Maslow's opinion.
117. Horney distinguishes, in accordance with W. James, between
    (a) the material self, a person's psyiological body *and* his/her possessions
    (b) "the actual self is an all inclusive term for everything that a person is at a given time: body and soul, healthy and neurotic. We have it in mind when we say that we want to know ourselves; i.e., we want to know ourselves as we are".
    (c) "the idealized self is what we are in our irrational imagination or what we should be according to the dictates of neurotic pride"
    (d) the real self, a self which "engenders the spontaneity of feelings . . . is the source of spontaneous interest and energies . . . the capacity to wish and will . . . is the part of ourselves that wants to expand and grow and to fulfill itself . . . All this indicates that our real self, when strong and active, enables us to make decisions and assume responsibility . . . Horney 1951, pp. 156—158.
118. This is one of J.S. Mill's classical argument in favour of utilitarianism.
119. The variables in the argument A_3 are: Sx = P's deficiency-needs are gratified, Tx = P's actions are directed towards gratifying P's self-actualizing needs, Px = P actualizes some characteristics X, Y, Z . . . , Qx = P has B-cognition, and Rx = P has knowledge of Y.
120. von Wright 1972, p. 37.
121. See, for instance, Copi 1978, pp. 277—279.

Chapter 3

1. Other attempts, but less ambitious, to describe the contents in peak-experience can be found in; Dennis & Povers 1974, Rosenblott & Bartlett 1976; Klavetter & Mogen 1967; Blanchard 1969a, Day 1975 and Grof 1976.
2. Maslow 1954, p. 164. Wilson asserts that Freud took over this term from W. Whitman; Wilson 1972, p. 203.
3. Maslow does not clarify what he means by religious terms. A contextual reasonable interpretation is that he primarily uses religious terms in connection with the assumption of a transcendent entity separated from the material world, mostly expressed in a theistic context, see Maslow 1976b, p. 106.
4. Maslow 1970a, p. 164.
5. The eximanees had to answer the following questions: "I would like you to think of the most wonderful experience or experiences of your life; happiest moments, ecstatic moments, moments of rapture, perhaps from being in love, or from listening to music or suddenly 'being hit' by a book or a painting, or from some great creative moment. First list these. And then try to tell me how you feel in such acute moments, how you feel differently from the way you feel at other times, how you are at the moment a different person in some ways. (With other subjects the question asked was about the ways in which the world looked different.) Maslow 1968a, p. 71; see also Maslow 1976a, p. 168.

184

6. These where sent to Maslow after the first publishing 1959; Maslow 1959a.
7. The quotation is from Lowry 1973, p. 14. See also Maslow 1979, p. 434, Knipper 1972, p. 112.
8. "In a word, to perceive an object abstractly means not to perceive some aspects of it. It clearly implies selection of some attributes, rejection of other attributes, creation or distortion of still others. We make of it what we wish. We create it. We manufacture it. Furthermore, extremely important is the strong tendency in abstracting to relate the aspects of the objects to our linguistic system. This makes special troubles because language is a secondary rather than a primary process in Freud's sense, because it deals with external reality rather than psychic reality, with the conscious rather than the unconscious. It is true that this lack can be corrected to some extent by poetic or rhapsodic language but in the last analysis much of experience is ineffable and can be put into no language at all." Maslow 1968a, p. 90.
9. Maslow 1962b, p. 13; Maslow 1968a, p. 105.
10. Maslow 1976b, p. 84—90.
11. Ibid., p. 89.
12. Ibid., p. 90. Compare also Maslow 1966a, pp. 45—46, 59, Maslow 1979, p. 799.
13. This does not only concern communication about peak-experience, but communication on the whole. See, Maslow 1966a, p. 45.
14. Maslow also makes this distinction, Maslow 1976a, p. 184; Maslow 1966b, p. 110.
15. Alston 1964, p. 22.
16. See Alston 1964, p. 23—25, Harrison 1979, pp. 26—37.
   Wittgenstein criticizes in *Philosophical Investigations* mentalistic theories of meaning of the type which ideational theory of meaning belongs to. Some of Wittgensteins critisism, exclusively the above mentioned can be found in §§ 316—362. Wittgenstein 1972, pp. 104—114.
17. "Det språkteoretiska postulatet innebär . . . blott att det är möjligt för både troende och icke troende religionsfilosofer att förstå de kristna utsagornas funktion och betydelse." Hedenius 1971, p. 20.
18. Stegmüller 1969, p. 266.
19. Wittgenstein discusses the problem of private language in §§ 243—315, see especially §§ 258—271. Maslow is certain that the contents in peak-experience cannot be defined intersubjectively and ostensively. "The problem here [the problem of cummunication] was not the usual one in teaching. It was not a labelling of something public that both could simultaneously see while the teacher pointed to it and named it. Rather it was trying to ge the person to focus attention, to notice, to name an experience inside himself, which only he could feel, an experience, furthermore, which was not happening at the time. No pointing is possible here, no naming of something visible, no controlled and purposeful creation of the experience like turning on an electric current at will or probing at a painful spot." Maslow 1976b, p. 85.
20. There is some research about mystical experience and physiological data, see, for instance, Anand et al, 1961, Kasamatsu & Tomio, 1966. Our opinion is that the content of consiousness in peak-experience have a much greater extension than mystical experience and are therefore much more difficult to correlate with some physiological data.
21. Maslow 1976a, p. 101.
22. "God the Father, as all-powerful, as the one who created the world and who rules the world of things . . . changes it and masters it and conquers it". Maslow 1976b, p. 106.

23. "This nonhuman reality is independent of the wishes and needs of human beings, being neither beneficent nor malevolent, having no purposes, aims, goals, or functions (only living beings have purposes), no conative and no affective tendencies. This reality that would persist if all human beings disappeared — a not impossible happening." Maslow 1970a, p. 7. See also Maslow 1966a.p.74f, Maslow 1968a, p. 201.

24. Maslow 1966a, p. 69, se also pp. 45—46, 78—79, 135..

25. Concerning the distinction between ontological and intentional object we are influenced by C.D. Broad's discussion in Broad 1980. However, Broad uses the term "epistemological object" instead of "intentional object".

26. Proximal stimuli are distinguished from distralt stimuli. "Distralt stimuli" designates the ontological object. This distinction is established in cognitive psychology, see Koffka 1935, p. 80; Neisser 1967, p. 3; Eriksson 1974, p. 16.

27. For the term representative realism, see Hospers 1970, pp. 496—505.

28. Phalén 1977, p. 14.

29. Maslow 1968a, p. 104, Maslow 1976a, pp. 63, 70.

30. Sartre 1976, p. xxix

31. Concerning an information-working-model in cognitive psychology, see Neisser 1976, ch.1.

32. Hirst uses the term "perceptual consciousnes" as synonym for our term "percept". Hirst 1967, p. 80.

33. See, for instance, Maslow 1968a, p. 202.

34. Dember 1969, p. 290; Eriksson 1974, p. 163.

35. Marc-Wogau 1945, pp. 151—166. In accordance with Marc-Wogau we use the relative interpretation of the terms determinable-determinat. This interpretation is different from the terms' introducer Johnson's determination of the terms, see Johnson 1921, pp. 171—185.

36. See Marc-Wogau 1945, p. 157.

37. Maslow 1970a, p. 205.

38. Maslow's examples are cancer, virus and mosquits, Maslow 1968a, p. 76.

39. Maslow 1966a, p. 114.

40. Maslow 1968a, p. 85. The so called field-theory in Gestaltpsychology, see for instance, Köhler 1975; ch. v, vi; Koffka 1935, p. 184; Eriksson 1974, p. 18.

41. Maslow 1970a, pp. 209ff, 226. It is the *concepts*, not the grammatical structures. These categories, constructs, etc., are not only learnt by language, but also by processes of abstractness. Maslow 1966a, p. 46. Maslow's view concerning the genesis of these categories can therefore be classified as a "mixed theory", see Bråkenhielm 1975, p. 130.

42. Maslow 1968a, p. 89.

43. Maslow1970a, p. 205.

44. Ibid., p. 203; see also Maslow 1968a, p. 75.

45. This problem also concern *how* and *why* the subject distinguishes between different intentional objects in the visual field. Some different answers are (a) by ealier learning (b) by properties of the ontological object, for example sharp contours, a common colour or similarity in the structure of the object's surface (c) by the laws of the Gestalt, see Katz, 1942, pp. 38—39.

46. Concerning this theory see Neisser 1967, pp. 43—47; Eriksson 1974, pp. 159—163

47. Maslow 1970a, p. 208.

48. Neisser 1967, p. 47. Maslow had a personal relationship with Neisser, see Maslow 1968a, p. x. "…. words and concepts are absolutely necessary for organizing and

ordering the welter of experiences and the ultra-experiential world of which they apprise us". Maslow 1966a, p. 46.

49. For a survey of different opinions in the history of philosophy, see Stegmüller 1969, pp. 68—70.
50. Maslow 1968a, pp. 89—91. A central article on this topic is" Cognition of the Individual and of the Genetic" reprinted in Maslow 1954, 1970a, see also Maslow 1962a. Rubrizing also takes place in other cognitive functions, for instance, memory, problem-solving and learning.
51. Maslow 1968a, pp. 74—96; Maslow 1970a, pp. 163—164, 205.
52. Maslow 1966a, p. 62; Maslow 1976a, p. 72; Maslow 1962a, pp. 49, 62, 67.
53. Maslow 1968a, p. 74.
54. Maslow 1976b, p. 60; Maslow 1966a, p. 81; Maslow 1976a, p. 67; Maslow 1968a, p. 89.
55. Maslow 1968a, pp. 89; Maslow 1962a, pp. 49, 51.
56. Maslow 1976b, p. 78; Maslow 1976a, p. 254.
57. Maslow 1976b, p. 61, Maslow names this from projection liberated process of cognition "object-centered" in constast to "ego-centered".
58. Maslow 1966a, pp. 53, 64; Maslow 1976a, p. 254; Maslow 1968a, pp. 87, 109.
59. Maslow 1968a, pp. 86f, 94.
60. Maslow 1968a, pp. 90, 94; Maslow 1966a, p. 75; Maslow 1970a, p. 203.
61. "Nous appelons ici intuition la sympathie par laquelle on se transporte à l'interieur d'un objet pour coincider avec ce qu'il a d'unique et par conséquent d'inexprimable" Bergson 1946, pp. 174—175. One author who has noticed Bergson's influence on Maslow is Steffen, see Steffen 1973.
62. Bergson 1946 and Bergson 1944, ch. 2—3
63. Bergson 1946, pp. 170—175.
64. Maslow 1976a, p. 102.
65. Maslow 1976a, p. 242.
66. Ibid., 241, see also pp. 118, 183; Maslow 1968a, pp. 75, 88; Maslow 1962a, p. 50—52, Maslow 1976b, p. 78. One illustrative example of suchness is Maslow's friend A. Huxley's description of his experience of van Gogh's "The Chair", see Huxley 1978, p. 24.
67. Maslow 1966a, p. 81, see also Maslow 1976a, pp. 125, 137, 273, Maslow 1976b, p. 78; "Self-actualizing people have been found more capable than the average population of a particular kind of cognition which I have called Being-cognition. This has been described in Chapter 6 as cognition of the essence, or 'is-ness', or intrinsic structure and dynamics, and presently existing potentialities of something or someone or everything." Maslow 1968a, p. 116.
68. Maslow 1976a, p. 241.
69. Maslow 1976a, p. 124, 200, 267; Maslow 1968a, p. 75.
70. A clarifying analysis of different theories about the self can be found in Evans 1970. He shows that substantial theories (for example, Kant's theory) and "cluster"-theories (for example Hume's theory) have wrongly analysed the self as an object, in terms of an unmanifested substance or as different conjunction of different qualities of experiences, see especially, p. 29.
71. Maslow 1976a, pp. 244, 259, 60; Maslow 1968a, p. 79.
72. Maslow 1976a, pp. 111, 273; Maslow 1976b, pp. 32, 68, 79, 103f, 116. Stevens hints at this type of peak-experience in his comparision between Maslow and Teilhard de Chardin. Stevens 1972, see also Day 1975.
73. Krippner 1972, p. 113—117.

74. Maslow 1976b, pp. 103, 116; Maslow 1976a, p. 48, 112.
75. Maslow 1976a, p. 247−248.
76. Maslow 1976a, pp. 259−260.
77. Maslow 1976a, p. 111; Maslow 1968a, p. 78.
78. Compare Anderson-Furberg 1974, p. 49f and Jeffner's term "changing Gestalt", Jeffner 1972, pp. 45ff.
79. Wittgenstein 1972, p. 193.
80. Maslow 1976a, p. 248, see also Maslow 1966a, p. 84f, 98, Maslow 1976b, p. 80f.
81. Hospers interprets Locke's secondary properties as: "According to Locke, secondary quality is not really a quality of the object at all; the object only contains within itself a power to produce in perceivers certain sense-experience ("ideas" in Locke's sense). The object itself has no color; it has, somewhere in its "insensible parts"−that is, the arrangement of molecules within it−only the power to produce in perceivers a certain kind of sense−experience". Horspers 1970, p. 497. See also Marc-Wogau 1935.
82. In spite of the fact that Maslow uses Bucke's term Cosmic consciousness we cannot find that Bucke's description of Cosmic Consciousness is similar to Maslow's description of Cosmic consciousness. See Bucke 1923.
83. Maslow 1976a, p. 124.
84. Ibid., p. 266, see also pp. 124, 126, 242, 249, 278, 263; Maslow 1976b, pp. 55, 59, 78; Maslow 1968a, p. 88; Maslow 1970a, p. xi.
85. The term "Pan-en-hen-ism" is taken over from Happold 1977, p. 43, see also Zaehner 1978, p. 28.
86. Concerning a discussion of the theory of relation *versus* a Gestalt-psychological theory, see Katz, 1942, pp. 56−58, 104−105.
87. Maslow 1976a, pp. 247−248.
88. Grof 1976, pp. 105−107.
89. Maslow and Grof met on several occasions. In some cases Grof visited Maslow's home, see Maslow 1979, pp. 882, 884, 887, 1093, 1104, 1196, 1298.
90. Maslow 1976a, p. 308; Maslow 1968a, p. 83.
91. Maslow 1976a, p. 313, see also Maslow 1963, p. 121; Maslow 1968a, p. 84, Maslow 1979, p. 110.
92. Maslow 1976a, p. 104.
93. Chiang & Maslow 1969, p. 50.
94. Maslow 1976b, p. 94, Compare Maslow 1976a, p. 105.
95. Marc-Wogau distinguishes between (a) the experienced space, that is, the space experienced by our five senses (b) the perceptual space, that is, the space experienced by our eyes (c) the physical space, Marc-Wogau 1980, p. 213.
96. Maslow 1968a, p. 80: Maslow 1976a, p. 60, 266; Maslow 1976b, p. 63.
97. Maslow 1968a, p. 214; Maslow 1976b, p. 63. The phenomenal time is distinguished from the physical time, see Goodman 1977, p. 258.
98. Maslow 1976a, p. 266.
99. Maslow 1968a, p. 73; Maslow 1976a, p. 169.
100. Maslow 1976a, p. 46; Maslow 1962b, p. 13.
101. The described characteristics are primarily described in the article "Peak-experience as Acute Identity-Experience" reprinted in Maslow 1968a.
102. Maslow 1968a, p. 114.
103. Maslow 1976b, p. 66f.
104. Maslow 1968a, p. 81, 87, 112−113; Maslow 1976a, p. 323; Maslow 1976b, p. 94.
105. Maslow 1968a, p. 84, see also Maslow 1962a, p. 56; Maslow 1976a, pp. 122, 131.

106. Maslow 1976a, p. 265, 271.
107. Krippner 1972.
108. Ibid., p. 117.
109. Maslow 1962b, p. 13.
110. Krippner 1972, p. 115.
111. Maslow 1962b, p. 16.
112. Ibid., 1962b, p. 18.
113. Maslow 1964b, p. xii, see also Maslow 1968a, p. 88; Maslow 1976a, p. 271.
114. Maslow 1968a, p. 102.

Chapter 4

1. Moore, 1929, p. 41.
2. Maslow 1968a, p. 77.
3. Maslow 1966a, p. 101, see also pp. 32, 48, 79, 100, 137.
4. Marc-Wogau 1967b, p. 137f..
5. We presuppose in our example objects which are relatively unchangeable and in this case that the car is one-coloured.
6. Moore, 1953, pp. 2ff; see also Moore 1902, Characteristics 1, 2 and 3 are necessary logical criteria see p. 9. Compare also Broad's description of the common-sense view, Broad, 1980, pp. 146ff. For a discussion of Broad's description, see Marc-Wogau 1967b, p. 189ff.
7. Maslow 1970a, pp. 7−8.
8. Maslow 1966a, p. 115.
9. For the term "representative realism". See, for instance, Hospers, 1967, pp. 496ff.
10. Maslow 1966a, pp. 76−77.
11. Goodman 1977, pp. 93ff.
12. Kaila uses φ-to designate intentional language i.e. "this looks red," "this feels hard," "this tastes sweet", f- to designate extentional language, i.e. "wood are combustible", "this body is a piece of chalk". Kaila, 1967; pp. 216−221.
13. Wedberg, 1970, p. 136.
14. See, for instance, Ayer, 1977, p. 52; Armstrong 1974, p. 137.
15. Maslow 1966a, pp. 45−46.
16. Maslow 1968a, p. 95, see also pp. 32, 48, 128; Maslow 1966a, pp. 46−48, 128.
17. Maslow 1968a, p. 79.
18. Russell, B. 1979, p. 760. Goudge, in the article "Bergson" in Encyclopedia of Philosophy 1967, interprets Bergson's term "matter" in terms of intentional objects. In this case Bergson becomes an ontological idealist.
19. Phalén, A. 1977, p. 84.
20. Phalén, 1977, p. 67. Compare quotation in Maslow, 1970a, p. 235.
21. Maslow 1966a, pp. 84, 98, 100, Maslow 1976a, pp. 67, 118.
22. For this classification, see Goodman, 1977, p. 96. For advocates of an optimal theory, see Ayer, 1973, pp. 77, and Hospers, 1970, p. 511.
23. Goodman 1977, p. 96.
24. Ibid., p. 96.
25. Maslow 1966a, p. 70, see also pp. 47, 74.

26. Maslow 1976a, p. 247.
27. Maslow 1979, p. 1221.
28. Kaila 1967, p. 33.
29. Bergson 1946, p. 206.
30. Ibid., p. 180.
31. Maslow 1976b, p. 77.
32. Bråkenhielm 1975, pp. 60—61.
33. Maslow 1968a, p. 71.
34. Maslow 1976b, p. 75; Maslow 1968a, p. 79, 210.
35. Maslow 1976a, p. 59, 75.
36. Maslow 1968a, p. 208; Maslow 1976a, p. 17.
37. Maslow 1979, p. 485. Compare "The most efficient way to perceive the intrinsic nature of the world is to be more receptive than active, determined as much as possible by the intrinsic organization of that which is perceived and as little as possible by the nature of the perceiver." Maslow 1968a, p. 41.
38. Lewis 1929, p. 39ff.
39. Ibid., p. 40.
40. Ibid., p. 42.
41. Ornstein 1975, see especially pp. 148—157.
42. Bergson 1946, p. 181 "des concepts raides et tout faits", p. 208" concepts figés, distincts, immobiles".
43. Maslow 1966a, p. 46.
44. Maslow 1976a, p. 102.
45. Maslow 1966a, p. 47, see also p. 70.
46. Maslow 1968a, p. 100.
47. Maslow 1966a, p. 48, see also Maslow 1968a, p. 99.
48. Maslow 1968a, p. 41, 97, 116.
49. Ayer 1973, pp. 4—7.
50. Maslow 1962b, p. 13, see also Maslow 1968a, p. 87.
51. Armstrong 1974, p. 152—161, see also Moore 1978, pp. 122—123.
52. Compare note 39 above.

Chapter 5

1. Maslow 1976b, p. viii; Maslow 1976a, p. 174. Maslow makes this distinction in the second edition of *Religions, Values and Peak experiences* but he does not apply this distinction in the rest of the book. This explains why Religion in the quotations in this chapter are spelled with small r. See also Maslow 1979, p. 405.
2. Maslow 1976b, 19—20, see also p. 59; Maslow 1976a, pp. 282, 328 "Peak-experiences can be considered to be *truly* religious experiences in the best and most profound, most universal and most humanistic sense of that word." Maslow 1962b, p. 10.
3. Maslow 1976b, pp. 26—27.
4. Maslow 1979, p. 844; Maslow 1970a, p. xii. Compare also section 1.1.
5. James 1979.
6. Maslow 1976b, p. 33; Hardeman, 1979, p. 24.
7. Maslow 1976b, p. 21.
8. Ibid., pp. 24, 29.

9. Ibid., pp. vii, 21, 29, 35.
10. See preface, Maslow 1964b; Maslow refers to James' book and to Larski 1961, see also Maslow 1979, vol I, p. 138. Larski applies James' over-belief-theory, see Larski 1961, pp. 14, 20, 295, 339. Maslow is also influenced by his personal contacts with Aldous Huxley and Erich Froom, see, for instance, Huxley 1978, Huxley 1946 and Fromm 1972.
11. James 1979, pp. 416, 428.
12. "It [critical Science of Religions] could never get away from concrete life, or work in a conceptual vacuum. It would forever have to confess, as every science confesses, that the subtlety of nature flies beyond it, and that its formulas are but approximations. Philosophy lives in words, but truth and fact well up into our lives in ways that exceed verbal formulation. There is in the living act of perception always something that glimmers and twinkles and will not be caught, and for which reflection comes too late. No one knows this as well as the philosopher. He must fire his volley of new vocables out of his conceptual shotgun, for his profession comdemns him to this industry, but he secretly knows the hollowness and irrelevancy. His formulas are like stereoscopic or kinetoscopic photographs seen outside the instrument; they lack the depth, the motion, the vitality. In the religious sphere, in particular, belief that formulas are true can never wholly take the place of personal experience." Ibid., pp. 437—438.
13. Ibid., pp. 416, 436.
14. Ibid., p. 436.
15. Ibid., 416.
16. Ibid., p. 414.
17. Ibid., p. 481.
18. Ibid., p. 481.
19. Ibid., p. 472.
20. Ibid., p. 484.
21. Ibid., Ibid., pp. 486—487, 462.
22. Ibid., p. 487.
23. Ibid., p. 491.
24. For a description of James' theory of consciousness, see Scheffler 1974.
25. Maslow 1976b, pp. 72—73.
26. Maslow 1962b, p. 12, Compare Maslow 1976b, p. 29.
27. Maslow 1976b, p. 19.
28. Maslow 1962b, p. 9.
29. Maslow 1976b, p. 44.
30. See for instance Katz 1978, p. 54.
31. Barbosa da Silva, 1982, p. 72.
32. Ibid., p. 72.
33. Maslow 1979, vol I p. 322.
34. See Maslow 1976b, p. 20, 28, 47, 55.
35. Maslow 1979, vol. I p. 6, compare p. 35.
36. Ibid., p. 146; see also Maslow 1976a, p. 282.
37. Maslow 1976b, p. 47, Compare also p. 28.
38. Ibid., pp. 36—37, Compare also p. 4.
39. Ibid., p. 5, Compare p. 45; Maslow 1964b, p. xiii.
40. Maslow 1979, p. 1266, Compare ibid., pp. 29, 136, 158, 890, 1035; Maslow 1976a, p. 247—248.
41. Stace, 1972, pp. 85—127

42. Maslow1976b, pp. 14, 20, 33; Maslow 1964b, p. xii; Maslow 1968b, p.8.
43. Maslow 1962b, p. 11.
44. Maslow 1976b, pp. xi, 28.
45. Ibid., pp. 12—14.
46. Ibid., pp. 21—24. Maslow's hypothesis that adherence to conventional religious beliefs is a hindrance gets some empirical support by a research done by Breed and Fagan, see Breed & Fagen 1972, see also Breslauer 1976.
47. Maslow 1976b, pp. vii, 24.
48. Ibid., pp. 15, 66, 100; Maslow 1976a, p. 108.
49. Maslow 1979, p. 159.
50. Compare note 36 above, see also Maslow 1979 p. 116, 241.

Chapter 6

1. Maslow 1966a, pp. 7—8.
2. Ibid., p. 14; Maslow 1970a, p. 12, Compare also Maslow 1966a, pp. 56, 60.
3. Ibid., p. 5. He is critical of the irrationalism he finds in some of the criticism of orthodox scisnce, ibid., p. xvi.
4. Bärmark 1976, p. 56.
5. Maslow 1970a, p. 1, 6.
6. Maslow 1970a, pp. 5—6
7. Bergström 1972, p. 15; Hermerén 1972, p. 12. Compare Maslow 1970, ch. 1.
8. Bergström 1972, pp. 31—32; Hermerén 1972, p. 12.
9. Bergström 1972, p. 15; Hermerén 1972, p. 12.
10. Maslow 1956, p. 20—23.
11. Maslow values Polanyi's work in Philosphy of Science very highly. "This profound work [Polanyi's *Personal Knowledge*] which is certainly required reading for our generation, does much of what I had planned to do, and solves many of the problems which had concerned me". Maslow 1966a, p. xvii; Maslow 1970a, p. 10.
12. Ibid., pp. 1—6, 57; Maslow 1970a, p. 296.
13. Maslow 1970a, p. 295; Maslow 1966a, p. 11.
14. Maslow 1966a, pp. 11—12.
15. Ibid., ch. 2; Maslow 1956, pp. 30—32.
16. Maslow 1966a, ch. 2.
17. Ibid., pp. 40—44.
18. Ibid., pp. 8—10, 40.
19. Ibid., p. 13; Maslow 1970a, pp. 11—18.
20. Maslow 1976b, p. 54—55.
21. Maslow 1966a, pp. 47, 74, 80; Maslow 1966b, p. 107.
22. Maslow 1966a, pp. 128—129, see also, pp. 47, 131, 133, 135.
23. Maslow 1956, p. 22.
24. Maslow 1970a, pp. 15—18.
25. Maslow 1966a, ch. 3,4, Maslow 1976b, ch. 2.
26. Maslow 1966a, pp. 73, 76; Maslow 1965, p. 197; Maslow 1956, pp. 30—32; Maslow 1968a, p. 15.
27. Maslow 1970a, pp. 8—10.
28. Ibid., pp. 11—18, Maslow 1966a, p. 57, 108; Maslow 1956, p. 24.

29. Maslow 1970a, pp. 11—18; Maslow 1966a, pp. 56—58.
30. Maslow 1966a, pp. 119—127; Maslow 1976a, p. 20.
31. Føllesdal & Walløe 1977, pp. 202—209.
32. Maslow 1976a, p. 20; Maslow 1976b, pp. 12, 16.
33. Maslow 1966a, p. xiv; Maslow 1976b, pp. 5—10; Maslow1970a, p. 10.
34. Maslow 1970a, pp. 20—21, 27—28.
35. Ibid., p. 33.
36. Maslow 1966a, pp. 102—103; Maslow 1976a, p. 14.
37. Maslow 1966a, pp. 95, 109.
38. Kluckhorn & Murray & Sneider 1959, p. 53.
39. The taoistic method is described in Maslow 1966a, ch. 10 and 11 note, also p. 52.
40. Ibid., p. 103, see also pp. 112—114, 50, 52.
41. Ibid., pp. 48—50.
42. Maslow 1976a, p. 17.
43. Maslow 1966a, p. 129, see also ibid., ch. 10 and Maslow 1976a, pp. 15—18, 104.
44. Maslow 1966a, p. 133 and see the whole of ch. 13.
45. Ibid., p. 68, see also ibid. pp. 78—79; Maslow 1956, p. 24; Maslow 1966a, p. 319; Maslow 1965, p. 197.
46. Maslow 1966a, pp. 72, 78.
47. Ibid., pp. 70—81, note p. 74 especially.
48. Ibid., pp. 69—70.
49. Ibid., p. 78.
50. Ibid., p. 76.
51. Ibid., pp. 73—80, 58, 145.
52. See, for instance, Barbour 1974, pp. 34—38.
53. Hempel 1966, pp. 77—82.
54. Bergström 1972, pp. 83—84.
55. Plato, Theaetetus 1952 (209e—210b), pp. 547—550.
56. The account is to some extent influenced by D.M. Amrstrongs's and G. O'Hare's discussions on this problem, see Armstrong 1974, pp. 151—161.
57. Naess 1968, pp. 1—35. Naess has strong symphaties for Pyrrhonism as depicted by Sextus Empiricus.
58. James 1956. Compare also Diamond; 1974, pp. 135—143.
59. Wittgenstein 1972, § 50.
60. Armstrong 1974, pp. 162—197, Moore 1978, p. 122—126.
61. Moore 1978, pp. 122—126.
62. Føllesdal & Walløe 1977, pp. 44—55.
63. Quine 1951, pp. 20—43.
64. Kierkegaard 1974, pp. 167—168.
65. Furberg precizates to some extent how our actions are "belief-impregnated"; Furberg 1975, pp. 89—101.
66. Neurath 1932, p. 201. The interpretation of this quotation is not an intentional interpretation of Neurath.

Literature

Alston, William P, 1964, *Philosophy of Language.* Englewood Cliffs, New Jersey. Prentice-Hall.

Anand, B.K. & Chhina, G.S., & Singh, B., 1961, "Some Aspects of Electroencephalographic Studies in Yogies". In: Tart, C. (ed), *Altered States of Consciousness,* 1969, pp. 503—506. New York—London—Sydney—Toronto. John Wiley & Sons.

Anderson, Jan & Furberg, Mats, 1974, *Språk och påverkan.* Stockholm. Aldus/Bonniers.

Antsyferova, L.I., 1973, "The Psychology of the Self-actualizing Personality in the Work of Abraham Maslow". In: *Soviet Psychology,* 1974, Spring, pp. 21—39.

Armstrong, D.M., 1974, *Belief, Truth and Knowledge.* London—New York. Cambridge University Press.

Aspelin, Gunnar, 1955, "On the Interpretation of Philosophical Texts". In: Regnéll, Hans (ed.), *Readings in Analytical Philosophy.* Stockholm—Gothenburg—Lund. Läromedelsförlagen 1971, pp. 154—165.

Ayer, Alfred J., 1973, *The Central Questions of Philosophy.* London. Weidenfeld and Nicolson.

— 1978, *The Problem of Knowledge.* Middlesex-New York. Peguin Books.

Barbour, Ian G., 1974, *Myths, Models and Paradigms.* The Nature of Scientific and Religious Language. London. SCM Press LTD.

Barbosa da Silva, Antònio, 1982, *The Phenomenology of Religion as a Philosophical Problem.* An analysis of the Theoretical Background of the Phenomenology of Religion, in General, and of M. Eliade's Phenomenological Approach, in Particular. Uppsala. CWK Gleerup.

Bay, Christian, 1980, "Human needs, wants, and politics: Abraham Maslow, meet Karl Marx". In: *Social Praxis,* 1980 Vol. 7, pp. 233—252.

Bergson, Henri; 1944, *Creative Evolution.* New York. Modern Library.

— 1946, "Introduction de la metaphysique". In: Bergson, H., *La Pensée et la Mouvant.* Genève. Editions Albert Skira.

Bergström, Lars, 1972, *Objektivitet.* En undersökning av innebörden, möjligheten och önskvärdheten av objektivitet i samhällsvetenskapen. Stockholm. Prisma.

Blanchard, William H., 1969, "Psychodynamic Aspects of the Peak-experience". In: *Psychoanalytical Review,* 1969 No. 56, pp. 87—112.

Boucouvalas, Maricie, 1980, "Transpersonal Psychology: A Working Outline of The Field". In: *The Journal of Transpersonal Psychology,* 1980, Vol. 12, No. 1, pp. 37—46.

Breed, G. & Fagan J., 1972, "Religious dogmatism and peak-experiences: A test of Maslow's hypothesis." In: *Psychological Reports.* 1972, Vol. 31, p. 866.

Breslauer, Daniel S., 1976, "Abraham Maslow's Category of Peak-experience and the Theological Critique of Religion". In: *Review of Religious Research,* 1976, Vol. 18, No. 1, pp. 53—61.

Broad, C.D., 1980, *The Mind and its Place in Nature.* London-Henley. Routledge & Kegan Paul.

Bråkenhielm, Carl-Reinhold, 1975, *How Philosophy Sharpes Theories of Religion.* An Analysis of Contemporary Philosophies of Religion with Special Regard to the Thought of John Wilson, John Hick and D.Z. Phillips. Lund. CWK Gleerup.

Bucke, R.M., 1923, *Cosmic Consciousness.* New York. E.P. Dutton & Co., Inc.

Bugental, 1964, "Basic Postulates and Orientation of Humanistic Psychology". In: *The Journal of Humanistic Psychology,* 1964, Vol. IV, No. 1, pp. 22—25.

Bühler, Charlotte & Allan, Melanie, 1972, *Introduction to Humanistic Psychology.* Monterey, California. Brooks/Cole Publishing Company.

Buss, Allan R., 1979, "Humanistic Psychology as Liberal Ideology: The Socio-historical Roots of Maslow's Theory of Self-actualization". In: *Journal of Humanistic Psychology,* 1979, Vol. 19, No. 3, pp. 43—55.

Bärmark, Jan, 1974, *Paradigm i Humanistisk psykologi.* Göteborg. Avdelningen för vetenskapsteori.

— 1976, *Världsbild och vetenskapsideal.* Några ledande temata hos Abraham Maslow. Göteborg. Avdelningen för vetenskapsteori.

Cofer, C.N. & Appley, M.H., 1968, *Motivation: Theory and Research.* New York — London — Sydney. John Wiley & Sons, Inc.

Copi, Irving M., 1978, *Introduction to Logic.* New York. MacMillan Publishing Co., Inc.

Day, John, 1975, *Platonic essences utilized as model for Maslow's peak-experiences.* Diss. United States International University. Ann Arbor. University Microfilms International.

Dember, I., 1969, *The Psychology of Perception.* New York. Holt, Rinehart and Winston.

Dennis, L.I. & Powers, F.J., 1974, "Dewey, Maslow, and Consummatory Experience." In: *Journal of Aesthetical Education, 1974,* No. 8, pp. 51—63.

Diamond, M.L., 1974, *Contemporary Philosophy and Religions Thoughts.* New York. McGraw-Hill.

Elmo, F., 1974, *The Concept of Self-actualization in the Theology of Paul Tillich and the Psychology of Abraham Maslow.* Diss. Fordhan University. Ann Arbor. University Microfilms International.

Eriksson, Sture, 1974, *Perception.* Stockholm. AWE/Gebers.

Evans, C.O., 1970, *The Subject of Consciousness.* London. George Allen & Unwin.

Fhanér, Stig, 1979, *Psykologi som förklaring, förståelse och kritik.* Om psykologins vetenskapsteori. Stockholm. Bonniers.

Franck, Isaac, 1966, *The Concept of Human Nature.* A Philosophical Analysis of the Concept of Human Nature in the Writings of G.W. Allport, S.E. Asch, Erich Froom, A.H. Maslow and C.R. Rogers. Diss. University of Maryland. Ann Arbor. University Microfilms Inc.

— 1977 "Self-realization as Ethical Norm; A Critique". In: *Philosophical Forum,* No. 9, 1977.

Frankena, William K., 1973, *Ethics.* Engelwood Cliffs, New Jersey. Prentice-Hall.

Freud, Sigmund, 1925, *Gesammelte Schriften.* Vol. II—III. Leipzig.

Froom, Erich, 1972, *Psychoanalysis and Religion.* Toronto—New York—London. Bantam books.

Furberg, Mats, 1975, *Allting en trasa? En bok om livets mening.* Lund. Doxa.

Føllesdal, D. & Walløe, L., 1977, *Argumentasjonsteori og vitenskapsfilosofi.* Oslo-Bergen-Tromsø. Universitetsförlaget.

Geller, Leonard, 1982, "The Failure of Self-actualization Theory: A Critique of Carl Rogers and Abraham Maslow". In: *Journal of Humanistic Psychology.* 1982, Vol. 22, Spring, pp. 56—73.

Globe, Frank G., 1975, *The Third Force. The Psychology of Abraham Maslow.* New York. Pocket Books.

Goldstein, K., 1939, *The Organism.* New York. American Book Company.

Goodman, Nelson, 1977, *The Structure of Appearance.* Dordrect-Holland/Boston-U.S.. A.D. Reidel Publishing Company.

Goudge T.A., 1967, "Bergson, H.". In: *Encyclopedia of Philosophy.* Vol. 1, pp. 287—295.

Grenholm, Carl-Henrik (ed.), 1981, *Metoder för religionsvetenskapligt studium.* Lund, Studentlitteratur.

Grof, Stanislav, 1976, *Realms of the Human Unconscious. Observations from LSD Research.* New York. E.P. Dutton & Co. Inc.

Hall, Mary H., 1968, "Conversation with Abraham H. Maslow". In: *Psychology Today,* 1968, No. 2, pp. 35—37, 54—57.

Halldén, Sören, 1981, *Nyfikenhetens redskap. En bok om kritiskt tänkande inom vetenskapen och utanför.* Lund. Studentlitteratur.

Hansson, S.O., 1982, "Självförverkligande — begrepp utan mening?" In:

Filosofisk tidskrift, 1982, Nr. 3, pp. 1—15.

Happold, F.C., 1977, *Mysticism. A Study and an Anthology.* New York. Peguin Books Ltd.

Hardeman, M., 1979, "A Dialoge with Abraham Maslow". In: *Journal of Humanistic Psychology.* 1979, Vol. 18, No. 1, pp. 23—28.

Harrison, Bernard, 1979, *An Introduction to the Philosophy of Language.* London and Bastingstoke. The MacMillan Press LTD.

Hedenius, Ingmar, 1971, *Tro och vetande.* Stockholm. Aldus/Bonniers.

Hempel, Carl G., 1966, *Philosophy of Natural Science.* London—Sydney—Toronto—New Dehli. Prentice Hall Inc.

Herméren, Göran, 1972, *Värdering och objektivitet.* Lund. Studentlitteratur.

Hirst, R.J., 1967, "Perception". In: *Encyclopedia of Philosophy.* Vol. 5, pp. 79—86.

Horney, K., 1951, *Neurosis and Human Growth. The struggle toward self-realization.* London. Routledge & Kegan Paul.

Hospers, John, 1970, *An Introduction of Philosophical Analysis.* London. Routledge & Kegan Paul.

Huxley, A., 1946, *The Perennial Philosophy.* London. Harper & Row Publishers.

— 1978, *The Doors of Perception.* London—Toronto—Sydney—New York. Granada Publishing Limited.

James, W., 1956, *The Will to Believe and Other Essays.* New York.

— 1979, *The Varities of Religious Experiences.* Glasgow. Collins.

Jeffner, Anders, 1972, *The Study of Religious Language.* London. SCM Press.

— 1973, *Livsåskådningsforskning.* Uppsala. Teologiska institutionen. (Mimeographed)

Johnson, W.E., 1921, *Logic.* Vol. 1. Cambridge

Jones, K.M. Jr., 1975, *The Construction and Validation of an Instrument to Measure Self-actualization as Defined by Abraham Maslow.* Diss. University, Southern Mississippi. Ann Arbor. University Microfilms International.

Kaila, E., 1967, *Den mänskliga kunskapen.* Stockholm. Utgiven av Universitetskanslersämbetet genom kommittén för akademisk kurslitteratur.

Katz, David, 1942, *Gestaltpsykologi.* Stockholm. Bonniers.

Katz, S.T., 1978, "Language, Epistemology, and Mysticism". In: Katz, S.T. (ed.) *Mysticism and Philosophical Analysis.* London. Sheldon Press.

Kasamatsu, A. & Tomio, H., 1966, "An Electroencephalographic Study on the Zen Meditation (Zazen)". In: Tart, C. (ed.), *Altered States of Consciousness.* New York—London—Sydney—Toronto. John Wiley & Sons, Inc. 1969. pp. 489—502.

Kierkegaard, Sören, 1974, *Either/or.* Vol. 2, Princeton.

Klavetter, R.E. & Mogar, R.E., 1967, "Peak-experience: Investigation of

197

Their Relationship to Psychedelic Theraphy and Self-actualization". In: *Journal of Humanistic Psychology*, 1967, Vol. 7, pp. 171—177.

Kluckhorn, C. & Murray, H. & Scheider, D. (ed.), 1959, *Personality in Nature, Society and Culture.* New York. Knopf.

Koffka, Kurt, 1935, *Principles of Gestalt Psychology.* New York. Harcourt, Brace & World.

Krippner, S., 1972, "The Plateau Experience: A.H. Maslow and Others". In: *Journal of Transpersonal Psychology,* 1972, No. 4, pp. 107—120.

Kuhn, T.S., 1962, *The Structure of Scientific Revolution.* Chicago. University of Chicago Press.

Köhler, Wolfgang, 1975, *Gestaltpsychology. An Introduction to New Concepts in Modern Psychology.* New York. New American Library.

Larski, M., 1961, *Ecstasy.* London. Cresset Press Ltd.

Lindström, Johan, 1973, *Dialog och förståelse.* Göteborg. Avdelningen för vetenskapsteori.

Lewis, C.I., 1929, *Mind and the World-order. Outline of a Theory of Knowledge.* New York-Chicago-Boston. Charles Sorbiner's Sons.

Litt, S., 1977, *Humanistisk psykologi och gestaltterapi.* Stockholm. Almqvist & Wiksell.

Lowry, R., 1973, *A.H. Maslow: An Intellectual Protrait.* Montery. Brooks/ Cole Publishing Company.

MacIntyre, A.C., 1976, *The Unconscious. A Conceptual Analysis.* London. Routledge & Kegan Paul.

MacKinnon, Donald W., 1972, "Maslow's Place in the History of Psychology". In *Journal of Creative Behavior.* 1972, Vol. 6, No. 3, pp. 158—163.

Madsén, K.B., 1976, *Allmän psykologi.* Stockholm. Esselte Studium AB.

Malmgren, H., 1978, *Förstå och förklara.* Lund. Doxa.

Marc-Wogau, Konrad, 1935, "Om skiljandet mellan primära och sekundära kvaliteter." In: *Festskrift tillägnad Axel Herrlin. 1935.* Lund. pp. 261—294.

— 1945, *Die Theorie der Sinnesdaten. Probleme der neuer Erkenntnistheorie in England.* Uppsala. Lundequistska bokhandeln.

— 1967 a, *Freuds psychoanalys. Presentation och kritik.* Stockholm. Bonniers.

— 1967 b, *Philosophical Essays.* Lund. CWK Greerup.

— 1980, *Filosofin genom tiderna. Del V. Filosofin efter 1950.* Stockholm. Bonniers.

Maslow, Abraham H., 1939, "Dominance-feeling, Personality and Social Behavior in Women". In: *Journal of Social Psychology,* 1939, No. 10, pp. 3—39.

— 1940, "A Test for Dominance-feeling (Self-esteem) in College Women". *Journal of Social Psychology,* 1940, No. 12, pp. 255—270.

— 1941 (Maslow, A.H. & Mittelmann, B.), *Principles of Abnormal Psychology:*

The Dynamics of Psychic Illness. New York. Harper and Bros.

— 1942 a "Self-esteem (Dominance-feeling) and Sexuality in Women". In: *Journal of Social Psychology,* No. 16, pp. 259—294.

— 1942 b *The Social Personality Inventory: A Test for Self-esteem in Women.* Palo Alto, California. Consulting Psychologists Press.

— 1949 "Our maligned animal nature". In: *Journal of Psychology,* 1949, No. 28, pp. 273—278.

— 1951 a "Higher needs and personality". In: *Dialectia,* 1951, No. 5, pp. 257—265.

— 1951 b *The S—I Test (A measure of psychological security-insecurity).* Palo Alto, California. Consulting Psychologists Press.

— 1954, *Motivation and Personality.* (1st edition.) New York. Harper and Bros.

— 1956, "A philosophy of psychology". In: Severin, F.T. (ed.), *Humanistic Viewpoints in Psychology.* New York. McGraw-Hill, 1965.

— 1959 a "Cognition of Being in the Peak Experiences". In: *Journal of Genetic Psychology,* 1959, No. 94, pp. 43—66.

— 1959 b (ed.) *New Knowledge in Human Values.* New York. Harpers.

— 1962 a, "Notes on Being-Psychology". In: *Journal of Humanistic Psychology,* 1962, No. 2, pp. 47—71.

— 1962 b, "Lessons from the Peak-experiences". In: *Journal of Humanistic Psychology,* 1962, No. 2, pp. 9—18.

— 1963, "Further notes on Being-Psychology." In: *Journal of Humanistic Psychology,* 1963, No. 3, pp. 120—135.

— 1964 a, "Further notes on the Psychology of Being". In: *Journal of Humanistic Psychology,* 1964, No. 4, pp. 45—58.

— 1964 b, *Religious, Values and Peak-experiences.* (1st edition.) Ohio State University Press.

— 1965, *Eupsychian Management: A Journal.* Homewood. Irwin-Dorsey.

— 1966 a, *The Psychology of Science: A Reconnaissance.* New York. Harper & Row.

— 1966 b, "Comments on Dr. Frankl's paper." In: *Journal of Humanistic Psychology,* 1966, No. 6, pp. 107—112.

— 1968 a, *Toward a Psychology of Being.* (2nd edition.) New York—Toronto—London—Melbourne. Van Nostrand.

— 1968 b "The Farther Reaches of Human Nature". In: *Journal of Transpersonal Psychology,* 1968, No. 1, pp. 1—9.

— 1969, (Maslow, A.H. & Chiang, Hung-Min), *The Healthy Personality: Readings.* New York. Van Nostrand, Reinhold.

— 1970 a, *Motivation and Personality.* (2nd edition.) New York. Harper & Row.

— 1970 b, "Peak-experiences in education and art". *The Humanist,* 1970, No. 30.

— 1972, *A.H. Maslow: A Memorial Volume.* Monterey. Brooks/Cole.

— 1976 a, *The Farther Reaches of Human Nature.* New York. Peguin Books.

— 1976 b, *Religion, Values and Peak-experiences.* (2nd edition.) New York. Peguin Books.

— 1979, *The Journals of A.H. Maslow. Vol. I & II.* Monterey. Brooks/Cole.

Misiah, H. & Sexton, V.S.S., 1973, *Phenomenological, Existential, and Humanistic Psychologies. A Historical Survey.* New York and London. Grune & Stratton.

Moore, G.E., 1902, "A Defence of Common Sense". In: *Contemporary British Philosophy.* Vol. 2. 1925.

— 1929, *Principia Ethica.* Cambridge. University Press.

— 1978, *Some Main Problems of Philosophy.* London. George Allen & Unwin Ltd/New York. Humanities Press Inc.

Moritz, M., 1967, *Inledning i värdeteori. Värdesatsteori och värdeontologi.* Lund. Studentlitteratur.

Morris, Frank S., 1972, *A Philosophical Examination of Abraham Maslow's Concept of Intrinsic Learning.* Diss. University of California, Los Angeles. Ann Arbor, University Microfilms International.

Murphy, G., 1947, *Personality.* New York. Harper & Row.

Naess, Arne, 1968, *Scepticism.* Oslo. Universitetsforlaget.

— 1969, *Hvilken verden er den virkelige?* Oslo-Bergen-Tromsø. Universitetsforlaget.

Naranjo, Claudio, 1974, *The One Quest.* London. Wildwood House.

Naranjo, Claudio & Ornstein, Robert E., 1971, *On the Psychology of Meditation.* New York. The Viking Press.

Neisser, Uric, 1967, *Cognitive Psychology.* New York. Appleton-Century-Crafts.

— 1976, *Cognition and Reality.* San Francisco-London. W.H. Freeman and Company.

Neurath, O., 1932, "Protocol Sentencse", In: Ayer, A. (ed.), *Logical Positivism.* London. George Allen & Unwin. 1959, pp. 199—208.

Nielsen, Kai, 1962, "On Taking Human Nature As the Basic of Morality". In: *Social Research,* 1962, Summer, pp. 157—176.

Nilsson, L., 1980. *Förklaringar inom psychoanalysen.* Lund. Doxa.

Nordenfelt, Lennart, 1974, *Explanation of Human Actions.* Uppsala.

— 1979, *Kunskap-Värdering-Förståelse,* Stockholm. Publica.

Ornstein, Robert E., 1975, *The Psychology of Consciousness.* New York. Peguin Books Inc.

Passmore, J., 1972, *The Perfectibility of Man.* London. Duckworth.

Pelletier, Kenneth R. & Garfield, Charles, 1972, *Consciousness: East and West*. New York—Evanston—San-Francisco—London. Harper & Row, Publishers.

Peters, R.S., 1974, *The Concept of Motivation*. London. Routledge & Regan Paul.

Phalén, Adolf, 1977, *Några riktningar i nyare kunskapslära. Ur Efterlämnade manuskript*. Stockholm. Natur och Kultur.

Plato, 1952, Theaetetus. In: *Great Books of the Western World. Vol. 7*. Hutchins, R.M. (ed.). Chicago—London—Toronto. Encyclopaedia Britannica, Inc. 1952, pp. 512—550.

Poelling, R.K., 1971, *A Developmental Study of Abraham H. Maslow's Self-actualision Theory*. Diss. Northern Illinois University. Ann Arbor. University Microfilms International.

Polanyi, Michael, 1973, *Personal Knowledge. Towards a Post-critical Philosophy*. London. Routledge & Regan Paul.

Quine, W.V., 1951, "Two Dogmas of Empirism". In: *Philosophical Review*, 1951, No. 60, pp. 20—43.

Radnitzsky, Gerad, 1968, *Contemporary Schools of Metascience. Vol. I. Anglo-Saxon Schools of Metascience*. Göteborg. Akademiförlaget.

— 1968, *Contemporary Schools of Metascience. Vol. II Continental Schools of Metascience*. Göteborg. Akademiförlaget.

Rogers, Carl R., 1975, *Becoming a Person. A Therapist's View of Psychotherapy*. London. Constable & Company Ltd.

Rosenblatt, Howard S. & Bertlett, Iris, 1976, "Some Phenomenological Aspects of the Peak Experience". In: *Southern Journal of Educational Research*, 1976, Vol. 10, pp. 29—42.

Russell, Bertrand, 1979, *History of Western Philosophy*. London. Unwin Paperbacks.

Ryding, E., 1979, *Jag och personlighet*. Lund. Doxa.

Sartre, Jean-Paul, 1976, *Being and Nothingness*. London. Methauen & Co Ltd.

Saussy, C, 1977, *A Study of the Adequacy of Abraham Maslow's Concept of the Self to his Theory of Self-actualization*. Diss. Graduate Theological Union. Ann Arbor. University Microfilms International.

Scheffler, Israel, 1974, *Four Pragmatists. A Critical Introduction of Peirce, James, Mead and Dewey*. London. Routledge & Kegan Paul./New York. Humanities Press.

Shaffer, John B.P., 1978, *Humanistic Psychology*. New Jersey. Prentice-Hall, Inc.

Siu, R.G.H., 1957, *The Tao of Science. An Essay on Western Knowledge and Easten Wisdom*. London. Chapman & Hall, Limited.

Smedslund, J., 1972, *Becoming a Psychologist. Theoretical Foundations for a Humanistic Psychology.* Oslo. Universitetsförlaget.

Smith, Brewster, 1973, "On Self-actualization: A Transambivalent Examination of a Focal Theme in Maslow's Psychology". In: *Journal of Humanistic Psychology,* 1973, Vol. 13, No. 2, pp. 17—33.

Stace, W.T., 1972, *Mysticism and Philosophy.* London and Bastingtoke. Mac-Millan.

Stegmüller, Wolfgang, 1969, *Main Currents in Contemporary German, British and American Philosophy.* Dordrect. Holland. D. Reidel Publishing Company.

Steffen, Alan, 1973, "The Active Tradition: A Convergance of Ideas". In: *Educational Theory,* No. 23, pp. 321—332.

Stevens, W.A., 1972, "The Sacred and Profane as Found in Teilhard de Chardin and Abraham Maslow". In: *Religious Humanism; a Quarterly Journal.* 1972, No. 6, pp. 15—19.

Sutich, Anthony J., 1961, "Introduction". In: *Journal of Humanistic Psychology,* 1961, Vol. 1, No. 1, pp. vii—ix.

— 1969, "Some considerations regarding Transpersonal Psychology". In: *The Journal of Transpersonal Psychology,* 1969, No. 1, pp. 11—20.

— 1976, "The Emergence of the Transpersonal Orientation. A Personal Account". In: *The Journal of Transpersonal Psychology,* 1976, No. 1.

Tart, C.T. (ed.), 1969, *Altered States of Consciousness.* New York—London—Sydney—Toronto. John Wiley & Sons, Inc.

Underwood, Ralph L., 1975, "Freedom and Dignity in A.H. Maslow's Philosophy of the Person". In: *Zygon, Journal of Religion and Science,* 1975, Vol. 10, No. 2, pp. 144—161.

von Wright, G.H., 1971, *Explanation and Understanding.* London. Routledge & Kegan Paul.

— 1982, "Om behov". In: *Filosofisk tidskrift,* Nr. 1, 1982, pp. 1—12.

Wahba, Mahmoud A. & Bridwell, Lawrence G., 1976, "Maslow Reconsidered: A Review of Research on the Need Hierarchy Theory". In: *Organizational Behavior and Human Performance,* 1976, No. 15, pp. 212—240.

Wedberg, Anders, 1970, *Filosofins historia. Nyare tiden till romantiken.* Stockholm. Bonniers.

Wilson, Colin, 1972, *New Pathways in Psychology. Maslow and the Post-Freudian Revolution,* New York, Mentor.

Wittgenstein, Ludvig, 1972, *Philosophical Investigations.* Oxford. Basil Blackwell.

Zaehner, R.C., 1978, *Mysticism. Sacred and Profane. An Inquiry into some Varities of Praeternatural Experience.* London—Oxford—New York. Oxford University Press.